SO FEW GOT THROUGH

SO FEW GOT THROUGH

BY MARTIN LINDSAY

Pen & Sword
MILITARY

First published in Great Britain in 1946 by William Collins
Republished in 2000 and reprinted in 2012 by
PEN & SWORD MILITARY
an imprint of
Pen & Sword Books Ltd
47 Church Street
Barnsley
South Yorkshire
S70 2AS

ISBN 978 1 84884 856 6

Printed and bound by
CPI Group (UK) Ltd., Croydon, CR0 4YY

Pen & Sword Books Ltd incorporates the Imprints of
Pen & Sword Aviation, Pen & Sword Family History, Pen & Sword Maritime,
Pen & Sword Military, Pen & Sword Discovery, Wharncliffe Local History,
Wharncliffe True Crime, Wharncliffe Transport, Pen & Sword Select,
Pen & Sword Military Classics, Leo Cooper, The Praetorian Press,
Remember When, Seaforth Publishing and Frontline Publishing

For a complete list of Pen & Sword titles please contact
PEN & SWORD BOOKS LIMITED
47 Church Street, Barnsley, South Yorkshire, S70 2AS, England
E-mail: enquiries@pen-and-sword.co.uk
Website: www.pen-and-sword.co.uk

To
THE INFANTRY COMPANY COMMANDER
British, Canadian and American,
who played a greater part than
any other individual in the
liberation of Europe,
1944–45

Contents

List of Maps

Introduction
by
Colonel Oliver Lindsay CBE FRHistS

My father, Martin Lindsay, was a soldier, explorer, politician and author. But his first love was soldiering. He came from a Scottish military family and was the twenty-second in descent from Sir William Lindsay 1st of Dowhill. Dowhill Castle near Kinross was sold by the family in the 1740s.

My grandfather, a Gurkha, died in 1914 when Martin was aged nine, as a result of trying to save a drowning soldier. His mother, with little influence or money, somehow saw him through Wellington and Sandhurst. He was commissioned into the Royal Scots Fusiliers in 1925.

Paying his Mess bills in Glasgow became increasingly troublesome and so, like the more enterprising of his contemporaries, he sought secondment to a more exciting life far afield. By 1927 he was with the Nigerian Regiment which gave him his first opportunity for exploration: he travelled across Africa through the Ituri forest in the Belgian Congo, enduring considerable hardship, and collecting pigmy artefacts for the British Museum.

Back in Britain his Commanding Officer, a somewhat characterless individual, objected to Martin volunteering to be the surveyor of the South-East Greenland expedition which sought to establish an Arctic air route to Canada. Nevertheless he went and such was the expedition's success that he received the

King's Polar Medal and wrote his first book – *Those Greenland Days* (1932).

Now fired with ambition, he subsequently took his own expedition, sledging over 1000 miles in 103 days, mapping 350 miles of mountains – with no radio contact, external support or air resupply: no wonder this expedition has subsequently been featured in the *Guinness Book of Records*.

Despite postings to India and Shanghai, peacetime soldiering offered no prospects, and so he sought a parliamentary career. However, Hitler and the Second World War put his political ambitions on hold.

We all have to be at the right place at the right time and on two fateful occasions Martin was. First, in 1940, in Norway, General Carton de Wiart (the possessor of 'one arm, one eye and one Victoria Cross') appropriated him and Peter Fleming, in the absence of any other staff; a better pair never existed, wrote the General. Consequently my father saw the disasters of that short, yet costly, campaign at first hand and, on return, briefed Atlee while still in his battle-stained service dress. His first-hand information helped to bring down the Chamberlain administration.

His second stroke of good fortune occurred in July 1944. Because, tragically, the casualties in the 1st Battalion Gordon Highlanders were greater than elsewhere, he was posted to that Battalion which he commanded in 16 operations, vividly described in this book which became mandatory Staff College reading for many years. My brother, sister and I are all delighted that Pen and Sword Books share our belief that this book is as relevant today as it was when first written.

After the war, the author returned to our family, a successful career in politics, more books and his share of honours and awards, including a baronetcy. Dying in 1981, he is greatly missed and remembered by his many friends for his courage, charm and panache.

Part One

France

1

It all began with a telegram.

About a month after D-Day I had been spending a few days with Bobby and Dolly near Ascot. Dudley and Eve Tooth were also staying there. He and I talked about our prep. school, where 'Tooth was swished by Beetle yesterday' was scrawled on a wall in the pavilion and reminded successive generations of small boys not only of the birching of the unknown Tooth, but also of that legendary, gouty old tyrant, Hawtrey. Dudley tried to teach me about pictures, Dolly tried to improve my bridge, which nobody will ever succeed in doing, and Eve inspired me to a birdie on the 18th at the Berkshire, the last hole I was to play for a long time. So I left Kingsmead that morning a much better man.

We all drove up the Great West Road together, in Bobby's little car. I saw some duck flighting very high and wondered what echo of war had disturbed their daylight siesta. We passed a long convoy – fresh landings on the French coast, perhaps? The porter at my Club handed me the telegram which I had been expecting: '*Major Lindsay posted to 21 Army Group as a second-in-command will join 12 repeat 12 July at Virginia Water and report to Major Wellington.*'

I savoured in full that last morning in London. I took a last look round the Club, pinched some notepaper, and promised Alan Lennox-Boyd to ask for news of his brother, missing since D plus 1. I had a military haircut at a fashionable and unmilitary barber. I left my best service dress with my tailor. Of course I had to tell Mr. Welsh that I was just off to France, and he was slightly sentimental. He showed me two tunics belonging to a young officer of the Rifle Brigade, which his mother had sent in to be cleaned before she gave them away. So I left him Joyce's address, in case I never called back for mine.

I walked very slowly up St. James's Street, sniffing the air like a young spaniel working up a hedgerow. A flying bomb streaked across the sky but everyone continued about their business: two taxi-drivers were haggling over the price for a bottle of black-market gin, an American aviator smiled into the laughing eyes of somebody else's wife, in the bay window of White's an old man was reading a newspaper.

At Claridge's I went to telephone for a car to meet me at Virginia Water. Scribbled on a message pad I read: 'Sally Lovelace has still not returned to her flat. They have not yet finished digging. We will let you know as soon as possible.' But the foyer was crowded. The restaurant was filling up, and soon there was not a table left.

There was another Alert at Waterloo Station, but the All Clear sounded at Twickenham. The train stopped for a long time in front of a village green. The slow left-hand bowler sent down two full pitches running. 'Dear Daddy,' had written Lindsay *ma*, 'I think I like crikket.' 'Darling wife,' I wrote then and there, 'if I do not return I want you please to remember that the boys . . .'

When we arrived at Virginia Water I asked the A.T.S. driver if she knew where 21st Army Group was to be found. 'No,' she replied, 'it's all so very hush hush. Nobody yet knows where anything is.' 'Well, Dolly told me at lunch that it's at the Wentworth Golf Club,' I said, 'so let's try there first.'

Major Wellington had never heard of me, so there was much telephoning and searching for files. A lieutenant-colonel came into the room and they talked *sotto voce* for a while about the crop of adverse reports which had come back from France, against hitherto successful battalion commanders and brigadiers who had lost their heads when the guns began to fire. There was some mention of a new colonel for 11th Scots Fusiliers.

'Why, what's happened to Colonel Cuninghame?' I asked, for he was just about my greatest friend. 'I'm afraid he's gone,' the major said. 'He was killed three days ago.' I felt very sad, for Sandy and I were in the same company at Sandhurst and joined the regiment together.

Wellington rang up France and tried to sell me to 9th Durham Light Infantry, but his opposite number over there was out. So he told me to 'proceed' and get myself fixed up when I reached the other side.

So, on a lovely summer evening in July 1944, I was a passenger in what was formerly a small Dover-Ostend Channel boat – one of a number of infantry reinforcements on our way to replace the heavy battle casualties that had occurred in the first weeks' bitter fighting in the Normandy beach-head.

We were a silent and sober crowd, standing at the ship's rails watching the slanting rays of the setting sun on the green fields of Hampshire and the Isle of Wight. I am sure that each one of us was speculating upon his individual destiny, wondering whether he would ever again see the coast of England – many never did. Most of that group were little more than twenty years of age, and had not been abroad before. As I looked at those fresh young faces I felt desperately sorry for them all. I myself was spared the more poignant emotions, for all this had happened to me before. Three times before had I put my affairs in order and made peace with myself before setting out on a venture, wondering whether it would be my good fortune to return safely from it.

My companions soon went below, and before long their shouts and laughter echoed up the companion-way. I turned up the collar of my khaki great-coat and stayed on deck for another hour or two, watching the yellow stabs of flak as a lone representative of the Luftwaffe streaked across the sky. The searchlights one by one went out and a pale moon rose higher and higher above the sea. Orion and Leo, Pegasus and Perseus became visible, starting their leisurely noctambulation round the Pole Star as if nothing unusual had happened and a new phase in world history was not being written in blood in the fields and orchards of Calvados just out of sight over the horizon.

We had a good view of the French coast as we steamed in towards it next day: rolling grassfields sloping down to the sea from a ridge behind, and few distinctive features. I was struck by the enormous quantity of shipping of all types riding at anchor: cruisers, cargo vessels, tankers, lighters and many smaller craft; more ships than I had ever before seen in so small a stretch of water. No wonder the Luftwaffe came over most nights to lay mines.

We left the *Prince Albert* in a tank landing craft, which steered for a large white pole not unlike a polo goalpost. At the foot of it a notice informed us that this desolate piece of featureless sand was King Beach. Stranded on the shore were several burnt-out craft which had blown up on land mines, and a few tanks which had bogged themselves in the heavy, clay-like sand. The only beach official appeared to be an elderly captain crouching like a cave-dweller in a lean-to made from ration boxes and tarpaulin sheets. He said that a car would be going to Second Army H.Q. in three hours' time.

So I went for a walk along the beach. The Navy were busy with jeeps and bulldozers salving derelict landing craft. There were no buildings to speak of in sight and they lived in dug-outs cut into the sandy hillocks just above high-water mark. The story of the D-Day battle was still written in the sand for all who could to read: the Germans occupying diggings at the

4

edge of the beach had not been a first-class field formation, for the weapons they had left there were a miscellany of British and French equipment, no doubt captured in 1940. On the approach of the landing craft they had run for it – there were no empty cartridge cases, but on the other hand much hastily-jettisoned equipment at the foot of their trenches.

Our men had been held up by heavy mortar fire short of these diggings, as could be seen by the number of holes, the edges of which were scarred in the path of the flying metal fragments and stained black from the bursting charge. One could see that there had been casualties, for in several places one saw a more or less complete set of British equipment – steel helmet, rifle, web equipment and so on. I could picture the scene: the men just landed, relaxing after the tension, loitering a bit, lighting a cigarette. So this is France; cushy, ain't it? Officers hustling around, sorting things out: 'Anybody seen the Company Commander?' 'Over here, No. 9 Platoon.' Then suddenly the fearful cracks of bursting mortar bombs all round, and as one man everybody went to ground.

It was a lovely summer day and I struck off along a path until I found what I was looking for – a Frenchman. He was an old man, leaning upon a hoe, and he told me that life had been hard during the occupation. German soldiers had been everywhere. Although the French along that coast had been all the time expecting us to land, the enemy were taken completely by surprise. Our bombing around here was very scattered and had killed few Germans, but nine French people.

I told him that I loved France, that we would liberate the whole country, and that perhaps next summer or certainly the one after I should return once again for my holidays. He straightened his back and looked away into the distance, towards the faint sound of the guns rumbling and banging away. 'Maybe,' he said. 'But I am a very old man. I have seen two wars and now I have lost faith. All life is uncertain. *Mais je prierai Dieu de vous protéger, mon ami.*'

I went on past a roadside cemetery. There were some twenty small white wooden crosses, mostly graves of officers and men of the East Yorkshire Regiment and Green Howards. Then I jumped a lift in a passing truck and came to a much knocked-about village, and there I found Ian Mackenzie, who had crossed on the boat with me, in a group of officers.

We asked about the fighting which had lately taken place. Then one of them said, 'Fifteenth Scottish Division is attacking tonight. They cross the start line at 1 a.m.' This was a nasty shock for Ian, as his posting was to a Highland Light Infantry battalion in that division. He hurried off to the Town Major's office to try to borrow a jeep, and I felt very sorry for him being pitched into a night attack within an hour or two of joining.

My staff-car arrived. The driver said that many Frenchmen were not at all pleased when we turned their countryside into a battlefield; one of them soused him with a bucket of water as he sat there in the driving seat. After dark we reached a small tented camp in an orchard. Just as I was about to turn in, there was a beautiful display of flares and fireworks as the Luftwaffe flew over towards the beaches.

After breakfast I went across to the appropriate tent and reported myself. Before my identity was established I had a narrow escape from being posted as a Town Major in mistake for some other Lindsay. Then I said that I was particularly keen to go to the 51st Highland Division.

'Yes,' said the Lieut.–Colonel, after thumbing through a file, 'the Divisional Commander has applied for you by name. 153 Brigade – a Black Watch and two Gordon Battalions – have lost a lot of officers in their last show. I think we can place you there.' He telephoned to the Division for confirmation, then showed me a map where I would find their H.Q. 'You have arrived at the right moment,' he said, 'for 153 have come back into a rest area this morning. I will send you over in my car.'

I walked across to the survey truck to get a map which would guide me to my destination. Second Army H.Q. was dispersed in the grounds of a château. The garden walls were of an attractive near-Cotswold stone, but largely fallen down. The road to 153 Brigade was choked with transport of all kinds, as was the air with dust. Their H.Q., consisting of a few caravans, tents and slit trenches, was in an orchard near Benouville. The Brigadier, 'Nap' Murray, a Cameron Highlander, had just begun to talk to me when there was a sudden swish and a bang, and a shell landed right in the middle of the orchard, causing nine casualties. Every three or four minutes for the next half-hour something landed pretty close. 'God Almighty!' I thought to myself, 'if this is a rest area, how can I ever stand the real thing?'

The Brigadier told me I would go to 1st Gordons. Their Colonel had been wounded two days ago and he had applied for Harry Cumming-Bruce (now Lord Thurlow), the second-in-command, to be promoted in his place, which would make a vacancy for me to step into.

At that moment Major the Hon. Henry Charles Hovell-Thurlow-Cumming-Bruce, to give him his full title, walked in. He seemed a charming chap; perhaps a slightly unorthodox military figure with his rather old-fashioned curly moustache, white-framed horn-rimmed spectacles and slight stoop. He wore the St. John's black medal ribbon, which caused much speculation among the troops when he arrived. He asked his servant what they thought it was, and the reply was, 'Well, Sir, we thocht that perhaps baith your parents were killed in the blitz.' I hoped to God he knew his job.

We went to the Battalion area. The companies were well dispersed and dug-in, in some fields and scrub on the high ground overlooking the River Orne. 6th Airborne Division were then holding the ridge beyond. All day they had been harassed by shell-fire in this so-called rest area, and Cumming-Bruce's visit to Brigade H.Q. was to ask for permission to move elsewhere. That evening we moved to some fields three miles away. It was quiet there and we could rest as long as it did not rain, but to keep the troops in good spirits a town or village was needed, a place where they could put on their best battledress and ogle the girls.

Cumming-Bruce had a small caravan made out of a captured ambulance and I had a long talk with him inside it. He gave me the low-down on the Battalion. They had lost twelve officers, including the Colonel, three company commanders and 200 men, in the thirty-five days since the start of the campaign, without achieving very much. Two days ago they were ordered to take the Colombelles factory area, but it was much stronger than anybody anticipated and the attack failed miserably. He was rather worried about the morale of the Battalion. The continual shelling had made a number of men 'bomb-happy'. ('Bomb-happy', meaning shell-shocked or nervous, was a phrase much in use out here. Others I had not heard before were 'duva' for dug-out or slit-trench, 'brew-up' for boil up or burn-out, and 'stonk' for a concentration of shells or mortar bombs.)

The Battalion had fought for thirty-four days and was now having three to four days' rest before the next show. Cumming-Bruce said that the Colombelles attack failed partly because the troops lacked offensive spirit as the result of being too tired, too much use having been made of the Division. He thought that the change of country would do everybody good. What they would appreciate most was that there were no trees there; everybody hated them as a shell explodes when it hits a tree and causes more casualties than when it bursts on the ground. Recently the Battalion had spent some time in woods the other side of the Orne where there was a lot of shelling and mortaring.

I was very proud to be in this Division. The original 51st was (except for one brigade) forced to surrender at St. Valery in 1940. A new Highland Division was then formed in Scotland and in due course made a great name for itself in North Africa and Sicily. It was brought back from Italy to England early in the year in order to take part in the present campaign.

The Division consisted (apart from the supporting arms and services such as R.A., R.E., R.A.M.C., R.A.S.C., etc) of the five Highland regiments: the Black Watch, Seaforths, Gordons, Camerons, and Argyll and Sutherlands. The three Brigades were 152 (5th Camerons and 2nd and 5th Seaforths), 153 (5th Black Watch and 1st and 5-7th Gordons) and 154 (1st and 7th Black Watch and 7th Argyll and Sutherlands). All five regiments have magnificent traditions.

One thing which particularly interested me was the way in which the men's feelings were considered in this Division. Twice in two days I had heard, 'The Jocks don't like raids. They prefer to attack with somebody on their flanks, as part of a big show.' And 'The Jocks don't like sitting still and just being shelled,' one officer said ponderously, as if this were a peculiar racial characteristic. 'The Jocks fight far better if it is under somebody whom they know.' And 'The Jocks are accustomed to being visited by celebrities,' by which were meant the Corps and Army Commander, etc. There was a good deal of annoyance because nobody from 1st Corps H.Q. ever visited us.

I decided to read up the history of the Gordon Highlanders. All I could remember was that the regiment was raised by one of the Dukes of Gordon whose crest, the stag's antlers above the ducal coronet, was worn as a cap badge to this day. His Duchess, Jean, is said to have allowed all would-be recruits to take the King's shilling from between her lips with a kiss.

They were Sir John Moore's favourite regiment, and when he chose his coat-of-arms he had the figure of a Gordon Highlander in full dress as one of the two supporters. When he was killed it was a bearer party from the regiment which carried him to the grave, and their white spats still have black buttons in mourning for this sad day. Most people must have seen Lady Butler's famous picture, 'Scotland for Ever', showing the charge of the Gordons, holding on to the leathers of the Scots Greys, at Waterloo. Later the regiment gained great renown in an attack on the heights of Dargai, on the Indian Frontier,

9

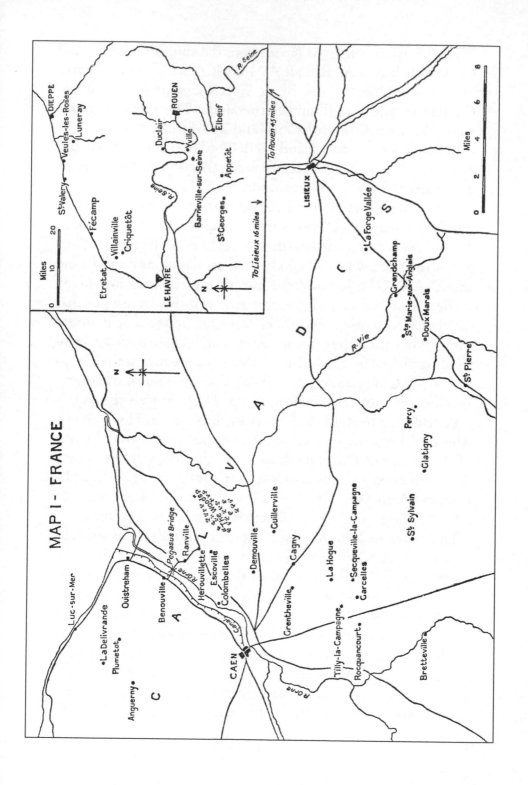

MAP I – FRANCE

in which Piper Findlater won the V.C. for playing the regimental march, 'Cock o' the North', after being shot through both legs. They are often known as the 'Gay Gordons', although this is actually a corruption of the Scottish word gey, meaning a true or, as the French would say, *un vrai* Gordon.

The Battalion had very fine material in it. At this time they were Scots almost to a man, and most, like my servant Graham, had seen a lot of severe fighting in Africa, Sicily, and now in Normandy. The officers appeared to be a fine type, though Harry said he was not sure about one or two of the younger ones.

It was about this time that they changed our name from British Western European Force to British Liberation Army. When we were the B.W.E.F. the wags said it stood for 'Burma when Europe finished'. Now they said B.L.A. meant 'Burma Looms Ahead'.

We spent several pleasant days in the fields. I slept in my bedding roll at the edge of the corn, a slit-trench beside me ready to roll into if there was any trouble. We sat in the sun. The Jocks gossiped, washed, read and wrote letters, mended their clothing and improved their dug-outs.

On one of these afternoons I ran over to Luc-sur-mer. A few French sat about on the beach, watching the troops bathing. All the time loads were being brought ashore. I was told they landed 2,000 tons a day on that beach alone. The little town had been knocked about by shelling, but apart from wired-off enclosures marked 'Mines' there was hardly a sign of four years of German occupation. There was not much for the troops to do there; only three shops were open, two of which sold vegetables (mostly onions) and the third children's toys. The 3rd Division had taken over a hotel and turned it into an excellent rest camp where men could bath, change their underclothes, write letters, drink beer, etc. The road back was very dusty. I spoke to a Tank Corps sergeant and for a moment I really thought he was an Indian or African, so black was his skin. It

11

was amazing what a lot of stuff we had got ashore: thousands of vehicles, and dumps of one kind or another almost every hundred yards.

Then came the news that we were to move forward next day, part of a big push.

It started with the arrival overhead of hundreds of Fortresses at 5.40 in the morning, and for an hour we heard bombs bursting in the distance and felt the tremor of the ground vibrating. Then our guns began to fire and kept up a steady barrage for four hours. Every now and then a German battery replied, and a dozen shells landed in an empty field two hundred yards away – all right so long as they would stay there. One admired these German gunners firing back in the face of this overwhelming display. I paid a visit to 43 Medium Regiment, not far away. Girls were driving the cows in for milking, past the guns as they were firing; the noise seemed enough to curdle any milk. The gunners told me that 660 guns were firing 200 rounds each in this fire programme, to say nothing of twelve naval guns of the Fleet.

I gathered that the grand strategy behind this operation was for the tanks to break through on the left of the line, through the gaps in the minefield recently made by the sappers. The armour was to be followed by 3rd British and 51st Highland Division. But we had been given only a limited objective, for this thrust was no more than a feint to draw off the German armour in order to enable the Americans on the right of the line to drive south and west along the coast as far as they could manage to go.

As we were not to move off until after dark there was nothing for us to do but lie about in the sun among the oats, hay, flax and potatoes of our fields. It was certainly an odd sight: 700 men scattered over the ground in little groups without a building anywhere near.

While we were waiting I wrote some letters, and in one of them I said that I knew I was going to be very happy in this little Battalion H.Q. community. The Colonel, or Harry as he had asked me to call him, was a dear. The other members were Alec Lumsden, the Adjutant, a member of Stock Exchange; Ewen Traill, our Padre; 'Bert' Brown, the doctor; and David Martin, Intelligence Officer. David was a tremendously hard worker and also a very lovable character. He came from Dundee, was an only child and had just left school when the war broke out. Ewen was a great character: a Church of Scotland minister in Glasgow who resigned in 1939 and in due course obtained a combatant commission, in which capacity he was posted to us. He was young, high-spirited and argumentative, and a Labour Parliamentary candidate though more from force of circumstances than conviction, I suspected. He was a brave chap and went into battle with the stretcher bearers instead of staying at the Aid Post, as most padres did. Bert Brown was a solid, sturdy chap with a grand sense of humour, the sort of man of whom one could make a friend for life. His pre-war practice was in Galashiels.

I wished that I were able to see through the months ahead and know what fate had in store for each one of us.[1]

At 6 p.m. I left for Ranville with a reconnaissance party consisting of one officer from each company, to act as guides for the Battalion when it arrived.

We were routed across the Orne at Ouistreham, captured by 4 Commando on D-Day. Several times we had to pull in to the side to make way for returning ambulances. At one of these halts I spoke to the Quartermaster of a King's Shropshire Light Infantry battalion, whose driver was mending a puncture. They had had 170 casualties that day, he said.

---

[1] To anticipate somewhat: of these six of us in Battalion H.Q. in July, 1944 – Cumming-Bruce, Lindsay, Lumsden, Martin, Traill and Brown – three got through unscathed, one was wounded, one killed and one died of wounds. The four who survived the campaign were between them awarded three D.S.O.s and two M.C.s.

13

Ranville had once been a nice little village. The Château was the first H.Q. of 5th Parachute Brigade, who landed all round it. A parachute still hung in the branches of a big elm, and I wondered if the luckless owner was shot like a sitting bird as he swung there, or whether he managed to get down safely. In front of the Château was a P.O.W. cage containing over a thousand, who looked a very scratch lot, dirty and dejected.

While waiting for the battalion, I bought two bottles of cider at six francs apiece from a very old lady who had been living alone for five years, all her relations being in Paris. I found her almost in tears because her best milking cow had been killed on a mine. She apologised for the cider. It was very poor stuff, she said, because some shell splinters had pierced the vat.

There was plenty of excitement before the battalion got in.

At 11 p.m., just as I was going to meet them, we had an air-raid. They came over low and lit up the whole countryside with dazzling clusters of parachute flares. Our A.A. was pretty in-effective and we had no night fighters up. They dropped five bombs very close to this farmhouse and two officers in my small advance party were hit. We lay on the floor of the dining-room for the first one or two, then ran outside to a dug-out.

When all was quiet again I went to look for the battalion, but missed them as they had been sent another way owing to the road being blocked by burning transport. Some artillery ammunition trucks had been hit and set on fire and the shells kept exploding. I had a nightmare ride on the back of a motor-bike, and was upset and annoyed to find that neither I nor the driver had a field-dressing when some gunners at the roadside stopped us and asked for some.

Eventually, tired, cross and sweating, I found the battalion, and the guides led the companies and transport off into the areas we had chosen. Then a young and rather shaken officer of the Fife and Forfar Yeomanry arrived to ask for assistance. Their transport had caught it badly in the bombing and three officers had been killed. It was too dark to assess how many men were killed, wounded or missing. None of them had dug slit-trenches. Incredible – and in the fifth year of the war! One would say it served them right were it not such a tragedy.

All through the night the fires burned and shells kept exploding.

I had a good sleep in pyjamas from 5 a.m. till 11, then went out for a stroll. In the yard a rabbit was eating a shirt, so I told some men to feed the animals. There were five bomb holes within a hundred yards, one of which was only six feet from the farmhouse. I went round the company areas. A were sharing some farm buildings with a party of Welsh Guardsmen, B were dug in alongside a wall, C were in the garden and cellars of a completely gutted house. The Jocks all seemed in excellent spirits.

I got back in time for the one o'clock news, to hear that the Russians were within thirty kilometres of East Prussia, and Stalin said he could not be responsible for the consequences. Ewen, our Padre, went to help the Fife and Forfar Yeomanry bury their dead.

It was difficult to find out what was happening in the battle. One gathered that several villages were holding us up, each with a few tanks in them which were costly to dislodge. One had to hand it to the German for being a tough fighter.

We were to spend three days in Ranville. There was sporadic shelling of the area; nothing very much, but the Brigade Signal Officer was killed one night. What a lot of people in the course of the war must have been killed by those odd shells which suddenly and unexpectedly arrived. A few landed near the mobile shower baths and there was a scurry of men, stark naked except for their steel helmets, to the nearest cover.

Meanwhile the Canadians captured Colombelles, and I went to view the scene of 1st Gordons' abortive attack of July 13th. I could not think how anybody could have expected a battalion to take such a strong position with no great fire support. All the houses were fortified and the ground was honeycombed with German diggings. Although nine artillery regiments were made available, Corps said this was not necessary and the programme was drastically cut down.

David Martin, the Intelligence Officer, pointed all the features out to me, so it was very interesting walking round the battlefield, though we did not feel very comfortable owing to the possibility of mines and booby-traps. David told me that two brigadiers were blown up walking the course after an action in Sicily. I saw a dead Canadian in his shirt-sleeves just beyond a wire fence and thought that I should collect his identity disc, then realised he could only have been killed by a mine. I wondered for what private purpose he had wandered off there on his own. Further on I saw an arm in a khaki shirt sticking out from under a groundsheet, and on investigating found it was a dead German. The ground was very heavily pitted with craters, for the Canadians attacked after the Fortresses had bombed it. We came to an abandoned German anti-tank gun and could see from the marks on the ground that the crew had come out of their dug-out (with several bomb holes very close to it) and turned the gun round more to the right and then fired fifteen rounds – brave chaps. Returning, we met a Seaforth subaltern who told us he was looking for the place where his brother was killed.

Harry was also touring the battlefield and I was quite relieved when he got back safely. Shortly afterwards, a very chastened party, consisting of Ewen Traill, our Padre, Alec Lumsden and one other, came in to say that they had blown up their jeep on a mine and that Robertson, a subaltern, would lose his foot and several fingers. They were following a truck when somebody said: 'This can't be right. And look at that brewed-up carrier. I bet it was a mine.' So they began to turn and, immediately, up she went. The tragedy was that Robertson might not have been badly hurt had he put sandbags on the floor of his jeep; they were taken out that morning for the car to be cleaned, and were not replaced.

My diary tells me that we had a good dinner that night: rabbit and some excellent white wine. Somebody had obtained a four-gallon container of this from a drunken Canadian in exchange for a Gordon cap-badge, which the Quartermaster would replace. 'Scrappy' Hay, who commanded 5-7th Gordons in this Brigade, came in afterwards. He said that his view of foraging was that he just did not enquire what happened to rabbits and hens in unoccupied farms. He told us he had heard a duologue between a staff officer and a Gordon who was plucking a fowl, as follows:

S.O.: 'You know you will be shot if anybody sees you with that hen?'

Gordon: 'Well, Sirr, we mae git shot ony time so it maks nae difference.'

S.O. (disgusted): 'I suppose you are one of those desert fellows.'

We sat about most of next day watching the tanks passing through: 11th and 7th Armoured Divisions, displaying their heraldic fauna. It was still as hard as ever to know how the battle was going.

We heard that night that 'Scrappy' Hay had been wounded in the head by shellfire while crossing Pegasus Bridge.

Next morning, July 22nd, the Brigadier came over after breakfast and told me to take command of 5-7th Gordons in place of Scrappy, until somebody who was on the way arrived. They were a T.A. Battalion which had always done well in action. He told me that the battalion was about to take up a forward position which had been reconnoitred the day before, and that I had better get down right away, contact the units on the flank, and meet the battalion when it arrived in the afternoon.

I had only about ten miles to go but it took a long time. First there was a traffic block in Demouville, and then we got bogged in deep mud on a tank track until a Welsh Guards R.S.M. in a carrier towed my jeep through. We went on until we came to some unmistakable Guardsmen.

17

'Are you 1st Grenadiers?' I shouted, and then there was a sudden swish and some cracks close by. I dived into the nearest hole and landed on the ankles of a subaltern. For the next ten minutes we sat facing one another with our feet tucked under each other's armpits, while mortar bombs landed in the orchard all round. He told me that it was a bloody place. Cagny just in front, and Guillerville a mile off to the left, both got shelled a great deal. So they were not sorry we were going to take over from them.

As soon as things were quiet I made my way over to the battalion command post. I walked fast, one ear cocked for the next lot of stuff coming over, and passing as close as I decently could to any slit-trenches on the way. The Grenadier Colonel also said that it was a bloody area. From his trench I could see our position away to the left, and as I looked through my glasses a salvo of shells landed right in the middle of it. The Grenadiers were to the left of and slightly behind the Irish Guards, and 5th Black Watch and 7th Argylls took over that evening from these two battalions. On their left was a gap of a mile until one came to the Warwicks in Guillerville and the K.S.L.I., the two right-hand battalions of 3rd Division. It was this gap that 5-7th Gordons had to fill.

From the Grenadiers I went on to the Irish Guards. They, too, said that it was a bloody place; there seemed to be complete unanimity on this point! What I particularly wanted to know was whether my area was under enemy observation, in which case I had to hurry back and stop the battalion coming in till after dark. They thought not, and this I was inclined to confirm when I walked round the ground, which consisted of several very large fields, with some thick hedges and trees, in a slight dip.

The battalion came in sight: a few carriers, followed by a column of marching men, a thousand yards away. Then there was the usual hum, quickly becoming louder, and down came twenty-four shells half-way between us, which greatly increased my anxiety lest we should get many casualties before we were dug in. This stonk was followed by heavy concentrations on Guillerville, Cagny and the road leading into it. However, the battalion arrived safely and lost no time in getting below ground.

I had felt rather jumpy all day and wondered if it was the result of smoking too much.

That night we were told to send out a reconnaissance patrol. I sent a young Canadian officer, Glass, with a corporal and a private. My orders to them were that they should return through the King's Shropshire Light Infantry on the left, whom we took good care to inform. The K.S.L.I. warned one of their companies, but the patrol strayed rather too far to the left, came in on the front of another and were shot up. Corporal Bruce was killed and the other man wounded.

Next morning I was up at 4 a.m. and round the battalion at 'stand-to'. At 5.30 the Brigadier arrived (to judge my form?) and walked round two companies with me. In a deserted Hun dug-out there was an opened bottle of Sauterne and, after tasting it rather tentatively, we both took a swig at it. It had gone sour but the bitter taste was oddly clean and refreshing.

Later a very heavy concentration, at least a hundred heavy-calibre shells, came down on the Warwicks in Guillerville. I was by this time quite confident that we were not under observation, and as the whole battalion was in open fields and away from features that would be marked on German maps, it seemed that we should not get much shelling. My H.Q. was a dug-out in the middle of some standing corn. After breakfast, just as I was going to turn in for some sleep, another patrol was ordered for that night. I used to hate sending out these patrols and wondered if this one was really essential. Did the higher command, before ordering one, carefully consider whether the information which might be obtained was worth risking the life of a good young officer or N.C.O.?

We had another air-raid about 11 p.m. The parachute flares

and A.A. red tracer were a most beautiful sight, and one felt pretty safe peering out at it from inside one's slit-trench. Later we were lightly shelled, most of it falling short.

I went round the battalion from 5 a.m. and returned to find that the doctor, Thom, was killed during the night. He was rather a lone wolf and always slept away from other people, and one shell landed inside his dug-out. Nobody knew about it until his servant went to call him. He had been with the battalion since the night before El Alamein and was immensely popular. We buried him that afternoon at the edge of the corn, with ten representatives from each company, and the Pipe-Major playing 'Flowers of the Forest', the customary burial lament. I breathed a sigh of relief when it was safely over, for sixty or seventy men bunched together was asking for trouble.

Next morning there was two hours' artillery preparation for the Canadian attack, followed by a Typhoon strafe. In spite of this the Germans fought hard and we heard a lot of small-arms fire, and once a Canadian officer on the R/T saying that he was held up by mortar fire coming from the far end of a village.

We had another air-raid just after dark but most of the bombs fell in no-man's land or on the enemy forward positions. About midnight the duty officer woke me to say that a squadron of enemy tanks were reported two miles in front of us and advancing towards us. Tanks are very blind at night so I had no anxieties for the moment, and thought that perhaps they were getting into position to support a dawn attack. I checked up once again on our mortar and artillery S.O.S. tasks and told the duty officer to wake me and all company commanders at 3.40 a.m. with a view to special alertness from 4 a.m., fifteen minutes before the normal time for 'stand-to'. Then I turned in again.

Every time one left one's dug-out it got full of mosquitoes, and once more I had to go through the drill of burning them up with a torch of paper; then, after singeing my eyebrows and almost setting my bedding alight, I closed the trapdoor and went round again with a torch, swatting a few hardy survivors.

20

This done, I got into my bedding roll and smothered my hands and face with mosquito cream.

No sooner was this elaborate ritual completed than the duty officer popped his head in to say that there were a lot of flares coming up from the enemy lines, so out I had to go again. And so there were, for the Hun was feeling jittery, but I could not order shelling where the lights were coming up from because our patrol was still out in front. Later the patrol commander came in to say that they had been caught in the bombing and one of the men with him had been hit in the head and stretcher-bearers were required.

In the morning we were relieved as the result of regrouping, and marched back to Ranville.

Soon after lunch there we got heavily stonked. Thirty or forty shells landed in a very small compass and we had nine casualties, including Dowson, second-in-command of D Company and a fine chap, badly wounded in the stomach. Luckily there was an Advanced Dressing Station within fifty yards of where Dowson was hit, and they had him on the operating table in no time, which saved his life.

It seemed a good moment to send four officers off on forty-eight hours' leave to Bayeux, one of whom was Ian Glennie, a magnificent young company commander, who had a narrow escape two days before when a shell splinter smashed his pocket-watch. Three weeks later he was wounded by mortar fire. Although bleeding from five or six different wounds, he refused to be sent back in a jeep, saying that others were in greater need. While walking back he collapsed from loss of blood. He has never been decorated.

On one of these evenings we had Retreat, with 'The Road to the Isles', 'The Skye Boat Song', and all my favourite tunes. It was a brave display, the pipe band marching and counter-marching in a tiny paddock beside the main road, with ammunition trucks and ambulances slowing down to see what they could while passing. Most of the time the guns in the field

21

beyond were firing over our heads. The officers of the battalion, in their kilts, stood on the mounds of earth excavated from trenches, and the men sat around in their shirt-sleeves. The only person who wasn't happy was myself because of the risk of a lot of casualties from the one odd shell.

For supper we had an excellent sirloin of a cow killed in the shelling, and a guest in the person of Maurice Burnett, who commanded 127 Field Regt. R.A., which had supported this Brigade since the start of the desert campaign. He was saying what a bad show it was that an Airborne and a Commando Brigadier, Kindersley and Lovat, had been badly wounded by one troop of our own artillery firing short, and how difficult it is to find out who is responsible when this happens as everybody checks and covers up on receiving the signal 'Report elevation fired.' It is the one unforgivable sin, but one must be philosophical when it happens and forgive the occasional human error as the benefit one receives from the guns is so immense. Colonel Burnett said that our superiority of artillery was about forty to one, and that most of the German guns were immobile as the enemy had only one tractor to about four guns, and a great shortage of petrol. If this were so, it was the R.A.F. we had to thank for it.

The new Divisional Commander arrived: Major-General Thomas Rennie. He was a Black Watch who escaped in 1940 after the Division had to capitulate at St. Valery, and subsequently commanded a battalion and then a brigade of the reformed Highland Division in North Africa. He was wounded commanding 3rd Division soon after D-Day. Everybody was delighted with the appointment.

We spent two days at Ranville. There was a good deal of sporadic shelling, so we were glad to move out, though only to the usual open fields: A Company in the mustard, B in the wheat, C in the roots, etc. There was no building in the whole area, but it would be all right if the weather held as it was further back. Everybody could relax, instead of wondering if they were going to be shelled any minute, which was always so tiring.

One wished that it were possible to arrange more recreation for the men. I felt sure all the rear H.Q.s and people far from the battlefront had plenty of mobile cinemas, concert parties, etc. The only pleasure resort was 'Nobby's Bar', where men could buy chocolate, soap, tooth-paste, etc., nothing very exciting. I sent parties off to the seaside, but there was nothing for them to do there except bathe. I also tried to buy some cider so as to get a reading-room and canteen open.

This gave me an excuse to visit Caen, and there I found a friend in Colonel Usher, a Gordon Highlander who was in charge of Civil Affairs there, who promised to provide some. There was awful desolation from our bombing. Usher said there were 1,000 killed and 2,000 wounded, and 600 bodies were still buried under the debris; there was certainly an unhealthy stench there.

Fortunately the cathedral was only slightly damaged – far less than St. Paul's – and we made a pilgrimage to the tomb of William the Conqueror, 1066-1087. Caen was then still under shellfire so the shops and restaurants were closed and all activities had come to a full stop.

A film show was organised in the rear and some of us went to see *The Lodger*, but it was not much fun. The marquee was not dark enough for a successful film show and the seats consisted of ration boxes. Even the unaccustomed smell of powder and scent that wafted back from a row of Canadian nursing sisters in front did not adequately compensate for my numb bum.

On July 31st the new Colonel, Blair-Imrie, arrived. He was five years younger than me but had had five times more battle experience, having fought through the desert campaign and out here since D-Day.

So after lunch I returned to 1st Gordons at Anguerny, and was delighted to be once more with Harry and Co. Some of them were off to Bayeux and I went with them. Never had I

seen a place so crowded with troops. It was far worse than
Salisbury on a Saturday night, and the cathedral not so fine. Hot
and dusty, we went to the Lion D'Or for a wash. It had been
taken over by the Press, but we found that even they were living
in some squalor and discomfort. When I saw 'Information' I
thought that a charming French girl would tell me what was
what, but the bureau was staffed by a military policeman. 'The
only place to eat in is the N.A.A.F.I.,' he said. However, I found
a small restaurant and shared a table with two young reinforcement officers who had arrived from England that afternoon.
They were very curious to know what war is like and I fear I
shot a bit of a line.

We drove back in an open jeep, racing the gathering darkness.
At Fontaine-Henry we passed a castle straight out of Grimm's
fairy tales, and it was something of an anti-climax to read a large
notice outside which said that it was now a dental centre.

Carrier

2

August 1st brought big news. The Highland Division was to be the spearhead of the coming break-through south-east of Caen.

I spent the first part of the morning inspecting transport, after which I attended one of Harry's twenty-minute talks to each company, a tactical discussion, and at 1.30 p.m. a talk by the Brigadier. Then after a hurried lunch I drafted some notes on battle discipline for Harry and went out to help judge the Regimental Games, as sports in a Scottish unit are always called. C Company won, and its commander, the handsome and charming Bruce Rae, looked the very personification of a Highland officer as he stepped forward to get his prize. The games were followed by Retreat, from which we all went to Brigade H.Q. for a drink. After supper I helped Harry write some citations for awards. A few more days like this, I thought, and I would be glad to get into battle for a rest.

Auguerny is a nice little village, or rather cluster of farms with a school and one shop. The weather was heavenly, which was just as well as nearly all the troops were sleeping out in slit-trenches. We had a visit from an officer of Corps H.Q., who asked if we didn't know that it was forbidden to use crops for camouflage purposes and to line the bottom of dug-outs (for warmth). The Adjutant tartly replied that he was our first visitor of any kind from Corps H.Q. They still seemed to think that we were out on an exercise.

A steady stream of British aircraft flew over and returned that evening. We wondered where they had been.

In company with several thousand others I had a bathe in the sea one afternoon. As far as I could see, total war or not, they all had a bathing dress on except two, of which I was one. On the way back I took David Martin to the dentist and so caught a glimpse of the two tented General Hospitals, 80 and 88. The nurses were very sensibly dressed in khaki silk shirts, drill trousers and bandeaux round their heads. There was an airfield next door, and many of the wounded reached England on the same day that they had been hit. We got back in time to see the end of the inter-company football final. While watching it we heard a mine explode not far away and wondered what unlucky chap had caught it.

We understood that things were going very well (though we were not quite sure what things), so well that some of the timings had been advanced, which meant that we would move next day.

The confidence we all felt in the future was wonderful. It was the produce of faith in the generalship, in our own Division and in Second Army. The Battle of El Alamein marked a turning-point in the fortunes of the British Army, a landmark in its history which will always be associated with the name of General Montgomery. Since El Alamein the Army had never doubted that each operation would end successfully. Nor could morale in any Division have been higher.

The strength of the Highland Division lay firstly in the regular Highland officers, 'from the oldest families in Scotland', as Ian Morrison wrote of the Argylls in Malaya. Coming as a Scots Fusilier from a Lowland regiment I cannot be accused of prejudice in holding the opinion that the pre-war Highland officers were, with the Foot Guards, Green Jackets and some cavalry regiments, the pick of the Army. This was due to the fact that each of these regiments always had the choice of a very large number of candidates for commissions. In spite of the losses of

26

five years of war, ninety per cent of the infantry commanders and principal staff officers of the Division came from these regular soldiers who went from Sandhurst into the Black Watch, Seaforths, Gordons, Camerons and Argylls.

The second source of strength was the fine type of pre-war Territorial officers who commanded most of the companies and batteries in the Division at that time. The quality of the company commanders is of immense importance as nearly every operation is a succession of company battles. Normally the battalion commander fights with one, or at the most two companies at a time, while the rest are firm.

The third source of strength was, of course, the magnificent type of man that you get from Scotland, whether he comes from the glens or the straths, the fields or the coalface, the towns or the cities.

Bert, our doctor, was confident that we should be in Paris in ten days. Certainly the Hun had failed to contain us in our little peninsula and the front he now had to try to hold was already doubled in length.

On August 6th we moved down to Grentheville, starting at 9.30 p.m. The men were in troop-carriers, which were followed by our own column of transport. It was pitch dark going through Caen and the dust made it worse. Except for a few traffic-control policemen, the streets were empty, and it was very hard to follow the little green lamps which marked our route. I thought what a mess up there would be if somebody took a wrong turning as everybody behind would follow. A mile short of the village we got out and walked, so as not to risk a lot of men being hit in a troop-carrier if the enemy shelled the village just as we were coming in. Battalion H.Q. was in a small, old farmhouse, tucked in among buildings and dark alleyways. It was too close to the cross-roads for my liking, though the ramification of walls and buildings promised some protection.

We took over from a Canadian battalion and they told us what they could of the form there. Most of the shelling was directed at a lone château three hundred yards away, they said, so this we decided to leave severely alone. I did a turn of duty officer from 3 a.m. till 5 a.m. and then went round with Harry at 'Stand-to'. Many of D Company had no equipment on, and A's and C's trenches few good fire positions. B had no latrines and two platoons no proper field of fire and no sentries. Harry, I thought, was too kind. On the other hand, everybody loved him so much that they always tried desperately hard whenever any test came, so he produced good results just the same.

We were sharply shelled several times next morning, then David Martin, the Intelligence Officer, spotted that this always happened when a car raised a cloud of dust coming into Grentheville; so he posted a sentry to tell them to take it more slowly, and it was quiet after that. But we expected a lot of enemy gunfire when the bombing of La Hogue and Secqueville-la-Campagne would take place, so we moved Battalion H.Q. three hundred yards back from the cross-roads. Our artillery superiority had altered the whole conduct of the war; without it we should not have been able to sit in these few obvious villages like we did.

The bombing started at 11 p.m. and our barrage at 11.45 p.m. that night. There was a little harassing fire; two or three shells landed in the village, killing one man and wounding two others. The bombing lasted an hour, and as the targets were only three miles from us we heard it pretty plainly, though the cotton-wool we had been given for our ears was unnecessary. Nor did any of it land amongst us.

The next day started with the news that the other two Brigades had got all their objectives except a village called Tilly-la-Campagne, which was still holding out. We left Grentheville in twenty-seven Priests (armoured troop-carriers), with everybody protected except one or two jeep drivers at the back.

Our route took us through the Polish Armoured Division, and there we stopped for a time, in the middle of an open plain. Then Harry came up and told me that we were to attack

Secqueville-la-Campagne at 4 p.m., that he was going to choose a start line behind Garcelles, which the Camerons had just captured, and that I was to bring forward the battalion.

So I drove off in a Priest with the company commanders to look for a place where we could debus and feed. We had a jolting journey across country, six or eight of us all standing with our elbows on the edge of the armoured cupola. We crossed another huge plain and saw mines and brewed-up tanks and carriers at the side of the track. In front was Rocquancourt, and we could see shells crumping down on it; we chose some cornfields, not too close to it, for companies to disperse.

On the way back a monster shell exploded only fifty yards from us, but nothing rattled against our tin hide; they say that the bigger the shell the poorer the fragmentation, and perhaps that is so. I was always nervous and unhappy when troops were bunched, as when they were getting out of trucks and forming up to move off. However, in spite of my anxiety, which was aggravated by periodical shelling of the area, they all got dispersed safely by about 1 p.m. and began to dig in. There had been a muddle over the H.Q. officers' food so I felt very hungry, but a Canadian officer insisted on giving me a bar of chocolate.

Then a message from Harry: Company commanders to be just short of Garcelles two miles away at 2.30 and the battalion to be there by 3.30. So at two I sent the company commanders and specialist officers off in two jeeps to get their orders, and soon after began to follow at the head of the marching battalion.

I led off out of the cornfield and on to the tarmacadam with my servant, Graham, and two signallers carrying wireless sets in contact with the companies, the leading one of which was at my heels. Down the main road we went. It was raised on an embankment and there were no trees or hedges on either side. The road and verges were much pitted by shell craters and I felt very naked. As soon as I could, I turned off left and across a field, five hundred fighting men, well-dispersed, following behind me. Then I heard the awful groaning of Moaning Minnie (multi-barrel mortars) and looked round to hear the crack and see the burst as some twenty smackers landed just about where we had left the main road. But, as luck would have it, they came down between two companies. The Camerons' carrier platoon, digging in just there, had some casualties.

We crossed the stubble and entered a leafy lane, and there in the middle of it I found the General: a tall, rather heavy figure wearing a tam o' shanter with the red hackle of the Black Watch. He pointed out ground where I could get the battalion dispersed and which had not hitherto been shelled.

The General was looking very glum. 'I'm afraid there will not be much artillery to support this attack,' he said. 'The Americans have bombed our gun lines near Caen and Colombelles with forty-eight Fortresses.'

I walked up the lane and found Harry giving out his orders in an empty garage beside a ruined farmhouse. I found a corner and sat down in it. The orders were of necessity somewhat complicated. The company commanders asked for the time to be put back till 5 p.m., and even then they were late.

My job was to bring up the mortars and anti-tank guns when Harry called for them, but he soon got out of wireless touch. I walked down into Garcelles to try to read the battle. There seemed to be a good deal of shelling coming both ways and I couldn't tell what was happening. So I nipped back, got a carrier and ran up to see Harry. I found him with his Tac H.Q. at a hedge junction just short of Secqueville. The earth all around was scorched, burnt out by our flame-throwers. He told me that all the companies were on their objectives except one and that I could send up the anti-tank guns, but that the most important thing was to see to the evacuation of our wounded who were now going back in jeeps, some sitting up, some lying on stretchers.

Back in Garcelles I found the Aid Post in a mill: a solid round tower standing alone in the middle of the village square. About twenty wounded were lying in the straw. The doctor, Bert Brown, the Padre, Ewen Traill, and the medical sergeant were working away quietly and efficiently, while two orderlies carried the stretchers in and out and gave cigarettes and cups of strong, sweet tea to those who were awaiting attention.

As I waited for a word with the doctor, who was putting a sergeant's leg into a Thomas's splint while an orderly gave him a sniff of chloroform, Ewen called me over. Mitchell, a sub-altern, terribly shattered by a Minnie shell, had just been brought in with one arm and one leg half severed. But such must have been the shock that he felt no pain. The morphia, which a chinagraph scribble on his forehead recorded, had not yet begun to take effect, and he chatted away as brave as could be. His leg had begun to bleed badly, one of the dressings having slipped, and Ewen bade me press a pad on it till more expert attention was available. Then, to my astonishment, he opened his jack-knife and quickly cut through the inch or two of sinew and flesh by which the arm was hanging. Mitchell felt nothing.

Bert said he was short of ambulances, and could I do something about it quickly? He whispered that some of the badly wounded would not live unless they could be got back speedily to where they could be operated upon. Nothing loath, for I wished to see no more surgery, I went outside and across to the Camerons, who lent us three jeeps for the purpose.

I found Battalion H.Q. digging rapidly in a corner of a field just outside Secqueville. Harry told me that the companies had reported twenty-seven casualties, very few considering what a lot of mortaring and shelling there had been. We took sixty-five prisoners. One said they had had no rations for five days; they certainly looked a poor lot.

It was a lovely summer evening and everybody was in excellent spirits.

It had been a great day for the Highland Division and all our objectives were taken. Only Tilly gave much trouble, and the

31

second of the two Seaforth battalions had to be put in to complete its capture. These two battalions had eighty-odd casualties between them in taking the place, but they killed a large number of Germans and took 150 prisoners, including five officers.

The Polish Armoured Division was in front of us, but we could not find out where they had got to. David said that they never sent back any information and only came back when they wanted to draw more rations.

At six next evening we were put at one hour's notice, while Harry and the Brigadier went off to recce St. Sylvain, though they were not able to do much as the Poles were still attacking.

At 11.30 p.m. the Priests arrived but we didn't move off till one. I shall always remember that moonlight drive through several ghostly, shattered villages. When I thought about it I was slightly apprehensive: only four hours left till daylight and we had to find our way to the place, take over, and be in position ready to repel a counter-attack in that time. But I did not let it worry me for long for I found these moves into battle, whether on foot or in a vehicle, strangely exhilarating. I only hoped that this would last.

Harry met us on the way. The Poles had reported a very tough fight but had captured St. Sylvain, he said. We were to debus three miles short of it, as he didn't want the noise of tracks to reach the enemy. He jeeped ahead with the company commanders, leaving me to bring up the battalion.

We reached the edge of the town at 3.30 a.m., but there was no sign of the company guides and the first light of dawn began to appear in the east. Eventually the company commanders arrived. The Poles were all drunk, they said, so there could be no proper take-over. We trickled into the place by companies, and by the time we began to dig in it was broad daylight. We worked feverishly to get the anti-tank guns and machine-guns into position and the mortars laid on to defensive tasks, but we might have saved ourselves the trouble for the expected counter-attack never came. There was a great clatter of transport and a huge column of dust as the last of the Poles, driving much too fast, left the town, and sure enough down came the shells.

As soon as we were more or less firm we began to breathe more comfortably and to look around us and adjust our positions. Battalion H.Q. had been hurriedly established in a cow-barn, almost the first building we found as we entered the town. We now moved forward to the former German H.Q., a biggish house in the main street. The actual command post, with the maps, wireless sets and telephones, was established in a big dug-out in the garden, and we used the house to feed and sleep in.

The first shell arrived while we were having lunch outside in the sun. I could not understand how nobody was hit as it burst in the garden about twenty yards from us. After that there was a lot of shelling and we wondered if we had been foolish to have chosen such an obvious place as the former German H.Q. While looking for a good house I walked all over the town north of the main street (the Black Watch were holding the south side of it) and saw no sign of the very severe fighting of which the Poles spoke. To be precise, I found four dead Huns and three dead Poles. The latter were a Platoon H.Q. – officer, sergeant and wireless operator, looking as lifelike as three wax figures. They were still sitting upright, leaning back against the wall, the operator holding the microphone in front of his mouth. They had been killed instantly by a shell which burst against the wall above them.

Then David Martin, who was always indefatigable, came in to say that with a telescope and from a roof he had seen Germans eating their dinners in a field 3,000 yards away, so we turned the gunners on to them. About the same time somebody pointed out an enemy observation post built in a tree. The Battery Commander said he would shoot it down; we all stood on the roof of the command post to watch this performance,

33

but the meeting was quickly broken up when shells began to come back at us.

Then somebody started a scare that the enemy were forming up to attack; they were coming through a cornfield 1,200 yards away. It was awfully hard to see as the sun was shining so brightly on the corn that there was a kind of mirage or heat haze. But we easily persuaded ourselves that the enemy were indeed advancing towards us. So we 'stood-to' and fired the artillery and mortars for all we were worth. Meanwhile I was going round Battalion H.Q. supervising the fighting positions of all the odd signallers, clerks, policemen and batmen, while the R.S.M. followed behind issuing grenades. Without any doubt, there was one German tank in the corn. We could see it as plain as a house and asked the gunners to fire a 'victor' target (every gun within range). So bang went several thousand pounds and down came the stuff and the tank withdrew. I don't believe there was ever anything there except this one tank doing a reconnaissance.

The Huns had evacuated all the inhabitants with them. Presumably it was thought that they knew too much about their dispositions. There had been a lot of enemy here, and their withdrawal was premeditated as they had left nothing behind, not even so much as a box of matches.

We 'stood-to' from 10 p.m. but no attack developed. We 'stood-down' physically at 11.15 p.m., and mentally also at midnight when 154 Brigade passed through us to attack the ridge beyond.

There was a lot of shelling during the night, especially at about 4 a.m., when about forty shells landed on top of our house and in the garden all around. The big elm beside the command post and the wall behind it were badly knocked about. The only casualty was the Battery Commander's signaller, who was sleeping in the armoured scout-car, hit in the foot by a splinter which went through the steel door. I felt very secure down in the cellar.

34

Shelling started again at 7 a.m. and continued intermittently.

The day proper started with the news that Nap Murray had got a Division in Italy, which meant that Harry was temporarily commanding the Brigade and I the battalion. This information galvanised me into immediate activity and I went round the whole battalion and had a good strafe about small points like alertness, camouflage and cleanliness.

When I got back for a late breakfast we heard that 154 Brigade's attack last night was most successful and that they took all their objectives, but 7th Argylls had fifty-six casualties, all handled by Bert in our R.A.P. Their doctor was a newcomer who had not yet learnt the form, and when the casualties occurred was on the move forward with nowhere to treat them. When last seen he was digging feverishly in a potato field.

The Poles made an awful mess of things that morning. Their Reconnaissance Regiment, which was milling about in front of 154 Brigade all night, turned round and fled back through them in disorder at first-light. This brought down a murder stonk on 154, and the Black Watch and Argylls had another sixty-five casualties, including seven officers.

At noon the news was not so hot. 154 Brigade had been counter-attacked and the enemy had got into one of their company positions. The next thing we heard, from a Canadian major who dropped in to lunch, was that the Canadians to the south had taken a bad knock from 12 S.S. Division and lost fifty-three out of sixty-five tanks. One regiment lost the C.O. and all its squadron commanders.

This tank reverse, by no means the first, was to add fresh heat to the tank-design controversy. One frequently heard how inferior our tanks were to the Huns'. Their Tigers and Panthers were so heavily armoured that they were exceedingly difficult to knock out, whereas our Shermans brewed-up with the first direct hit. The result was that our tank crews had a definite inferiority complex, and who could blame them? Dick Stokes had raised the matter time and again in Parliament and had always been snubbed.

I was up early and round the whole battalion at 'stand-to' except A Company, who were back in bed by the time I got there.

There had been more shelling that day and the Colonel of the Divisional Anti-tank Regiment was hit driving through the town in his jeep. We had a discussion as to how many shells had landed in St. Sylvain in two days, and the general estimate was about 2,000. Yet there were less than fifty casualties among the 2,000 troops in the place.

That morning James Oliver, who commanded 154 Brigade, took me up in his armoured car to see the two Black Watch battalions on the wooded ridge in front. We found that 7th Black Watch H.Q. was overlooked from a ridge 1,000 yards away to the left, and a few snipers on it were making a nuisance of themselves, so the Brigadier ordered an artillery shoot along the top of it. The two battalions were well dug in. I could not but notice how nice the red hackle of the Black Watch looks. That little touch of scarlet on a tam o' shanter has every metal cap-badge in the service beat. Hardly anybody in this division wore a tin hat except when actually attacking, and then not always.

From 7th Black Watch we went to 1st Black Watch, and found the Colonel stark naked, having a bath in front of his command post. They had a lot of shelling during the night, but only one casualty, caused by a direct hit on a slit-trench. Some tanks were hidden among the trees, and the Brigadier had a chat with Cracroft, their Colonel, who was killed by shell-fire half an hour after we had left. There was a small German cemetery in the area: about twenty large Maltese crosses with the swastika in the centre of each. Most of the dates were of a fort-night earlier. One very seldom saw German graves; it was said that they are not thought good for morale so the Hun usually cheated, burying half a dozen in each individual grave. As we

36

walked around we talked to some of the men, who were shaving or breakfasting; one was washing in a German steel helmet. We passed a gruesome sight, a corpse half-buried but with the two arms sticking out of the ground in a supplicating attitude.

On August 15th we got orders to move out and occupy Glatigny, about two miles away, the armour being some distance beyond it. I went on ahead to choose the company areas.

I saw 154 Brigade H.Q. and stopped to pass the time of day. It was about this time that the Lancasters started to bomb the gun lines behind us. For one hour this went on and everybody was powerless to stop it.

Glatigny seemed to be under enemy observation because first the tanks on the far side of the village and then the village itself, just after we had entered it, got heavily and accurately shelled, though I was hanged if I could see where the observation was from, unless it was a village, one of the many Le Mesnils, on the left.

I took some of my party down a lane running along a ridge leading out of the village. Suddenly there was the usual whistle in crescendo which signalled a covey of shells on the way. With one accord we all lay flat and heard them landing all round us. Then there was a particularly loud crack as a shell burst twelve feet away – I paced out the distance later. I thought it was in the road beside me, for the dust was such that we were in pitch darkness for what seemed a minute, and our nostrils were choked with cordite – or whatever the bursting charge may be – so that it was some hours before I could rid myself of the acrid smell. I could hear somebody whimpering in the darkness behind me and Donald Howorth shouting, 'Lie still, you bloody fool.' When I could see I found that the Signal Sergeant, Rae, was dead, and the R.S.M., Thomson, slightly wounded in the head but bleeding profusely, and Howorth was tying him up. He himself had a few punctures in his thigh. Only Petrie, second-in-command of C Company, and myself were untouched.

I went back along the track to where there were, most conveniently, some empty slits dug by 2nd Seaforths, who had just moved out. I told the company commanders to put their men into them, and that we would not occupy Glatigny until dark as I thought it was under enemy observation.

The companies moved off successively, starting soon after 9 p.m. There had been no shelling for three hours, which I took to mean that the Germans were moving their guns back. Of this I was glad, because 152 were about to attack on our right.

Whenever any unit was involved in battle I always thought of my friends and hoped to God they would come through safely. Thus I thought of Richard Fleming and Charm and their three young children, as I plodded along in the gloaming across the stubble that led to Glatigny, and wished that any other battalion but 5th Seaforths were attacking that night. Most people seemed able to accept casualties, which was just as well; but for my part I could never overlook the tragedy that each one meant to some far away, stricken home. The sadness of it all was always with me.

About eleven the Luftwaffe paid us a visit. They dropped a cluster of parachute flares and then started anti-personnel bombing. Each Aircraft let loose a thousand or so of these tiny bombs, each hardly larger than a stick of shaving soap. One could hear the swish as the shower came through the air, and then the steady drumming as they exploded. Unfortunately D Company, the last to arrive, had only dug down about eighteen inches by this time and they had twenty-three casualties. Most were only lightly wounded, but two were killed and one of them was Glass, a young Canadian officer who had come to us ten days before.

After breakfast I laid on a plot to clear Le Mesnil, so that there should be no more doubt about observation on Glatigny, but had to cancel it on getting orders to concentrate 1st Gordons at Percy for an attack that afternoon. Just as we were moving off we got word that we had lost thirteen out of sixteen trucks in the R.A.F. bombing, though luckily no men.

The absurd thing was that there was no direct ground to air communication which could have stopped it at once. The channel of communication was Division – Corps – Army – Army Group – Supreme H.Q. – Air Ministry – Bomber Command – Group – R.A.F. Station (or something very like it), so no wonder it took over an hour to get through. Like the bombing by the Fortresses on August 8th, it was quite inexcusable for we were still close to the great industrial city of Caen, which stands up like Manchester in the middle of the Sahara, and visibility had been perfect each time.

In Percy the companies dispersed and got under cover in farm buildings. I was talking to Harry at the main crossroads when there was a stupendous bang fifty yards away, and the whole church tower came crashing down in a huge grey cloud of smoke. Out of it, after a few minutes, emerged Maurice Burnett, the Field Regiment Colonel, looking like I don't know what – smothered in grey dust from head to foot. He had been standing in the porch, the arch of which fortunately held, and he was untouched. Alan Brockie, another gunner officer, had blown himself up on a booby-trap when he went up the tower to get a better view. It was very sad as he was one of the old sweats who had gone the whole way through the desert with the Division and everybody was fond of him.

I tied up everything with great care and we got off at 5 p.m.: A Company, under Jim Robertson, in the lead with a squadron of tanks, then myself in my carrier with the wireless sets, and B following behind.

Our orders were to go as far as we reasonably could, though it was thought that we should be held up before very long by one or other of a series of bridges being blown. The column went on and disappeared down a long, tree-covered lane. I had been unable to see anything when I had tried to recce earlier, and now all I could see were the backs of the last men of A Company H.Q. halted in front of me. I heard Spandau fire, then the Brownings of the tanks, then silence, and I called up Jim and said, 'Why can't you get on?'

The leading tank reported that the first bridge was blown, then all the tanks started to get ditched until seven out of ten were bogged. I asked the squadron commander to send a troop off to recce another bridge to the right.

There had been mortar fire in front, and now the wounded began to come back in jeeps: some men with blood-soaked dressings on their stomachs, and their privates exposed where the trousers had been cut away. Wounded always came back like this down the axis of advance, to encourage as it were all the others waiting their turn to go up into battle. After an hour the tank troop had got nowhere, and the squadron commander admitted to me that the troop-leader was windy and useless. So I sent off a section on foot, who soon came back to say that this bridge was also blown.

Then Harry came up on the air and said that we should be moving in another direction next day, so we could come back to Percy. So we returned and I put everybody in barns and buildings with only one sentry in each company area. I then went down the village street to Brigade H.Q., intending to tell Harry that everybody was exhausted, having had little sleep last night at Glatigny since most of it was spent in digging, and that I hoped there would be no move tomorrow after all. But Charles Napier, the Brigade Major, forestalled me by saying that the other two battalions had had a worse time but were quite fit to go on next day. I thought he seemed very unsympathetic as I felt utterly exhausted, but there was no doubt that we had to keep cracking on, whatever we felt like, now that we had the Huns on the run.

August 17th was a tremendous day.

Troop-carriers arrived at 7 a.m. and I had them and all our own transport marshalled in a big meadow. Then, leaving Jim Robertson to bring on the battalion, I rushed off in my carrier, following Harry in his jeep. We seemed to be going a long way and in a south-east direction. Passing through St. Pierre, we saw French for the first time since Ranville, and they all waved madly at us. Beyond St. Pierre we stopped at a cross-roads just behind the Black Watch. At that moment the General arrived and Harry and he went into a huddle over the map.

Then Harry came back and told me that 1st Gordons' objective was St. Marais-aux-Anglais, a hamlet about four miles away to the east; we were to clear Deux Marais and some woods on the way there. As the tanks were still behind, I went on with a section of carriers as an escort, to recce the first part of the route.

All the French we passed came running out with garlands of flowers, milk and wine. They all tried to be very helpful with information about the Germans. They pointed out a farm with three soldiers in it, but *pas méchants*, they said, and we collected them on the way. Soon we were stopped by two dead horses blocking the line, so, leaving two carriers to clear them away, I returned to give out orders near the cross-roads. Just as I had begun to do so an old Frenchman thrust himself upon us. There was a dead Mongolian German on his farm, he said, and was it permitted to bury him?

One or two shells were coming down around us, and once or twice we flattened ourselves for a moment or two. Then the Luftwaffe came over, about twenty fighters streaking back to the Fatherland just as fast as they could fly. They were very low overhead, and I managed to fire off the best part of one Bren magazine at them as they passed.

In due course we started off. Deux Marais was just a church, a school and a farm or two, and once through it we shook out into three parallel company columns, each with a troop of tanks for the wood-clearing we had been ordered to do.

Soon afterwards I heard firing on the left, and, after a lot of difficulty as the country was so close, managed to find D Company H.Q. Murray Reekie was upset as he had lost the whole of one platoon. It had been caught by cross-fire from two light automatics, the platoon commander, Sergeant Walker, had been killed and the three section commanders wounded. The men, leaderless and with several killed and wounded, had disappeared in the undergrowth and had not been seen since. The woods were much thicker than we expected and the tanks were finding difficulty in getting through. There was still quite a lot of small-arms fire but we did not stop.

In a little while, rather to my surprise, I found myself leading the advance in my carrier, with my finger very much on the trigger of the Bren, driving up the approach to the Château of St. Marais-aux-Anglais.

As quickly as possible the four companies moved out into defensive positions, while awaiting the arrival of the vehicles. The ground rose sharply to a wooded ridge beyond the Château and I felt somewhat insecure with two companies perched precariously on the edge of it and the rest of us below. Moreover, I felt sure that the enemy must have observation from that ridge, and sure enough down came repeated heavy concentrations upon the track through the wood along which all our mortars, anti-tank guns, machine-guns, jeeps, carriers and the ambulance had to come. I felt desperately sorry for them, but there was nothing I could do about it except tell the gunners to shoot at every known enemy battery. I have no doubt that there was a good deal of quiet bravery on the part of certain officers who kept the column trickling forward down that bad and difficult track.

Meanwhile there were still a few pockets of Spandau boys in the woods we had passed through. We had to send out one or two small parties of tanks and infantry to round them up. Gallop, the mortar officer, and his platoon sergeant were unfortunately both wounded in taking some prisoners. They played the old trick of waving white flags, then shooting when those two began to walk over towards them, though indeed they should both have known better.

It was a relief when I felt that things were sufficiently far advanced to be able to enter the Château and sit down. It was a lovely place. There was an old tower built in the 15th century by the English who occupied Normandy during the Hundred Years' War until Joan of Arc turned us out, hence the name 'aux Anglais'. The tower was modernised with running water and electricity, and a 200-year-old farmhouse was built on to it.

Inside we found a large family and a number of refugees, and it was difficult to know who belonged to whom. They were very kind to us with gifts of wine, butter and eggs. Unfortunately one or two French working in the fields were hit during our advance, and they were carried into the Aid Post and evacuated along with our own wounded through our medical channels.

War is full of strange contrasts. I had to pass through the Aid Post on my way up to bed in the tower, and noticed a little ginger kitten asleep at the foot of a stretcher on which lay a corpse shrouded in the usual Army blanket.

In the morning we buried our dead under a tree in front of this beautiful château. I knew the graves would be well tended by these kind people. But I wished they could all be left to lie where they had been so tenderly placed by those who loved them, near where they fell. I hated the idea of their being dug up and reinterred in some military cemetery, where the grave-stones would remain for posterity and their bodies would be dressed by the right, regimented in death. Left where they now lay, they would have served for as long as was necessary as a reminder of the price that Britain paid to free Europe. Many would disappear in course of time, and that, too, was not to be regretted; thank goodness most of the graves of those who died more than a hundred years ago have long been obliterated.

That afternoon Harry gave out his orders at the side of the road. We broke up very quickly when an aircraft was heard about five miles away, for everybody was scared stiff of the R.A.F. All day the Typhoons had been strafing the roads behind us. The General and Harry twice had to get into a ditch that morning, and Jim Cassels had his Brigade H.Q. brought down on top of his head and his Brigade Major, John Thornton, killed.

The orders were for an assault crossing of the River Vie by 153 Brigade that night. 5-7th Gordons were to lead, then 5th Black Watch were to pass through and get on to a hill, the code name for which was Ben Nevis, then they were to occupy another piece of high ground on their left, Ben Lomond.

I got back to find a great scare at the Château as the gunners, God knows why, had fired one or two smoke-shells into the garden and somebody suggested this was to mark a bomb line for the R.A.F. While I gave out orders we all drank champagne, produced by our kind hostess.

There was a lot more champagne at supper and, feeling in mighty good form, I got into my carrier and went up to Harry's H.Q., in a concrete gun emplacement which looked more like a garage. The subsequent battle as I heard it over the R/T during the night was most dramatic. First the Colonel of 5-7th Gordons, Hugh Blair-Imrie, came up on the air and reported that the tanks were blocking the road. Then we heard that there was a lot of small-arms opposition in the area of the blown bridge, then that 5-7th Gordons were getting across all right. After this there was silence and I slept for half an hour. I woke up to hear Harry talking to the General on the phone.

'The one thing I cannot afford is to have the R.A.F. operating anywhere within fifty miles of me,' I heard him say.

Then an officer of the 5-7th came up on the set and said that Blair-Imrie had been killed. This was followed by the news that the bridging material was blocked on the road behind the tanks. I felt dreadfully sorry for Harry. He got up and went off to see what could be done. An hour later he returned to say that they had started to build the bridge and that he had just launched the Black Watch.

We heard some pretty heavy shelling and all went outside to listen. It was pitch dark. There was no doubt that it was coming down where the Black Watch were, and soon afterwards the news came over the air that their Colonel, Bill Bradford, was wounded, and the Battery Commander killed in addition to a number of others in Battalion H.Q.

Harry was not prepared to release us until 5th Black Watch were more or less firm, but as daylight was approaching I begged him to let us go so that we could cross the very open river valley under cover of darkness. At 6 a.m. we were put at thirty minutes' notice, and I rushed back to the Château and had the quickest shave and breakfast of my life, then back to Harry's H.Q. to get final orders while the battalion followed.

Here I met the General, who told me to cut transport down to the very minimum – two mortars, one anti-tank gun and an ammunition carrier was his suggestion – in order not to risk blocking the narrow lane leading down to the bridge if something was hit by a shell and brewed-up. So I peeled off a few superfluous vehicles into a field and off we went, Bruce Rae and C Company in the lead, then myself in my carrier. The wireless sets to companies were so unreliable that I always had to use despatch-riders, so two cocky wee Gordons, Lance-Corporal Hogg and Private Nichol, were following close behind me on motorbikes. Little did I know that both were to be killed before this foul day was over.

To my relief there was a thick ground mist and C Company got across without any trouble. I followed at their heels, but stopped in the lee of a small barn a hundred yards beyond the river, to await the other companies who had been told to start ten minutes after C.

There were a few Black Watch round the building and one of them moved a yard or two in front of it. There was a sharp crack, and he fell writhing on the ground in such agony that after a moment or two he had fainted, the bullet having hit him in the forearm and broken the bone. He is the only man whom I have ever seen in pain from a wound, the shock being normally so great that nothing much is felt for some hours.

I told the tanks to brass up the general direction from which

45

this shot had been fired, and sent the other two companies through as quickly as possible. Then, as soon as I had reported progress on the wireless to Brigade and ordered up the rest of the fighting vehicles, I jumped into my carrier and went up to the companies, passing a herd of eleven dead cows on the way.

Before long I came upon A and B Company Commanders, who were having a confab in an orchard, and they said that there were Spandaus firing to their left. Neither had heard any word of C Company. I told Jim Robertson that I would take one of the tank troops and go and look for C, and that he was to take the other and help A and B; the I.O. would remain with my carrier and follow on with the vehicles. Of course, the tanks should have started out with the companies instead of trying to catch up afterwards, but they had found it difficult to cross the river. I made an error in going off with this one troop of tanks. I had little enough control before, with the wireless to companies working so badly, but now I lost it all. I got the troop commander to let me ride in the co-driver's place. The inside of the tank was full of apples which had been knocked off the branches and fallen through the open hatches.

In due course we found C Company on their objective. Bruce said that there was an awkward Spandau firing away on the right, so I told him to take these tanks and deal with it. He pointed out that he was the only officer in that company, so I told him I would look after it until he came back, another error since I was supposed to be commanding a battalion and not a company. I collected them into a rather smaller area and started them digging.

Then B Company arrived, and Bill MacMillan said that A had been badly shot-up, and Johnny Grant and Needs had both been killed. Soon afterwards A Company arrived under Murray Reekie (A having absorbed the remainder of D two days ago). A and B now began to dig in alongside C on a razor-edge ridge.

At the bottom of a steep slope, and not much more than a

hundred yards behind the centre company, was a quarry into which I put Battalion H.Q.; the vehicles dispersed themselves all round the valley. Then, starting at about 2 p.m. and lasting for about thirty minutes, there was very heavy shelling of this area behind the crest. Three of our carriers were soon blazing away merrily. Unfortunately the driver of one was trapped in his seat, presumably wounded, and terrible were his shrieks as he realised that he was beginning to burn to death. The British soldier is always willing to take a big risk to save the life of a comrade, but so murderous was the shelling coming down at this time that all knew it would mean certain death to move from the slits and ditches in which they were lying, and nobody attempted it.

We lost Gordon Stewart, the anti-tank officer, killed, and nearly twenty N.C.O.s and men in this shelling. For a time we thought that Gordon Birss, who commanded S Company, had gone too as he had not passed through our Aid Post with the wounded, and there were five bodies which were unrecognisable as the result of the tree under which they were crouching receiving a direct hit. Later it transpired that he had gone through the Black Watch Aid Post.

The battalion seemed to me to be very shaken. I went to the wireless and asked Harry if I could have a company of 5-7th Gordons under my command, to thicken up the front. He said this was not possible, but that he could offer me an anti-tank battery instead. I said I would be glad to have them, provided that they came with their light automatics and rifles and left their guns behind, as the going was pretty bad.

I sent a dispatch rider back for various good types who at the moment were out of battle: the Padre, Pipe-Major, Pioneer officer and the Orderly Room Sergeant, who would be useful at Battalion H.Q. I had heard that the division on the left had been counter-attacked and to some extent driven back, and I was determined that this should not happen to us, so I went round the officers and told them that this was a test of character and we had to get a proper grip of the men. They were all excellent fellows and I soon realised that this was just what they were doing.

With some difficulty we hauled one or two anti-tank guns up the hill to supplement a troop of three Shermans who were already there, and which I was keeping in spite of an order to send them back to the rest of the regiment concentrating in rear.

Harry arrived just as I was beginning to feel neglected. He said that he had been very busy with 5th Black Watch, who had had a rather sticky time. Bill Bradford's wound was in the arm and not too bad. Harry was very upset about us having nearly fifty casualties, but said that everyone was very pleased with the Brigade.

The command post was in a cave fifteen feet wide and ten feet deep, with a wall of sandbags across the entrance. It was most comfortable, and I turned in, dead tired, for a night which would be all too short with 'stand-to' at 5.30 a.m.

There was a bit of a flap during the night as Bill Bradford, commanding the Black Watch, came up on the air at about nine to tell me that an attack was coming in on his left, i.e. between our two battalions. I thought it was probably no more than a German patrol, but took the precaution of firing the artillery. From just outside our command post we could see a tank on the crest of the hill, firing tracer at the Black Watch. They were all firing back like blazes but I told our companies not to do so unless they were actually attacked, so that the Hun would not be able to pin-point our positions. A little later we heard a succession of heavy stonks coming down not far off, and for a few moments I thought we were being fired at in preparation for an attack. However, it soon became clear that it was our own guns firing a programme for 'friends on left', as we said on the R/T when anxious not to give away an identification.

Next evening I was ordered to capture a hill three miles away by mid-day. Patrols sent out at first light all reported no enemy seen, so we moved off at 10.30 a.m. Meanwhile Harry had sent 5-7th Gordons through with some tanks, and before very long I came upon Colonel Jolly, who commanded 144 Regiment, R.A.C. I was a bit nervous on meeting him as I had disobeyed orders in not sending back that troop of tanks two nights ago; so I got all my excuses ready, but he did not refer to it. Then Harry arrived and told me to pass through 5-7th Gordons and take La Forge Vallée, two miles beyond, with a squadron of tanks in support.

I arranged for an artillery concentration and told the tanks that I wanted them to shoot at the objective from the right while we attacked from the left. Allan Jolly said he didn't want to interfere but he had seen lots of clever plans like this before and it wouldn't work. So when I gave out orders it was for the tanks and infantry to move together in sight of each other the whole time. We put in a tremendous attack, to find there was nobody there. As we were consolidating round the position there was a slight scare when enemy were reported coming round our left rear. I moved the reserve company towards that direction, but it proved to be only some Germans trying to give themselves up. Unfortunately somebody fired at them and they disappeared.

Apart from a couple of small farms and some cottages, La Forge Valleé consists of a large stud farm and training establishment. To my surprise, I found a note in Harry's handwriting pinned to the door of the office, which read, 'This place belongs to an Englishman. Respect it.' I went inside and looked at the photographs of horses and close finishes on the wall, and the saddles, bits and other tackle. A pile of bills (or maybe receipts) stood on the desk and I was intrigued to see that they were all made out to one Sam Ambler.

Meanwhile Battalion H.Q. was digging trenches in and around the yard and loose-boxes, and the mortars were setting themselves up in the stallion paddock. The command post itself was dug deep in the tan of the riding school. There was a

German equipment store here but no watches or field-glasses; only useless stuff like machine-gun parts, mortar tripods, anti-gas kit, pack saddlery. In fact it was all so useless that we thought we would do the right thing for once and get credit for reporting its location.

A young Frenchman who claimed to have taken fourteen German prisoners in the last two days came in after tea. He said he brought a message from Mr. Ambler, who with his French wife was living underground in a cavern not far away, to the effect that he was expecting me to visit him. I was so intrigued by this impertinent cave-dweller that, later in the evening, David Martin and I went to visit him.

Our guide led us to a narrow slit in the ground half-way down a steep slope. As we squeezed through it we saw a twinkle of light deep down in the bowels of the earth below. Gradually the passage opened wider till we could stand upright, and soon we found ourselves in huge halls and passages. There, living like Eskimos, in groups each of about half a dozen families, knee to knee, were fully a hundred people. In the central position, sitting like an Eastern potentate on a divan (of horse rugs) and sultan of this odd community, but blinking through the thick lenses of a pair of steel-framed spectacles, was the fabulous Mr. Ambler, once of Hoxton.

He promptly produced an excellent bottle of champagne which he said a German officer had given him to share with the first Englishman he met. We were not actually the first he had seen as five prisoners, the crew of a tank, and one of them badly burnt, had been confined for three days in his yard. His wife pushed food, including a roast chicken and two bottles of calvados, through the fence to them, he said. He was manager for an American called Strasburger, and the bloodstock in his charge was worth a quarter of a million. The horses were all out at grass, hidden away on small, obscure farmsteads. He had also some pedigree cattle which had not been so fortunate. The Germans had killed them all; sometimes they had only taken the shoulder off a beast, leaving the rest to rot.

That night it rained for the first time for weeks. Always will I remember and give thanks for the wonderful weather of that momentous summer.

We had a day of rest at the stud-farm with not a shell in the battalion area all day, though 154 Brigade in front were stopped by very heavy shelling and three times it came crashing down on the railway line half a mile to our left, where we had absolutely damn all.

Ten men had deserted from A Company the day before, just before we left for what looked like another battle. They had seen their company continuously reduced by casualties, including nine officers, three of whom went during the last three days. Now we heard that they all marched back together under a corporal carrying their arms and kit, so of course everybody who passed them on their way back thought it was quite in order. I wondered how far they would get.

August 22nd was my thirty-ninth birthday. That afternoon there was another surge forward and 1st Gordons, tailing rather behind, were told to find a place in a given area where we could rest for three or four days. We found a delightful spot consisting of small fields with nice leafy trees all round and a few pleasant orchards. I ordered the transport to come up and arranged for a distribution of N.A.A.F.I. packs, and applied for the mobile baths. There were lots of new potatoes and runner-beans there, and we managed to get a few eggs and negotiated for a goose. I lay on the grass in the sun, drinking gin while supper was being prepared. The weather once more was perfect and we thought we were going to have a lovely time there.

3

But the next day turned into one of the most miserable that I have ever known.

David as duty officer woke me at 4.30, and I thought a Panzer division at least was breaking through. He said that a message had just come in that I was required to meet Harry at the bridge in Lisieux at seven, and have one company down there at 7.30, and another at thirty minutes' notice from that time. This was because 5-7th Gordons, who were in the town, were having a spot of bother from snipers and an additional company or two might be a help to them.

I went down there at seven and found that the town had been badly bombed. All the centre of it was flat. Later in the day I heard that we bombed it on D-Day to prevent the Huns bringing reserves through it, after dropping leaflets to warn the inhabitants. But most of the leaflets drifted elsewhere and few took any notice of those that did arrive. Lisieux is a famous religious centre; the British will never bomb such a place, the French said.

I met Harry on the bridge which the sappers were just finishing, and we walked through two-thirds of the town without a shot being fired. The French told us that the Germans were holding a ridge on the far side of it, about three hundred yards from the last row of houses. Certainly we saw five of them running across in front of a bungalow on the hill four hundred yards away. I took a standing pot at them with a rifle.

Harry gave me some tanks and told me to take that high ground. So I told Jim Robertson, whose company had just arrived, to meet the tanks at the station and then move on to the hill. I sent some carriers back to fetch C and told Bruce to occupy the row of houses immediately facing the high ground, from which I hoped he would be in a position to support B company. I also sent back for A, and no sooner had it arrived than Harry gave it a job to do, to clean up another sector of the town. This took away my only reserve, though I am quite sure Harry would not have done so had I pointed this out.

The guts of the matter was that the 5-7th had walked into the town and occupied two-thirds of it with nothing more than slight opposition from snipers, and I did not appreciate that there was any change in the situation and that a full-scale battalion attack might be required of us. So in this way the battle got off on the wrong leg, and when this happens it is always difficult to retrieve the situation.

B and C Companies soon reported they were in difficulties, so I told Harry that I was going forward to see what was happening. There was a Corps stop on artillery firing beyond a certain grid line as 7th Armoured Division would be coming that way, and this in effect meant that we were forbidden to shoot at our objective. Harry now said I could use the guns, and I pointed out that this would mean withdrawing B and C, who were too close. He said I wasn't to do this as it would take too long, and that the important thing was to hurry.

I then set out in my carrier along the railway line, the route that B Company had taken. Before long we came to some points and the carrier got stuck, so, telling it to return and come round by another route, I walked ahead, feeling very naked going along the top of the embankment in full view from our objective five hundred yards away.

In front of the railway station I found two Sherman tanks. One was the squadron-commander's which had broken down, and the other belonged to his second-in-command. The latter had just come back to report, and he told me that B Company had got a foothold on the edge of the ridge but that only one of his tanks had been able to get up there. I could hear a lot of firing and was anxious to reach the company as quickly as possible, so jumped into his tank. I then found he was unwilling to move back up the hill he had just come down until he could get another tank to accompany him, and I had to give him a direct order to do so.

I found Jim and B Company in a quarry half-way up the hill, with C Company in the row of houses just behind. Jim told me that they had been stopped by very heavy light automatic fire, that a subaltern named Donald had been killed and nearly half the company were casualties. Moreover, most of them were lying out somewhere in front, which meant that there was now no possibility of using artillery. I said that I would get the tanks round to the right and on to the ridge, and that with their support C Company would advance. I sent the Intelligence Officer back to bring up A Company, and my carrier with the wireless sets.

The next hour was spent in futile attempts by the tanks to get on to the ridge. I got so angry that I jumped into the co-driver's seat in the tank belonging to the second-in-command, who was in charge in the absence of his squadron-commander still down at the railway station, and ordered him to proceed. We went about twenty yards and then it broke down. (7th Armoured Division found no difficulty in getting up there when they arrived two hours later.) Soon afterwards Harry ordered us to stay put.

David Martin arrived, driving my carrier himself. He said that they had been shot up on the way through. Both the driver and little red-haired Chamberlain, my wireless operator, were hit, and also a dispatch rider following behind. Beardwell was bringing his platoon up the street at the same time and was hit in the stomach.

Murray Reekie came to report where A Company was. I told him to take care going back; but, when only twenty yards from my H.Q., he was hit in the shoulder. C.S.M. Muir was in a bomb crater and shouted, 'Come down here, sir,' but poor Murray, distraught with pain, ran round in a circle instead. A burst of automatic fire caught him in the face and jaw and he died.

One or two people were both gallant and aggressive in going for these snipers. David got two, and C.S.M. Muir another, though not until he had received a nick in the neck, a bullet through his battledress blouse and a third bullet had hit his rifle. Meanwhile the Hun got a light mortar into position and we had yet a few more casualties, bringing them to five officers and forty-six O.R.s for a most ineffective day's work.

7th Armoured Division arrived on the scene about 3 p.m., sweeping over the ground with a mass of vehicles and men. It now began to rain hard and the ground soon became a bog. We were told we could withdraw to some buildings on the edge of the town, but this was cancelled when a German R/T message was intercepted to the effect that a counter-attack with tanks was being mounted. I now had to tell the Jocks that we were ordered to get ourselves firm where we stood, which meant that they had to dig themselves in, and spend the night in the open, in the mud and rain. They took the disappointment very well.

So there we were, in some sort of defensive position, what was left of us. We had lost fifteen officers and about 150 other ranks since the break-through started on August 8th. Being under strength before we started, we were now very short-handed indeed. In fact, we had only one subaltern, Williams, left. The remnants of the four rifle companies were now amalgamated into one composite company. I brought up the Pipe Band, the Pioneers and as many drivers and clerks as could be scraped together, under the transport officer, to thicken us up. In spite of an excellent hot supper, cooked in rear and brought up in thermos containers, which put new life into all of us, I felt very low indeed as I thought of the day's miserable failure.

Just before I turned in, a new draft of thirty, under a very young subaltern, Chappell, arrived. They were all as young as he was; I should think their average age was barely nineteen. I was able to find a place in the perimeter for them to hold. They were so keen that they 'stood-to' all night and managed to collar a few German deserters, which was an encouraging beginning.

In the morning we moved a few miles out of Lisieux, and Harry was back in command as the new Brigadier, Sinclair,[1] a Gordon Highlander, had arrived. Battalion H.Q. was in a small Château with some fine old panelling, though, like almost every house we had been in, it had been sadly looted by the Boche. No wonder the French were all so pleased to see us.

Here we had three days' rest, during one of which I ran back in my jeep to 88 General Hospital, near Caen, to get a new pair of spectacles. On the way there I crossed a plain where I counted twenty knocked-out German tanks. Coming back I had a look at the two cathedrals in Lisieux. One is very old and quite charming, and as it is down in the town it is a miracle that it had not been hit. The other had been completed a few years before and is a hideous white affair that looks like a cross between an Indian temple and a sugar cake.

Even after eleven hours' sleep on two consecutive nights, I was awfully tired and felt bruised all over. I was hoping that we might be staying here a week. And we needed time to get things sorted out. We received a good draft of men, but only two officers, which is what we needed most. One of them arrived and told the Padre that he was glad to find himself with this battalion as he had a friend there already, Donald. Poor Ewen had to tell him that he had just buried him. I spent much of the

---

[1] Later the Earl of Caithness.

time writing to next-of-kin, and found to my sadness that the two young officers most recently killed had both left widows.

August 28th was a grand day, for we advanced over twenty miles behind the armour: through St. Georges and over the river to just short of Boissey. Rouen was on the same map-sheet. We heard that fifty-six squadrons of medium bombers had visited it the day before, and that we were to by-pass to the north and go for St. Valery, where three-quarters of the Division had to capitulate in 1940. The Canadians had Dieppe to avenge, so it was also very suitable that they should be routed there. I feared we looked like missing Deauville, but anyway St. Valery and Dieppe might be fun.

We stopped the night in the usual fields and orchards near a village called Appetôt, and as the armour was in front of us we did not have to be very tactical. There was a brewed-up Covenanter tank, blown up on a mine, just beyond Battalion H.Q. It was in an awful mess and judging by the contents all the crew were killed, certainly the driver and co-driver.

I wished we knew more of what was happening at the Seine crossings. I was afraid that most of the Huns would have got across as we had seen very few prisoners coming back. I feared that this meant a pretty stiff campaign to break into Germany. But I did not much mind what happened so long as we first got a real good rest at the seaside.

Another small advance took us to a tiny hamlet called Burneville-sur-Seine, though it is not quite on the river as the name would suggest. It is a pretty little place among small hills and woods. On our way up we heard that the other two battalions were having some trouble and there was a long wait at the roadside. I was somewhat reassured when no casualties came back, but we later heard that each battalion had about thirty.

Our area did not look too healthy, as quite a number of shells and mortar bombs had landed there. There was a charming little farmstead in 'our' orchard, and the family gave us calvados, eggs, milk and butter, though they appeared to be in a very small way of business. I always regretted that we had to dig hundreds of slit-trenches on people's land and rarely had time to fill them in, since they were usually needed until the last moment.

Moaning Minnie came down in the night, though fortunately it caused no casualties. But it set part of the hamlet alight and the R.A.P. had to turn A.R.P. and put it out. Twenty-two rabbits were killed, which the morning's rumour turned into twenty-two people; also two cows belonging to our new-found farmer friend.

The day started with some patrols, all of which reported that the Hun had gone during the night. I went out with one of them and came to a little gem of a château on the escarpment, from which I had a wonderful view of a loop in the Seine that looked a long way below us. The enemy had been living there and the house had been stripped bare; one could see that there had been some lovely things inside.

Harry came back from Brigade after lunch to say that 5-7th Gordons were held up at the village of Yville and we had rather a difficult operation to do: to pass through them and occupy some high ground about two miles beyond. We were going to do it as a night attack.

The Brigadier, Charles Napier, the Brigade Major, and another officer named Aldridge got shot up when they motored too far down into Yville trying to find the 5-7th. Apparently a policeman who had been sent out to put up a 'Stop' notice was wounded. They were fired on at very short range by an anti-tank gun and Aldridge was killed, though the other two and their drivers and signallers managed to scramble out into a ditch. So the Hun was now in possession of the two jeeps and a wireless set.

At dusk we moved in transport to a debussing area just outside Yville, five miles away. As usual, Harry was on ahead, leaving me to bring up the battalion. I went rather too fast for the trucks and was horrified to find that half of them had taken the wrong turning, so I had to send dispatch riders to scour the countryside for the battalion. Meanwhile I had some anxious moments at the bottom of a ditch when a couple of Moaning Minnie salvoes came down in what was to be the debussing area. My anxieties increased when the lorries arrived and we had an awful hold-up at the cross-roads while they and some tanks and a 5-7th truck all tried to go in different directions at the same time. As quickly as I could I got the men out and the companies dispersed, and told them to dig slits.

We left there at 11.20, Zero Hour being midnight. Harry was afraid we were going to be late and that our artillery concentration would get too far ahead of us.

Down the hill we went, down a long and rather ghostly avenue, under bright moonlight with clouds, the best light you can have for night work. On we went, advancing in column along the side of fields and down a track through the woods. We were following a succession of artillery concentrations on the copses and woods astride our axis, which were lifted to advance at a rate of 100 yards every two minutes; three times we checked for a little when we were too close, and finally reached our objective without any opposition.

Now we were among heather and pine-trees and in some respects it was an ideal position as we could see nothing, therefore nothing could see us, and we were in consequence unlikely to be shelled. Most people seemed to like this type of ground but for my part it reminded me too much of my schooldays.

Twenty-odd deserters surrendered to us, but Poles, Mongolians, Jugo-Slavs and an Eskimo or two, not a Hun amongst them.

The Reconnaissance Regiment reported no enemy this side of the Seine, so I went off swanning for some eggs. I came to another nice château with a beautiful view of the river. They told me that twenty Germans crossed in a boat that morning.

I ran on to the ferry site at Duclair and found a lot of abandoned German vehicles head to tail. There were about a hundred, and most kinds seemed to be represented. Tanks, guns, stores and workshop trucks, armoured cars, and so on. The Master Race evidently fled across the river in an unpremeditated order of march. Our medium bombers caught them, but surprisingly few were burnt out. There were not many dead, though one saw a few gruesome sights. Soon there were quite a lot of us looking for anything which might be useful. I had brought Reid, the officers' mess cook, who did not often get a day out, and we got two cases of brandy, six bottles of red wine, a wireless set and an alarm clock.

It began to rain hard and it was pretty miserable in a dug-out. We had supper in a large captured Boche truck, but the roof did not really keep the water out.

The news was mainly of air-raids on Kiel and Bremen. We could not understand why the R.A.F. was not sent all out to rout the retreating columns. We felt that all our bombers ought to be turned on to the German field army (though preferably not just in front of the Highland Division).

There seemed nothing to do next day so I went in my jeep to Rouen. We began by following the river, then came to some branches across the road. I thought of trying to move them, but

Kangaroo

remembered that eight of our sappers became casualties that morning in clearing a similar roadblock which was booby-trapped. There was an encouraging amount of abandoned German transport on the road to Rouen, including several self-propelled guns which presumably ran out of petrol. All the Rouen bridges were blown except one. The outskirts of the town had been badly bombed, but the centre, with its famous cathedral, was untouched.

I was glad that we did not seem able to hit cathedrals. Caen, Lisieux and now Rouen were all undamaged. I found a bar with a bad type of Frenchman against it. He kept saying how much he liked the Germans, expecting a laugh each time. I only had an hour there as Harry had asked some guests to supper. On the way back I stopped at a cottage to collect some washing. The woman was very bitter as her son, taken by the Germans to work in Paris, had a throat infection and died of neglect.

On September 2nd we covered nearly our greatest distance in one day since the start of the campaign, to Veules-les-Roses, on the coast between St. Valery-en-Caux and Dieppe.

Reveille was at 4 a.m. on our miserable heath, and we washed and shaved in darkness and the rain. It was still very black at 5.30 and we had a job to get out of the wood. At the first corner I saw an 87 sign (the Brigade number) pointing left, and down there I went with a large part of the column behind me. The Brigade Major afterwards said it was 57, not 87. I soon found myself behind the polar bear signs of 49th Division. Our subsequent adventures were not very interesting, and it was some hours before we caught up with the Highland Division column, and even longer before we joined the Battalion, just after crossing the Seine at Elbeuf. The Brigade had been told to concentrate round Pissy Po, but en route orders were received for the Division to go straight to the St. Valery area, the Germans having withdrawn.

All along the route the population threw flowers at us, waved and gave the V sign, and whenever there was a halt we were

61

offered refreshment. All the little boys came up and asked for cigarettes for papa. The countryside was completely untouched by war, which had moved too fast across here. We passed through a village called Limesay and I wondered whether it was from here that my ancestors the de Limesays (hence 'Lindsay') came nine hundred years ago. If so I could not blame them, for it is a very dull little place. Everybody was very elated at this dash forward, and the convoy went much faster than the regulation 15 m.p.h.

In Veules-les-Roses I found two Fife and Forfar Yeomanry officers, who said they embarked here in 1940. I walked a little way along the top of the cliff to inspect the Hun defences and was intrigued to find some shells tied up head downwards at the edge of the cliff, so that they would fall and explode on the beach below when the wire was cut. All the front was blocked and mined, so we could not go down to the sea.

We heard that Commandos had liberated Dieppe, so I went there after tea. There were surprisingly few people there, considering that it had been very little bombed, though it was much knocked about in the 1942 raid. The Casino on the front had been blown up, and I was told that this was because our men fought from behind it.

I walked right through the hotel where my mother and I spent a week just before Munich. It had been a German H.Q., and in the principal room a sand model was laid out for a tactical exercise. The Canadians were thronging the streets. I could not stay long in Dieppe as Harry had a discussion fixed for 9 p.m. It was chiefly about smartening ourselves up, saluting and better discipline. Rather an anti-climax after the rest of the day.

The next day was September 3rd. Like no doubt millions of other people, I thought of that September 3rd five years before, when I woke up.

How vividly I can still remember that day!

We had kept a scrapbook in the Mess and it included an extract from Battalion Orders of August 4th, 1914, which read,

'Officers will send their swords to be sharpened by the armourer-sergeant.' Many of us had smiled at it in the intervening years. But now the hands of the clock had turned a full circle and the scrapbook had gone. With the regimental colours, our pictures and plate, it had been sent to store the week before. The orders now read, 'All officers will draw battledress from the Quartermaster', and I for one was thankful that I should go into action in this very practical and inconspicuous uniform, and not, as in 1914, sword in hand.

For a week we had been hard at work mobilising. I was in the company store trying to differentiate between pouches web basic, pouches web supporting and pouches web compass for carrying, when somebody came in and said that the Prime Minister was speaking. The storeman slept there and had a wireless set. I turned it on to hear '. . . and I have to tell you that no such undertaking has been received. A state of war therefore exists . . .'

A few minutes later the first air-raid warning sounded. As I put down the inventory and seized my steel helmet and respirator and ran to my post, I told myself that we should be doing this several times a day from now on. How, I wondered, would we ever get mobilised, how would anybody ever be ready for anything again?

But by September 3rd we had nearly finished. In the week we had almost completed the complicated changeover from a peace to a war footing. Ammunition, service bayonets, cooking utensils and field dressings had been issued. Ledgers and accounts were now closed down. Our respirators had been tested in the gas chamber, our weapons on the range. We had completed innumerable 'returns' and compiled many long lists: of 'those proceeding overseas' with the company; of those under nineteen who were to be relegated to Details and who, in military terminology, would also 'proceed', but only to the band block on 'Zero plus seven'; of clothing and equipment, weapons and stores.

We were medically examined, the men in line in the barrack room, the officers in the comparative privacy of the billiards room. 'The army hasn't changed much during the three years that I have been out of it,' I thought to myself as the Medical Officer listened to his stethoscope placed over my cigarette case.

We kept pace with the day's schedule and in addition solved several new problems which were not catered for in the 'mob-scheme', such as where to dispose of property varying from the company typewriter to the regimental beagles. Those of us who had not been on active service before learned many new things during that week, such as that the second of the two identity discs is intended for one's grave!

There were many strange faces in the Mess on September 3rd, 1939. The reservists had arrived the night before, mostly former officers who had hurriedly left their businesses, farms and estates. We now numbered amongst us a brewer, a stockbroker, a haulage contractor, a remittance man, a Parliamentary candidate and several farmers, all with one thing in common – uniform that was now many inches too tight. The Chaplain was the busiest of us all, performing more marriages in a day than he ever did before in a month, since many men at that time were getting married on a capital of about a couple of pounds. The young doctor, in a brand-new uniform, was instructing the band in stretcher drill.

There was certainly no lack of keenness. Derek Dodson, just nineteen, was genuinely frantic when ordered to India, as he so wanted to become an Old Contemptible. And nobody envied the Major (still with a piece of 1917 shrapnel in his spine) who had been sent away to command an internment camp.

Everybody wanted to jump off in front of the start, for we did not then realise how long the race was to be. Buying kit assumed a certain urgency when, for all one knew to the contrary, one might be in action a week hence. So officers snatched an hour off here and there and dashed down to the town, returning with queer-shaped parcels. Most had some fancy, perhaps for a shooting-stick, a balaclava helmet or a patent shaving brush which turned into a fountain pen. 'Socks are the things,' Ian kept saying. He went out as a reinforcement officer in May, 1940, with eighteen pairs and was killed within twenty-four hours in the one in which he landed in France.

War brings incomparable misery to all classes, but can there be any doubt at all that far the greatest burden falls upon the devoted shoulders of the private soldier? I was very conscious of this then, as indeed I am today. I had just left a wife and three young children, but had the comfort of knowing that they were provided for in things material. It is often not so with the men.

As a company commander at that time, I listened to some pathetic stories from reservists who were called up at a moment's notice, leaving sick wives at home with nobody to look after them. Even when all was well, unlike the officers, they could not in most cases afford to send for their wives to share those last few days with them. In every disaster it is the poor who suffer most, for at the best of times the security margin is slight, and when things go wrong that margin simply disappears.

At British Legion meetings I had heard ex-officers say that nothing is too good for the private soldier. Now I realised just how true this is. I realised also that, though the future seemed as if it could scarcely be more unpromising, I wished to be nowhere else than with those men of mine on that fateful day in 1939.

September 3rd, 1944, started with a memorial service for those of the battalion who had fallen in this campaign. It was most moving, and especially when Harry read out the list of 133 officers and men who had been killed or died of wounds.

The names seemed to go on for ever, and I feared that this long casualty list would come as a shock to the large new draft that arrived a few days before. At the end the buglers blew last

Post and Reveille most beautifully, and the Pipe-Major played the Lament. It was held in the courtyard of the principal hotel, and all the remaining standing room was taken up by the French. All through the service a little old *gamin*, very frail and wearing a sailor hat, sat on the steps of the terrace from which Ewen, with Harry at his side, took the service.

Harry and I called upon the Mayor, who was also the village doctor. He was exceedingly moved as he gave us an account of how he tended three hundred British and French wounded on June 12th, 1940. Most of them belonged to the Duke of Wellington's Regiment, he said, and he produced a list of those that the village had buried. Every grave had one French family responsible for its upkeep.

St. Valery also hid six prisoners for eight months. They were smuggled away to Paris and beyond, but unfortunately one of them was caught in a train smash, from which he was taken to a German ambulance and on his person was found the address of the woman in Veules-les-Roses who had hidden him. The Gestapo arrived and two women and the local barber were arrested. All three received the death sentence, though it was later commuted to life imprisonment; one woman died in prison, one was still there, and the barber, in ill-health, had been released after three-and-a-half years. The Mayor's two sons had both been prisoners since 1940. There was not one collaborator in the village, he told us, not one.

After lunch I ran over to Luneray, where I had once been *en pension*. I found that old Pasteur Grenier had died ten years ago, but his widow had remarried and was still there. Mme Grenier told me that the young *pasteur* who succeeded her husband was arrested for sending information to England by carrier pigeon, but escaped on the way to Germany when his train was *bouleversé* by the R.A.F. She said that many flying bombs passed over Luneray and that a large number came down in the fields and in the Channel.

In the middle of the afternoon dancing started in the village square, and soon the place was crowded out by people of all ages from seven months to seventy. They said it was the first time that there had been dancing since 1940. It was stopped at five for Harry and the Mayor to make speeches. Harry said just the right thing: how pleased we were to be there and how grateful for the succour they had given our wounded four years ago, how brave they had been under our bombing, how much we admired de Gaulle's resistance movement and how, with their help, we were going to liberate the last metre of French soil and give the German his deserts. He had a very good delivery – acquired by much practice in reading the Lessons I fancy – and it went down in a big way.

This was followed by Retreat, and of course the Pipes and Drums received a terrific ovation as they marched and counter-marched. In the middle of it an American tail-gunner turned up. He had been shot down in June, 1943, while returning to England from a raid, and had lain doggo in the same village ever since; somewhat unenterprising, but no doubt he had a good reason.

After this we had a big dinner party in the hotel, entertaining the Mayor and a few other local worthies. It was rather spoilt when the Brigadier whispered that we were going west to Le Havre, where 10,000 Germans were still resisting. It was not much fun to be going backwards when the big news was all of the drive forward into Belgium and Holland, and it looked as though we should be out of the hunt for some time.

I remained depressingly sober for the rest of the evening.

In the morning I had to preside over a Field General Court Martial at H.Q. 5th Black Watch, which was in another lovely château also largely ruined by the Germans. We tried two de-serters whom we sentenced to five years and eighteen months, and reduced a C.Q.M.S. to sergeant for giving away Army rations.

After a picnic lunch in the garden, I followed the battalion through St. Valery, Fécamp and Etrétat to a small place called

Villainville about ten miles east of Le Havre. On the way we passed a large notice-board which said, 'Honour the Black Watch Regiment who fought here with courage in 1940', and I wondered that the Germans had not ordered it to be taken down.

All this coastline was covered with minefields and fortified with sunken pillboxes for several miles inland, and nearly every field was obstructed with poles connected by wire and with a powerful charge on top of each. I could not but think how wise we had been to land where the defences were not nearly so formidable.

At Battalion H.Q. I heard that 49th Division had had a bad time trying to capture Le Havre from the south, so there was to be a pause while a big attack by the two divisions was mounted.

During our four days at Villainville, I went to the dentist. Each Field Ambulance had one, to give first-aid for jaw injuries from wounds and ordinary treatment at other times. On the way back I called in at Fécamp and left Harry's spectacles to be mended, one branch being broken, as the French so delightfully put it. It is a small industrial town and port, more famous for its Benedictine than anything else. Etrétat, on the other hand, is a residential place and has a golf course, though I had no doubt it was now mined like that of Dieppe. I hoped that clearing up the minefields would be the first task of German prisoners after the war.

We had dinner one evening in the hotel at Criquetôt. Somebody said that Churchill had once stayed there, so I optimistically took a towel and some soap, but of course it was not that sort of a place. The dining-room was reminiscent of the Naughty Nineties and reminded me of Rules in St. Martin's Lane.

The attack against Le Havre was being prepared with great care. Harry said that 1st Gordons had a reputation for dash, so we could afford to take things carefully this time. I reminded him how he had hustled me when I was commanding the Battalion at Lisieux, and he replied, 'Yes, and I have never regretted it more.' He had told the General that our abortive attack there was his fault for trying to go too fast. Not many officers would have done that.

The Huns in our objective were said to be full of fight, and their commander a fanatic as his wife and children were killed in Berlin. The Gloucesters in 49th Division had had 300 shells in their battalion area in the course of one day. Nevertheless we were on a far better wicket than the enemy. I would not have cared to have been in their shoes, being bombed and shelled every day and knowing that there was the hell of an attack to follow.

The general idea was that 49th Division would take the high ground on the left, then 152 Brigade breach the minefield, through which we were to go. Our marching troops would cross the forest beyond the minefield, then the armour would follow up and would support us over the open ground beyond. We should have fifty-four fighting vehicles. I hoped to goodness they would mark the route well, and especially through the minefields, so that we could not go wrong in the dark. Our column was to be led by a sapper sergeant, Whitfield, in charge of a scissors bridge to put across the first anti-tank ditch. One snag was that we were very short of artillery ammunition, having only about 200 rounds per gun. The wonder to me was that we had any at all, considering the length of our communications. Everything we possessed had been landed on the beaches of Calvados and brought 200 miles by road.

We moved into an assembly area, open fields somewhat congested by our guns and tanks, to say nothing of ourselves. After lunch I went to have a look from a gunner observation post. It was in a very Victorian house with rich mahogany fittings and a profusion of aspidistras and hydrangeas. I went up to the attic and stood on a table to look through the periscope sticking through a hole in the tiles. The gunner was full of information of what was to be seen, but the panorama did not convey much to me.

I got back and sat in the sun in my jeep, watching the bombing of Le Havre's outer defences and also a leaflet raid; we presumed that the leaflets had been printed in red for it looked like some strange pink cloud descending. Two pathologists came up and talked to me. They wanted to take specimen organs of Germans killed by flame-throwers, as some had been found dead without a mark upon them – fear or carbon-monoxide poisoning? So I told them to follow us next day and we would do our best to oblige.

We borrowed a room in a small cottage to feed in. The French were very good about this sort of thing, and a few tins of bully and packets of biscuits could not have been much compensation for the way we cut up the grass and dug slit-trenches everywhere. We turned in for a somewhat short night (my shaving water being ordered for 2 a.m.), Harry in his caravan, Alec and David in the dug command post, Ewen, Bert and I on the floor in the cottage.

A message came through from Brigade at 3 a.m., saying that we should start as soon as possible. Harry with his H.Q. and the companies managed to leave at four, with a bit of a scramble. Then I walked over to the tanks and climbed into my armoured car. We set off by the artificial moonlight of the searchlights.

The sky was clear so it was very cold, and I was glad of my greatcoat. The silhouette of those great black tanks, rumbling slowly westwards towards a glow low down on the horizon where something was on fire, the stars above and shoulders of mist at ground level, the indistinct shapes of beasts of the field and their tracks across the dew, together with the chat from the battle ahead that came through my earphones, all made a thrilling and romantic setting. Riding thus into battle, I felt an exhilaration such as I had seldom known before.

At the bottom of a valley we had to stop. From what I could hear, things were not going too well. Harry was complaining that the axis was blocked by vehicles of 2nd Seaforths. The Brigade Major told him to pass them with his marching companies. Harry asked why, if they were supposed to be ahead, then let them be ahead, he said; that way he would lose all control.

There appeared to be a lot of confusion over the three gaps, Ale, Rum and Gin, through the minefield; two were by no means through and the third was blocked by three flails which had blown up on mines. Two scissors bridges which were supposed to be over the anti-tank ditch had fallen sideways, and the sappers were trying to put another across. There was quite a lot of shelling coming down.

Meanwhile we brewed up tea at the bottom of our valley and watched the dawn turn into daylight. In a flash four hours had passed.

Eventually it was decided that the battalion should go through Rum, and Harry and the companies went that way. The men got through all right, but some of the few carriers they had with them blew up. As soon as we could, we moved up close behind Rum, and there waited while the sappers did some more mine lifting. I heard over the air that B Company was doing well. They had captured the final objective of 5th Camerons and 150 prisoners as well.

Soon they reported that they were on Pike, the code name for the edge of the forest, and had yet another 100 P.O.W. I gathered from this that the enemy were giving up rather easily, though several heavy stonks coming down in different places prevented any tendency towards complacency. Later I heard that there was quite a lot of opposition and it was not at all as easy as it sounded over the R/T, and that Chappell's platoon of nineteen-year-olds showed tremendous dash in this attack. As somebody remarked, they now only knew the thrill of battle and had yet to learn the danger. B Company had three killed and fourteen wounded in this attack down the hill into the wood, our only casualties in the day.

We were ordered through Rum about noon, as soon as the anti-tank ditch had been filled in. We passed down a very

71

narrow passage, marked with white tape, through the minefield, then down a steep slope and through a village at the bottom of the valley. It had been bombed flat, and later we heard that there were fifty French killed in what was hardly more than a hamlet.

The bulldozers were doing good work clearing a way through it. I walked on foot at the head of the tanks, across a field and into a ride in the woods, where I found Harry, who had just come back from looking at the far side. He said that all he had been able to see beyond was an A.A. gun with a white flag sticking out of the muzzle. He sent the companies down to their start-line at the forward edge of the wood, and the tanks down the ride after them.

Meanwhile a lot of prisoners were coming back, and it was most encouraging to see that they were being led by their officers. They lined up in front of me. 'There you are,' I said to the men who were near me, 'the Master Race. Help yourselves.' They soon had a fine collection of watches, fountain pens, pocket knives, and not a few French francs. Then I put the prisoners on to improving the track.

Some of them had our pink leaflets on them. They seemed very good propaganda to me. On one side was printed, 'Why die in the last week of the war? You are between two Allied armies and the sea, and your holding out will help no one.' On the back were set out briefly the terms of the 1929 Convention, stating that P.O.W. got seventy-five cents a day and could save it up to buy alcoholic liquor, and that they got papers, games, wireless sets, etc. But the main purport of it was to be safe conduct, for in largest print of all, above the signatures of Eisenhower and Montgomery, it said, 'This man is to be well treated and sent back from the front as soon as possible.'

The companies crossed the start-line and their news on the R/T was all very reassuring. Soon we heard that there was no opposition and they were all on their objectives. So I went through with the anti-tank guns and mortars. The batteries we had taken were in very strong concrete emplacements with many deep underground rooms and passages. We put our H.Q. mess in one of the gun-pits, just behind the gun itself, where there was much more light than down in the dungeons as well as the air being fresher. The whole place had been ransacked before I arrived, but I got three hurricane lamps for the mess. All the Jocks were smoking cigars.

We must have taken well over 500 prisoners in the day.

At 10.30 p.m., just after I had got to sleep, orders arrived for us to clear up a large area next morning. We breakfasted at 6.30 (not too good) and started off an hour later, for what proved to be a most entertaining day. I was riding in a carrier behind one of the companies. Every wood and gun-pit we came to produced its quota of Germans, till eventually we had about 300, and there was not a Jock in the company without a nice wrist-watch, most of which had been looted from the French in the first place.

It was the heavy bombing which had had such a demoralising effect upon them. I had never seen such large craters; some of them being nearly 100 feet deep. They said that not many were killed, perhaps an average of two or three in each position out of fifty or seventy, but I suppose a direct hit sometimes caused a real holocaust. It was this which made them give up so quietly. The R.A.F. had done a good job.

I found two Frenchwomen in one position, and they looked so pleased with themselves that I told them they would be handed over as collaborators and have their heads shaved. Whereupon one of them promptly went inside and produced six bottles of champagne. I said, 'Thank you, but it won't make any difference.' Later in the day we heard that 5-7th Gordons got fifty cases of bubbly in the Le Havre fort, lucky chaps. I still had not got any German field-glasses, which was my principal war aim.

I ran into Le Havre, where a few snipers were still popping off odd shots in the port area. The back and centre of the town was undamaged but most of the port was bombed flat. All the restaurants and cafés were closed and I could not help feeling that the French were rather wet; we should never have allowed bombing of one part of a town to have closed down all life in the rest of it. It had made us highly unpopular. We had none of the rapturous welcome there that we had received elsewhere, and when Ewen made a few tentative enquiries about getting up an officers' dance he was told that the whole town was in mourning and they would have nothing to do with it.

Le Havre seemed a poorish place with neither the cultural history of Caen and Lisieux nor the modern shops of Rouen.

On the way back I got lost in the dark among the bombed and shelled-out houses and blocked lanes, and was glad of the occasional bursts of fire from the port to give me my direction.

We returned to Villainville and there we were grounded for a fortnight, which was a sad blow. First they took our transport from us, to help get supplies up to the rest of the army now mainly in Holland, and then most of our tins of petrol. This came as a surprise to us as we had just got posting orders for twelve new officers, the significance of which would normally be unmistakable. We greatly feared that the war in Germany might be over while we were back there and out of it. Having travelled so far since 1939 we all wanted to be in at the death.

We spent most of the time training: tactical schemes, field-firing exercises, competitions, route marches, and so on.

David and I went to Paris one day. Late the night before we started an order came putting Paris out of bounds, but Alex Lumsden, the Adjutant, was decent about it and said that it was after office hours and he would not officially open it until the morning.

So we set off at 7 a.m., taking the officers' mess corporal, Robb, as well as my jeep driver, Ackers. It was a lovely drive as soon as the sun came through the mist. Perhaps the most striking thing about the roads in France was that at every twenty yards along the verge of every main road there was a hole dug to give cover from the R.A.F.

At Pontoise we found the bridge down, and crossed by ferry. While waiting for it, the first of many English-speaking Frenchwomen came up and said how pleased she was to see Scottish soldiers. She gave us some peaches. We asked about Paris and she said it was normal; she could not have given us better news.

We went on through St. Denis and the suburbs and down to the Rue des Capucines. Looking for a place to park the car, we saw a lot of jeeps and trucks outside the American Red Cross. We went inside and I asked the charming and sophisticated woman who was running it if we could make use of it, and leave the jeep in their car-park.

Then a Mme de Montague came up with her daughter and asked for news of someone in the Black Watch. David and I promptly asked them both to lunch. They said, 'No, you must come and lunch with us at the flat, but have you any tins?' We thought this a bore, so insisted that they should lunch with us. It was a bad lunch at the Ritz – the stew was German Army rations and not as good as our compo – but the martinis were excellent and it was all extremely cheap.

After lunch we went round the shops, almost the first we had seen as most of the others had been blitzed. To us it seemed a wonderful and quite pre-war display. It was a lovely afternoon and we had a lovely time. Paris as usual seemed very gay, and we wondered if it had been equally gay during the occupation. The restaurants were all going just as well as in London. We each had a luxury haircut, but spent most of the time just sauntering down the boulevards. Our kilts were a tremendous success, the first seen in Paris since 1940.

At five we assembled at the Red Cross and I was horrified to find that the jeep had disappeared. The American lovelies all thought it very funny. I went to the British H.Q. feeling that it was all rather tricky, with Paris out of bounds. However, the Lieut.-Colonel to whom I had to report was in the Blues with my brother-in-law.

He said he felt rather uncomfortable about Paris being placed out of bounds, and I was able to assure him that nothing caused more ill-feeling than the current system whereby the fighting troops captured a town, then some rear H.Q. arrived, settled themselves in comfortably, and then placed it out of bounds. Or so it seemed to us, for Rouen, Le Havre and Paris were all in the same category.

He fixed us up with passes to stay in the hotels that had been requisitioned, David and I in the Bedford in Rue de l'Acade, and Robb and Ackers in the Metropolitan in Rue Cambon; he also told us of a truck going to the Division next day, and that it might first be worth while visiting the barracks where picked-up American vehicles were taken. The Americans lost ten jeeps a day in Paris, he said.

I had a somewhat gloomy evening in the Bedford, feeling very guilty about losing the jeep and over-staying the one day's leave which Harry had given me. The barracks were packed with American vehicles of all descriptions, but alas not our jeep. The HD truck had come to fetch two Argyll absentees, so we travelled back in suitable company.

After a few days all the officers (except Harry, who had to set a good example) had now been to Paris or Rouen – in fact, I think all the officers in the Division – and all said they had a wonderful time, and none had been caught.

While at Villainville I had the strange experience of attending a board meeting of the electric light company in Fécamp, to try to get the electricity turned on. As the result of this several of us had a hot bath, though the light was still rather temperamental.

For several days we had a pleasant, idle time. There were lots of parties. I remember a very good dance given by Brigade H.Q. in Etrétat. Before it the Brigade Major said: 'I think we should open the case of wine I got in Le Havre. I believe it is very good stuff. The name on the box is "Encre".'

We even had Gertrude Lawrence with a concert party. The

officers of 5-7th Gordons gave a supper after it, at which the following duologue was heard:

Mike: 'Don't call me Major, Gertie.'

G.L.: 'Don't call me Gertie, Major.'

On September 28th we started the long journey eastwards to catch up with the war.

After the others had gone I went round the company areas to see if they had been left clean and tidy, and was pressed to have a glass of cognac with several farm families who all seemed sorry to see the last of us. The battalion left a good name in this district, though earlier on a soldier was found with the back of his head bashed in. As this was on the main thoroughfare we put it down as a road accident, but there were no signs of a smash, so it would seem that he was murdered, probably for womanising.

I followed the convoy, taking my time. We passed a lot of abandoned German artillery and armour which presumably had run out of petrol. The country was like Cambridgeshire or the Borders: open rolling fields and small woods. I stopped for lunch at a cottage by a large house, exchanged greetings with the lady of the manor, and was given some fruit. All the people at the roadside waved to us. Battalion H.Q. was in the usual château with the usual countess, but here it was neither old nor picturesque, just a big red house. As I had to do the three stages in two days, to get to the far end ahead of the battalion, I decided to go straight on. So, after a hasty meal, we drove on: four officers in two jeeps.

After dark we pulled up at the lodge of a large house. The massive gates were opened for us by a very old retainer. It was the Château de Saveuse, he said, and the owners the family de Hauteclocque. We drove into the courtyard and up to the front door, and asked if we might put up for the night. The Countess said that, except for her room and her daughter's, the whole house had been stripped bare by the Germans. She showed us the ground floor and every room was as empty as when the builders left it. They had brought huge vans, she said, and what they could not take out through the doors they removed through the windows: all the treasures of the family.

While the lodgekeeper fetched water and wood for a fire, she took us into her room. She was very ashamed that except for some apples she could offer us nothing but plates to eat off. She told us that General Beck had been taken prisoner in the house on August 29th, that he had turned her and her daughter out of the two rooms that had been left to them, and that he and his staff officer used the floor of the little recess that was ten feet from the dining-table as a latrine. She told us much about the atrocities committed by the Germans, and how essential it was that we be harsh to them this time if we did not want another war in a decade or two.

We were up at six and off at eight, and drove through many places with historic names: Amiens, Cambrai, Valenciennes, Mons. Several towns along the route of the retreating German armies had been bombed, and I doubted whether this policy had justified itself, for many humble houses had been laid waste for probably no great gain.

We stopped to look at some of the 1914–18 war graves. The entrance is under a Lutyens-style archway, and the names were kept in a book in a small cupboard with a copper door in the porches, but the Germans had stolen the books.

The stone crosses themselves are of a simple but beautiful design and each has the regimental crest on it, with the name, regiment and date beneath. Many of the graves were of unidentified remains, thus, 'An Officer in the Wiltshire Regiment', or 'A Sergeant in the Royal Artillery', or 'An Australian soldier of the Great War'. At the bottom of each of these crosses was inscribed: 'Known unto God'. Further on we came upon the memorial to the 9,000 killed in the Battle of Cambrai *who have no known grave*.

The war graves country is very open with long, straight

avenues, all of young trees. In places I could see the earthworks of 1914-18 trench systems near the road.

The Belgian frontier ran half-way down the main street, and immediately we were over the other side we had coffee pressed on us, a welcome change from the cider of yesterday and a very generous gesture in view of the shortage. Flags were festooned everywhere, and notices: 'We thank you soldiers for our liberation'. Portraits of the British Royal Family were much in evidence. One household was doing its best with a picture of Edward VII, fished out of the attic, no doubt.

Except in Mons, we had seen no war damage in Belgium. Brussels was untouched. It is a lovely city with many buildings finer than those of London or Paris. The railings in front of the Royal Palace were garlanded with bouquets and bunches of flowers. Belgian flags and drapings in Belgian colours were everywhere.

I spent an hour looking for the Field Cashier and another in a queue before I could draw 1,000 francs. Then, after lunch at the Palace Hotel on Army rations disguised, we set out along the tramway line to Haecht. On the way we passed two airfields from which the R.A.F. was going full blast. A squadron of medium bombers was just taking off, while some fighters cruised overhead awaiting permission to land.

The country north-east of Brussels is flat and Dutch-looking. At Haecht I could find nobody who could speak anything but Flemish. After waiting two and a half hours, I left a message that I would be back at 11 next morning, then turned round and drove back to Brussels.

After parking the jeep in the military police barracks (running no risks) I established a firm base at the Palace Hotel. Then I went out and joined up with an amusing young Belgian who was recovering from a wound received with the Maquis. His fiancée had dark-green eyes, pale red lips and hair like spilled honey. Together the three of us spent an amusing evening.

The battalion duly arrived in the morning. Our H.Q. was just getting settled down in the Catholic Girls School when orders arrived for us to move on again.

We were to take over the St. Oedenrode sector of the line from 15th Scottish Division, guarding the left of the corridor that ran up to Nijmegen. Then, as soon as the supply situation permitted, we were to attack northwards and clear up to the Maas.

So we had caught up with the war at last.

Part Two

Holland

4

We took over from 10th Highland Light Infantry on October 1st, in what, they assured us, was a quiet part of the front.

Three airborne divisions had been put down ahead of us a month before to secure the four bridges: over the Rhine at Arnhem, the Waal at Nijmegen, and the Maas at Grave and Mook. All three divisions took their objectives. The follow-up formations succeeded in relieving the American divisions who had secured the Maas and the Waal crossings, but they did not manage to get through to the bridgehead of 1st Airborne Division on the far side of the Rhine at Arnhem. Now we were holding, somewhat precariously, a narrow corridor connecting our three river crossings, with the Huns on either side of us.

The take-over went without a hitch, except for some gunners who drove down a lane into no-man's-land and blew up on an anti-tank mine; they were lucky to escape without serious casualties. We set fire to the jeep with three H.E. rounds from one of our anti-tank guns, to stop the enemy recovering it after dark. This was very flat, wooded country, and one could only see from one hedgerow to the next.

The companies and platoons were, as far as possible, based on

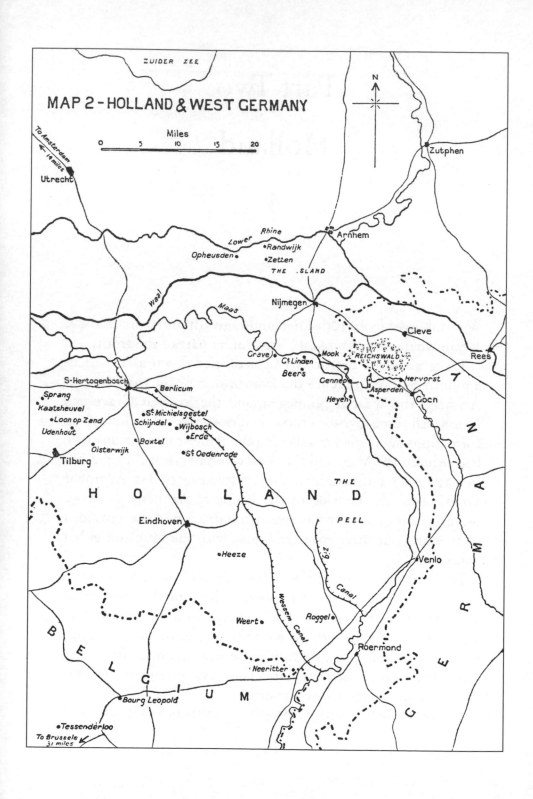

MAP 2—HOLLAND & WEST GERMANY

Miles
0   5   10   15   20

ZUIDER ZEE

N

To Amsterdam
14 miles
Utrecht

Zutphen

Lower Rhine
•Randwijk
Opheusden•   Arnhem
•Zetten
THE ISLAND

Waal
Maas   Nijmegen

Cleve

Grave•   •Mook   REICHSWALD   Rees
Ct Linden
Beers•   Gennep•   Hervorst•
S-Hertogenbosch   •Berlicum   Asperden•   Goch
•Sprang   Heyen•
•Kaatsheuvel
•Loon op Zand   •St Michielsgestel
Udenhout   Schijndel• •Wijbosch
          •Boxtel   •Erde
•Oisterwijk
Tilburg   •St Oedenrode

H O L L A N D   THE
                              PEEL

Eindhoven
          •Heeze

•Roggel   Venlo

Weert•   Wessem Canal
                Zig Canal
          Roermond

B E L G I U M   •Neeritter
                G E R M A N Y

•Bourg Leopold

•Tessenderloo
To Brussels
31 miles

farm buildings. In Normandy, to avoid mortar and shell-fire, one used to try to choose positions as far from isolated buildings as possible, but then it was summer. By now we felt that the weather was the greater enemy of the two. The Dutch had nearly all cleared off but they would come back daily to milk their cows. Battalion H.Q. was in a small farm. At one end was a barn in which we had the command post. Our drivers and mess staff lived in the centre, from which all the animals had been evicted, and the family was still in the house at the far end. All these Dutch farms seemed to be built on the one-storey housebarn plan.

At St. Oedenrode we spent three weeks without a move, almost a record.

The Huns in front of us were very quiet and we could walk from one of our positions to another without being shot at, although the enemy were only 400 yards away at the front edge of the wood opposite. Lying about were a few dead pigs and cows, clean killed by shellfire. There was an orchard with a bumper crop of delicious crimson apples; also the tail unit of a Typhoon. Our predecessors told us that most of the fuselage landed in the enemy lines and that the Huns had built a three-man dug-out beneath it.

Harry arranged a 'bashing-party' to beat up a position opposite. This is what is known as 'dominating no-man's-land'. When he suggested the operation I, too, thought that it was a good idea. Afterwards I was not so sure. At dusk we stropped up the front edge of that wood with our artillery and then sent a couple of platoons across under Clay, the second-in-command of D Company. The raiding party went through the near side of the wood like a pack of hounds and think they killed at least six enemy, though it was too dark to be sure. They brought back one prisoner, a pimply little rat-faced boy. But it cost us Clay, shot through the chest, though he was not to die, and a couple more casualties, and maybe we were lucky to have got off so lightly.

Our command post in the barn soon began to be comfortable. At first it was both dark and cold; but our Pioneers took a large slice out of the barn door and replaced it by talc which gave us more light, and we carpeted it with two feet of straw and rigged up tarpaulins to keep the draught out. The only snag was the habits of a cat which lived in the straw above our heads.

Every night we were there, one or two German deserters came over to us. It suggested that we had a very poor type of enemy opposite us. They were always examined by our Austrian interpreter, Private Likvornik. He was a small, thin, meek lad with a family background of Nazi persecution, and it did us good to see him stand up, with his hands on his hips, and fairly put it across the prisoners that were brought in to our H.Q. They said that they were commanded by a Lieutenant Bauer, and that his dug-out was very far behind and at least three metres deep!

Harry, Alec Lumsden the Adjutant, David Martin the I.O., Bert Brown our doctor, Ewen Traill the padre and I had now been together for three months, and a happier family would have been hard to find anywhere. Harry is a unique character. I had never met a colonel who was less feared yet so much respected and adored, nor one for whom people would go to such pains to produce good results. Our little company had lately had three additions. One was a friend of Harry's: David Scott-Moncrieff. He had not done much soldiering, having been on the staff of a Polish H.Q. for three years, but was intelligent and we knew he would be an asset. His hobby was pictures and his post-war ambition was to document all the Gainsboroughs in the world. Another was John Frary, the Signal officer, whom we called the Dormouse as he had a phenomenal capacity for sleep, in addition to a great sense of humour. The third was Jack Johnston,[1] the mortar officer, who

---

[1] Now Sir John Johnston, K.C.M.G.

arrived with a draft six weeks before and had been asked to join our mess because he was also a charming chap, though I told him that it was because he was the only officer who possessed a Tilley lamp.

We used to get about twenty shells or mortar bombs in the battalion area every day, but happily had very few casualties. Sometimes a stray bullet came through the roof of the command post and rustled at great speed through the straw above our heads.

The Division started a Rest Camp at Antwerp. Harry very sensibly offered to provide a major to run it, at a time when no one else was willing to part with one. Bruce Rae, Bill MacMillan and Jim Robertson had been through every action since El Alamein, except during brief absences recovering from wounds. This meant that we should be able to keep one of them out of battle in future.

We started a forward leave policy of our own. It would have been ages before everybody got a turn at the Rest Camp, so we sent off one officer and twelve O.R.s unofficially every day for thirty-six hours, and nobody found any difficulty in arranging his own accommodation.

While we were here the Division lost one of its best-known characters, Mike du Boulay, second-in-command of 5-7th Gordons, who was sent to lecture in America. He had been through every action with the Division since Alamein, and as he had a young wife with three children, I was delighted he was now out of it. There were so many good men being killed every day that one had to brace oneself to read the daily Roll of Honour in *The Times*. I had just seen Donald Howorth's name in it. He joined us with a draft soon after D-Day, and proved to be the beau-ideal of a fighting platoon commander. In the Colombelles show he killed eight enemy with his own pistol, and when Bruce Rae told him that he was to withdraw his platoon, he replied: 'Well, you must take full responsibility.' We had heard that he had returned to his own regiment, the

85

Rifle Brigade, after getting over the wounds that he received on August 15th at Glatigny. Now he, too, had been killed.

It had rained hard for three days, which made it miserable for the troops who were standing-to in trenches, most of which filled up with water very quickly. Our dozen deserters who were awaiting trial had been living back in comparative comfort while their more honourable comrades had been manning the positions, an intolerable situation. So I had them marched up and put in one of the forward positions each night.

On one of these days we heard that Harry had been awarded the D.S.O. for when he was commanding the Brigade, which delighted us all.

I enjoyed a run over to Antwerp, though it was rather an anti-climax after all the stories I had heard about it. Two of them made us laugh. The first was of two officers who went round the town talking broad Scots and saying: 'We speak vera leetle English'; this, they considered, put them in a better position to discuss the various attractions of Antwerp in public and to ignore the hotel notices about lady visitors in bedrooms. The second was of a young girl who gave an officer her photograph inscribed '*à Peter avec toute ma sympathie*', after her parents had declined to give her permission to sleep out!

Antwerp is a port and industrial town and might be said to compare with Brussels as Glasgow does to Edinburgh. There seemed to be plenty of drink *au marché noir* (a small gin 75 francs, about eight shillings (40p)), but no food so all the restaurants were closed. But all those on leave were enjoying themselves wildly. I was disappointed to find that the golf links were in the front line, so had a haircut and bath and saw a film. All the usual welfare organisations, such as N.A.A.F.I., Church Army, E.N.S.A. and Y.M.C.A., had reserved buildings and were evidently about to arrive to entertain the troops. I thought that by that time Antwerp would probably be out of bounds.

This peaceful interlude could not last for ever, and soon we were studying the maps and air-photos of Schijndel in preparation for an operation on the 23rd.

The plan was for 5-7th Gordons to attack and capture Wijbosch, a small village to the east of it, the night before. 5th Black Watch would then pass through at first light and capture the south-east end of Schijndel, including a large factory which appeared to dominate most of the town. Then we should attack from the south-west and take the rest of it. There was a very big building in our objective marked 'Klooster', which we took to be the same as 'Cloister', or in other words a monastery or nunnery. Bruce's theory was that it might with luck turn out to be a girls' finishing school.

At the beginning of this campaign we used to 'stand-to' at 4 a.m. each morning. Now we did so from 5 a.m., so the season was advancing. The leaves had nearly all fallen from the trees (which made camouflage much more difficult), and the fields were already in that sodden state which we had to expect for the next six months. A month before Harry was told by the General that the Higher Command expected us to be bogged-down for the whole winter. Yet now we were about to attack. A great deal would depend upon how the tanks managed to get over the ground. If they could compete with the mud and if this next operation were a success, I could see no reason why the coming winter should stop us.

So we handed over to our old friends, 10th H.L.I., and moved to a concentration area behind Erde. We were still in the same flat country in which one could never see more than two fields ahead. However, the whole battalion was under cover, in farms, barns and outhouses. This was a typical bit of the old, catholic, South Holland countryside: clogs, grannies in the traditional white lace head-dress, barges on canals, windmills. The beds in the small farms are all bunks let into the wall, and the chief ornaments are Madonnas and other coloured saints under glass cases. Although the principal living-room always opens directly into the cow byre, each house is scrupulously polished and clean.

There was a nice bitch in this house, of the Dutch barge-dog breed. Dick, our interpreter, said: 'She is going to have kittens.' Harry said: 'How very peculiar!' He bred these dogs at home and promised to return and buy one of this litter.

The operation looked like being fairly simple, but you never could tell. Colombelles and Lisieux looked easy enough until the shooting started. And other attacks, which had every appearance of being thoroughly sticky parties, went very well. It was odd to think that we had not fought an action since we captured Le Havre on September 11th, nearly six weeks before. I had almost forgotten what it was like to feel frightened.

In the afternoon I went for a solitary walk along the canal bank. It reminded me of another afternoon ten years before, on another Dutch canal many miles to the north: the ice crackling and bending beneath our skates, Joyce in a saucy little fur cap, her cheeks pink with excitement, a great bowl of yellow tulips in our bedroom. What was she doing at this moment? I wondered.

All went well next day. We advanced three miles, occupied our objective and then at least one company took part in an impromptu dance! There was no battle as by the time we got there the Huns had all pulled out.

5-7th Gordons started at midnight. It was to be a silent attack. We stood outside in front of our farmhouse for half an hour, listening for the non-existent sounds of battle. Douglas Renny, in command, had plenty of artillery at call and it was a good sign that he appeared not to need it.

Just as I was climbing into my bunk in the wall, David came in to say that there was a lot of Spandau fire from farther to the left. In the morning we head that this must have been when two companies of 5th Camerons were caught crossing the railway embankment, silhouetted against the searchlights behind them. They had nearly fifty casualties from this fire, including, I believe, as many as ten officers. David Scott-Moncrieff was acting as liaison officer with this Brigade and had a very lucky escape; he missed a mine going down a lane in his carrier and another carrier behind him blew up on it, killing the driver and co-driver.

We started off soon after 8 a.m. After being held up once or twice by formations in front of us, we found there was nothing to stop us moving straight ahead into Schijndel. The klooster turned out to be part monastery, part nunnery. It had been knocked about by shellfire and all the glass was broken. I was surprised at the warmth of our welcome, considering what a lot of damage had been done to the town. Afterwards we heard that the Huns had systematically looted every room in the town before withdrawing.

A few small groups of paraboys came out of the houses and gave themselves up; we got twenty-seven in all. We heard that 7th Armoured Division were a long way in front, so consolidated our positions rather half-heartedly. Later some dozen solid shot came whizzing down the line of the main street, overs from a tank battle ahead of us. Meanwhile the Black Watch behind us discovered that the big factory in their area made silk stockings.

We installed our command post in the Father Superior's small house in front of the klooster. The walls were covered with oil paintings, and the fat and jovial abbot slapped his stomach in front of each as he said: 'Yes, I make him.' But they made David Scott-Moncrieff wince. It gave the abbot great pleasure to show us his wireless set hidden under one of the floor-boards. He had made it too, he chuckled.

Next afternoon Harry sent me forward to reconnoitre a concentration area for the battalion in the St. Michiels Gestel area. Dark thunderclouds were banked up on the skyline, so I decided to try another klooster marked on my map. It only took a moment to see that there was accommodation for a brigade, let alone a battalion, in this huge place, part of which had already been taken over for a Casualty Clearing Station for the armour. I sent a despatch rider back to give Harry the O.K.

and went round the building. There was a wing for each company, and most of the men would have beds; judging by the number of bars and billiards tables, the Hun had used it as some kind of rest centre.

I walked across the lawns and up a lane, to be stopped by some men of our Reconnaissance Regiment. 'Spandaus ahead,' they said. This surprised me as it was only three hundred yards from the main road along which I could at that moment see a convoy of three-ton R.A.S.C. lorries.

The battalion arrived. I reported our location to Brigade, in code over the air. 'But have you turned the Germans out?' came back the startled voice of the Brigade Major. There seemed to be some confusion of thought.

We found a lovely mess-room, with fruit and flowers on the table. As we sat down to supper somebody remarked that there was none of the usual Boche kit lying about, so it had obviously been a planned withdrawal, and wasn't this just the very room in which to place a time-bomb?

Then in strode a squadron-leader of the Reconnaissance Regiment. He proceeded to point out that there was only his very attenuated squadron between us and some fairly hostile enemy no more than half a mile away. When Harry replied he would warn one company to be ready to turn out at short notice, the officer rather dryly pointed out that what he was interested in was having men on the ground *just there* – a nicotine-stained finger pointed to the map. Harry said that we had a battle to fight on the morrow and he wasn't prepared to do more; later he compromised by opening up the company R/T sets, and by making everybody sleep with their boots on.

After a quiet night I was sent off early, with my usual party of company representatives, to find a battalion concentration area north of Boxtel, which was the Brigade objective.

While driving down the road I wondered whether the Duke of Wellington's Regiment still had Boxtel on their Colours. It may have been replaced by some more illustrious battle honour, yet this little-known action in an obscure Dutch town is as richly associated with the traditions of the British Army as Waterloo or Mons, for it was here that the first Thomas Atkins gained his immortal renown.

It was almost one hundred and fifty years ago, in September, 1794, that the 33rd Foot under Arthur Wellesley repelled a savage French attack at Boxtel. Thomas Atkins, a soldier of twenty years' service and the right-hand man of the Grenadier Company, lay with a bayonet wound in his chest and a bullet in his lungs, his course almost run. Wellesley moved to the side of the dying soldier who, seeing the grief on his young colonel's face, gasped out: 'It's all right, sir. It's all in the day's work.'

Half a century later the aged Duke of Wellington stood on the ramparts of Walmer Castle with an officer who had come down from Whitehall with papers for the signature of the Commander-in-Chief, among which was the proforma of a new document relating to soldiers' pay which, as a matter of courtesy, was to be referred to the Duke with the request for a name typical of the common soldier to be inserted as the specimen signature. Could His Grace suggest a name?

The Duke moved forward to the ramparts and stood for some time in silence gazing out to sea. Perhaps those dimming eyes looked back across the blood-drenched slopes of Waterloo, the broken mountains of the Pyrenees, the ragged sierras of Spain, the olive groves and cork woods of Portugal, and the torrid plains of India; but it was on none of these that his memory lingered.

After a long pause, he turned and replied: 'Private Thomas Atkins.' His mind had gone back, as the minds of old soldiers often do, to the early days of his campaigning, to Boxtel; where Private Atkins himself had now returned, once more to conclude 'the trivial business of dying' and win anew his immortality.

It did not take long to choose company areas, based on some

very nice houses from which the Hun had hurriedly withdrawn during the night. Soon after the battalion arrived we received word that 5-7th Gordons had entered Boxtel without opposition, and later 'no move today'. We had chosen a charming modern house for the command post, and Harry immediately gave orders for the bath water to be heated.

On our way there we had passed what looked like a golf course, which Bert and I now proceeded to investigate. There followed one of the most comic games that can ever have been played. Incidentally I wonder when golf has taken place so close to the front line as, all the time we were playing, shells or mortar bombs were crashing down less than half a mile away.

There were only four holes, the others being in a minefield, and we had only three clubs between us, as the Germans had stolen all the rest. There was a brigade H.Q. set up a hundred yards from the first tee, and as I teed up my ball I wondered what the penalty was for hitting a brigadier. The fairway of the second was bordered by the tanks of 7th Armoured Division, and the crews all stood on them and kept up a running commentary of criticism or advice. The third tee we shared with a charging engine. A full colonel (medical) came out of a tent, looking very pompous and displeased, and proceeded to stand in the middle of the fairway. I suppose he thought we were not taking the war seriously. 'By Jove, it does me good to see golf again!' said a young Yeomanry half-colonel (as the Americans would say), striding by in his jodhpurs. 'Very well, then I'll call you at my court-martial,' I replied, before drawing breath to yell 'Fore!' at the Assistant-Director of Medical Services. But just in front of the fourth green the Divisional General was holding a conference of all his commanders, and this was too much for us.

We returned to our H.Q. to find David Martin and David Scott-Moncrieff planning a fishing trip – 'a 36 grenade is not big enough' – and Harry about to leave the house with a gun under his arm, when up drove the Brigade Major with orders for us to move off in an hour's time, preparatory to carrying out a night attack.

Harry and I rushed off to Brigade H.Q. in the hell of a hurry, to get the orders. It was to be a night operation to drive the Huns out of some woods so that the armour could go through into open country next day; tanks do not like woods until they have been cleared, as it is so easy for enterprising infantry to shoot them up from close range with bazookas. Harry then went off with his company commanders, to choose the start-point for the attack, which was on ground held by 7th Black Watch, while I brought the battalion forward.

The plan was for the companies to take successive objectives in the woods. Harry chose a small two-room cottage on the axis for his Tac H.Q., from which he could send each company forward when its time came.

All went well for a while. B Company, under Ronald Davies, silently filed past. 'Noo then, nae indiscriminet shootin'. Mind thur watches and founten pens,' I heard an N.C.O. shout, and gave him full marks for trying to relieve the tension of those men walking into battle. But the copse they had been given as their objective proved to be unoccupied.

Then, as previously arranged, there was a thirty-minutes' fire programme upon the objectives of the other companies. This had the effect of bringing down enemy fire, and, as I half-expected, it was upon the area of the level-crossing 400 yards ahead. I pointed this out to Jim Robertson, who was commanding A, the next company to go, and suggested that he should avoid it. He said he must go straight down the road and over the level-crossing, or he would get lost. I told him that this was rot, that he should use his compass and cut across the fields and join the road beyond it.

We stood there in the doorway of the cottage, watching the searchlights, smelling the dew-drenched honeysuckle and clematis, and arguing half-heartedly for the five or ten minutes that remained. Then, with a loud shout of 'Come on, you lucky lads,' Jim led off his company – straight down the road. I remained there and felt very miserable when I heard the stuff crashing down soon afterwards, but fortunately the Hun seemed to have lifted his fire a trifle, and it all landed behind A Company and away to a flank.

We heard no small-arms fire from A, so, in due course, Harry started off D, and later C. For a time there was no news as the wireless was screened by the trees, but a series of coloured-light success signals had been arranged and the Signal Officer was following the companies with a line party. Between the lights and the line we soon got the information that B, A and D Companies had reached their objectives without opposition. We could not hear any firing from C, and Harry and I agreed that it looked to be a walk-over. 'We can do with bags of attacks like this,' I heard one of the signallers say.

Soon afterwards a jeep came back with Heath, a subaltern in B Company, wounded by a shell splinter in the thigh. The medical orderly said it was one of our own that had dropped short. All seemed quiet in front, so I accompanied him back to the Aid Post, a mile away on the main road.

When I returned to the command post half an hour later I found Harry looking rather disturbed. Jim had telephoned from A Company to say that he could hear a lot of firing from the direction of C, and that there was a rumour that Bruce Rae, the Company Commander, had been killed.

A jeep arrived from C Company with another subaltern, Gray, shot in the foot, and several more wounded. Gray said they had been attacked simultaneously by two parties of enemy, each about thirty strong. He had no news of Bruce. The next event was the arrival of a corporal and eight men from C Company. They said there was confusion in front and they thought that somebody had shouted: 'Back to the command post to reorganise.'

Then Jim rang up to say that Bruce had been shot through the head and was on his way back on a stretcher. In a few

94

minutes the jeep arrived, but of course he was unconscious. Sergeant Honor, a platoon commander, wounded in the shoulder, was with him. He was very plucky but could not give us much information. By this time a lot more of C Company were to be found in the ditch outside Battalion H.Q.

Harry and I then went into a huddle. I offered to go forward and take command of C Company, but he said he would send for Alec Lumsden. Two days ago it had been arranged for Alec to take over this company and Bruce was to have gone to D. So now I spoke to Alec on the wireless and told him to come up.

But we had still not captured C Company's objective, which from the map appeared to be a large country house with extensive stables and outhouses and the equivalent of a home farm. I said:

'For God's sake, let's wait till daylight and then attack with some tanks.'

Harry agreed.

So at dawn the next day we gave the place the hell of a plastering with the artillery and heavy mortars, and then C and A Companies, supported by six tanks, attacked. It was a great success and they took it without any further casualties. Over sixty Huns surrendered, nearly half of whom were wounded, which was very satisfactory.

We moved Battalion H.Q. forward to the house. Unfortunately, it had been badly knocked about by our shelling. The owner and his wife were still living there and, as one would expect, were very sad about the damage, but took it well. 'This is the price of liberty,' the Baron said, 'and it is worth it.' The house had many old English sporting prints and some good heads of chamois and red deer. There was a gaping hole through the drawing-room wall and through the sixteenth-century tapestry that hung there.

Like every good Dutchman, he had kept a few bottles hidden away from the Huns, and over one of them he suggested that we might like to arrange a pheasant shoot in the park, as if we had not done enough shooting already. We all tactfully refrained from asking for news of his sister – Frau Von Ribbentrop!

The night's casualties had been six killed and seven wounded, including three officers. Amongst the dead was my first servant, Graham; we had parted company for our mutual good a month before, after which he went to Bruce Rae. We were all very sad about Bruce, though Bert said that he had a fifty-fifty chance of pulling through. He had been shot twice in the chest and also in the jaw, and his life was saved by the stretcher-bearers who got him back.

He was such an attractive chap: gay, handsome and brave – he nearly always led his company himself, and rarely deigned to take cover. This was the third time that he had been wounded since El Alamein. He could still speak when they got him back to his Company H.Q. He gave out some orders and his last words before collapsing from loss of blood were: 'Don't forget, whatever happens, C Company must take their objective.'

We moved to Oisterwijk, and as nobody knew how long we should be there we began to make ourselves very comfortable in a leather factory. The managerial offices were most sumptuous and we were just settling down to champagne and cigars with the directors, and about to initiate tactful enquiries as to the prospects of a bath, when orders arrived for us to move on. We were to go to a forward assembly area beyond Udenhout and attack Loon-op-Zand by night.

As usual, I went on ahead to choose the area. There were not many buildings, so it was mainly a case of allotting each company a field, where in due course they had tea. As soon as it began to get dark the first two companies, followed by Harry and a small H.Q., led off. Then I heard that a scout-car had blown up on a mine on the road ahead, although three tanks and several carriers had got safely through. So I ordered our Pioneers to clear it.

Unfortunately Ayres, the Pioneer officer, had been sent on a month's course, and Sergeant Campbell had gone to Antwerp with the last leave party. The next thing I heard was that the Pioneers had blown up their 15-cwt. truck, so I asked Brigade for some sappers. In due course Sergeant Urquhart arrived with a section, and they soon taped a safe lane through the mines.

Meanwhile I could hear a good deal of shell-fire in the distance and took a compass bearing to the sound. Plotted on the map it showed me that it was Loon-op-Zand that was receiving attention, and I felt restless and concerned on Harry's behalf. It was a consolation to know that the enemy could hardly be holding the town if he was shelling it now, so we were likely to be spared street fighting in the dark. Soon a message arrived from Harry for me to bring everything on.

I jeeped on ahead of the column, which consisted of the anti-tank guns, mortar carriers, a dozen trucks with the more essential stores and ammunition, and the Aid Post. Standing in the middle of the main street was Harry: a slightly stooping, unmilitary figure, wearing spectacles with a near-white frame above an old-fashioned fair moustache, a tam o' shanter and a short gaberdine coat with a black sheepskin collar: the unique, inimitable Harry.

He was in very good form, partly because we had got into Loon-op-Zand with only two casualties, and partly because he had knocked at the door of a house to ask a question, to find seven perfectly good German soldiers inside who surrendered to him. There had been no shelling for half an hour, he told me. The companies were now digging-in in their respective areas. They were in close contact, he said, and this I confirmed when I visited them, for there was a lot of sniping going on and Spandaus were firing from not far off.

We were only about four miles from the Maas, and I imagined that the Huns would be streaming back across it all night.

I was duty officer from 2 a.m. to 3 a.m. Then I woke David Martin and got into bed. For some time I could not sleep as I felt uneasy. The small-arms fire had died down, suggesting that the enemy had withdrawn, but there was a recrudescence of shelling. In particular, a gun was firing in our direction. We could hear the distant poop, followed almost instantly by the whizz-crash as the shell arrived and exploded not far away. We were in a council school, the usual one-storey affair with acres of glass. David said it was stupid of me to sleep under the window, and I replied that if a shell landed just outside I would probably be better off there than in the centre of the room, since right under the wall I was at least sheltered from ricochets.

After a little I dozed off, to be woken up by one or two particularly loud crashes. Some glass fell on my bed and I told David that he was quite right. He walked across the room to wake up John Frary, who was next on the duty roster. At that moment there was an even louder crash and a shower of plaster came down from the ceiling. I saw David stagger and fall, saying: 'I've been hit.' John and I pulled him, practically unconscious, on to his safari bed, which made a good stretcher, but he was heavy to lift. Both the others in the room, John Inglis, the Battery Commander, and Waters of the Intelligence Section, were sitting down, very green about the face and obviously wounded.

The Aid Post was in a doctor's surgery only 100 yards down the street and we soon got David inside. There was a hole about the size of a five-shilling piece high up in his buttocks; he had been bending over to wake up John when the splinters came through the ceiling. We hurried back to help the other casualties out; there were half a dozen more in the room next door. John Inglis had a piece in the chest, but Bert said it had not pierced the lung, and Waters was not too bad. The command post, when one had time to look at it, was indescribable: plaster on top of everything, blood all over the floor, and John and I as white from head to foot as a couple of millers.

That one shell destroyed for all time my faith in a house, at any rate one without a good solid floor overhead. In that school

98

the ceiling consisted of an inch or two of laths and plaster under a tile roof. Harry blamed himself for having chosen such a place for the H.Q., but it was already dark and he had been told to leave the best building for Brigade. As soon as it was light we moved into the klooster across the road, turning all the nuns into two rooms and leaving Brigade to find their own home. Every few minutes one of the nuns waddled past towards a cupboard, saying 'Goodbye' as she did so, which many Dutch seemed to think was the same as 'good-day'.

After breakfast we got orders to move on. Just as we were about to leave the town another signal arrived, saying: 'Stop where you are. New plan, Friends coming through.'

We had over twenty casualties there, thirteen from the direct hit on the school and eight or nine from mortar fire, mostly in C Company. Bert said he feared that a high proportion of them would be fatal as they were nearly all serious cases, including several stomach wounds.

Harry and I and the company commanders all went up the church tower at Kaatsheuvel to study the ground leading to Sprang. It was a fine day, and the land looked very fresh and green and peaceful. So it did not surprise us when some Dutch boys arrived on bicycles to say that the enemy pulled out of Sprang about midnight. We climbed into our vehicles and motored in. Chalked on a wall in the main street was: 'We will come back, Tomy.'

Harry gave me permission to take his carrier for a run down to the Maas. In the next village we met an octogenarian who said that there were twenty Huns in a café on the river bank. He was certain that they wished to surrender and offered to come as guide, so to the delight of the assembled crowd the old man was allowed to climb up inside. Going round the next corner, we almost knocked down a German soldier coming out of a public urinal; he, too, was put on board. Hastings, the signaller, asked him if he had lost his ferry ticket.

We set off down the mile of straight road leading to the river.

The tracks of the carrier seemed to be making a terrible noise on the cobblestones. There was no cover whatever and I feared there might still be some Huns on the dyke in front. We had to go slowly so as to be able to watch for mines. I felt naked and heartily wished we had not started out on so foolish a trip, but we got to the end of the road and under the high bank in safety.

There was a canal just this side of the dyke with the bridge across it blown, and beyond it the café, quite obviously empty. But one girder, about six inches wide, still spanned the canal, and after much hesitation I crossed by it, followed by Hastings and the driver. The old Dutchman was left in the carrier, guarding the prisoner with my pistol. I also left the Bren-gun behind for fear of dropping it into the water.

We crawled up behind a pile of logs, and through my glasses I began to study the far bank, eight hundred yards away. Suddenly Hastings tugged at my sleeve. I looked down and there, to my astonishment, were twenty fat Huns just starting to row clumsily across in a great, heavy boat.

It was the target of a lifetime. I shouted: 'Get the Bren.' I think we showed ourselves in our excitement, for there was at once a stream of bullets overhead. There must have been at least ten Spandaus firing at us, for it was just like being in the butts during a machine-gun classification practice.

After some minutes the firing slackened and then stopped altogether. I was just about to begin crossing back again, when there was a zoom and a bang as a small H.E. shell hit the far end of the bridge fifty yards from me. I nipped back pretty quickly and into a funk-hole.

In the next quarter of an hour about twenty more shells landed all round us. Three hit the café behind and two a small cottage close to the carrier; one hit the middle of the bridge and the rest landed among the rushes on the canal bank. I thought: 'This is frightful; they must have seen me trying to cross; Harry will get so worried, for we shall have to wait here until darkness, and then we'll get shot up by our own people.' However, after half an hour we crossed over, on our hands and knees, and got back somewhat late for lunch.

Bert heard that David Martin was going along well, and Bruce was strong enough to be flown from Eindhoven to Brussels, which was also excellent news.

Bruce Rae was the last remaining of the twenty rifle company officers who came out with the battalion on D-Day. That is what was so superlatively gallant about these chaps. They would go into battle time after time, knowing perfectly well that they were dicing against the mathematical odds, which indeed they sometimes jocularly observed. For an officer to go into a dozen actions without being killed or badly wounded was like a coin coming down heads six times running. He knew that his luck could not possibly last, yet he would die of shame were someone else to take his place.

We captured a prisoner with a remarkable letter upon his person.

Here is a translation:

State Office for Increase of Birth Rate,
Berlin.
Dear Sir,

As many men have died during the war, it is the responsibility of the living to care for the women and girls, in order to have a steady rising birth rate.

You are thought to be very fit and we kindly ask you to accept this honourable German duty. Because of this your wife will not have a right to divorce you but must take it as a necessary consequence of war.

You are detailed to the 12th District (of Berlin) comprising nine women and seventeen girls. Should you feel unfit for this task, you have to send the name of a good substitute (*eines tuechtigen Ersatzmannes*), together with a certificate of incapacity signed by three doctors.

Should you be able to take over another district too, you

become a Breeding Officer and also receive a breeding re-muneration; you receive, too, the birth medal, 1st class, with red ribbon. You are also exempted from all taxes and have the right to a pension.

We will soon send you a list of persons to be visited by you. You should start your fruitful work at once and report the results to this office after nine months.

With German greetings,
Personnel Branch of the War Ministry, I. A.

This was a letter which had been infiltrated by our intelligence, to rot enemy morale.

Our next move, later in the day, was to 'S-Hertogenbosch. This was due to a sharp counter-attack south-east of Eindhoven. All we heard was that it came in against 7th American Armoured Division, who were very thin on the ground, and that it gained three miles in the first day. 15th Scottish Division and the Guards Armoured had been used to stop it. It was only eight miles from Second Army H.Q., where there had no doubt been a boom in the price of tin hats.

So we moved and were soon installed in – what do you think? – another klooster! The amount of money these people had invested in kloosters seemed fantastic, and we rather resented it. The Dutch certainly had a very high standard of living, at our expense. In two wars had we saved their freedom, and not least by spending money on armaments while they had invested in kloosters, schools and houses. Or so it seemed to us at that time. But it is only fair to add that they have taken their full share of responsibilities in the peace.

We took over here from a Welsh battalion and they were a dirty crowd; all their tins were lying about unburied and the latrines were choked, though it was not fair to blame their new colonel, who had been in the chair only thirty-six hours.

'S-Hertogenbosch means 'duke's wood', with the apostrophe in front; 'bois du duc' is still printed on some maps. It is an attractive old fortress town, which played a big part in the history of the Middle Ages. The moat round one side of it was still visible. There was also a big sheet of flood-water round the rest of it, and I did not see the Germans doing much good here unless they brought up their navy. The town had been held by a S.S. unit until recently and had been badly shelled.

There was a metalled road, raised high up on a dyke with water on each side of it, leading out of the town to the north-west. B Company were in the Wilhelmina Barracks astride it. I visited them, and was glad to see the S.S. murals glorifying bloody war had been much spoilt by our predecessors' fire programme. B Company had a platoon post 500 yards up the road, commanded by Chappell, aged nineteen. I always felt very sorry for youngsters, whether they were officers or N.C.O.s, when they were stuck out on their own, a standing temptation for an enemy identification raid such as had been brought off here against the Welsh the night before. So I trotted up the road to see that his dispositions were as good as could be. In the fore-most trench, the nearest man to the enemy was young Ackers, aged eighteen, his shiny, round boyish face as cheerful as usual.

With darkness coming on, I felt very sorry for him and horribly responsible. A fortnight ago he became the driver of my new jeep and promptly smashed it up. This I did not mind. But when he rang up to report it I told him that he was to mount

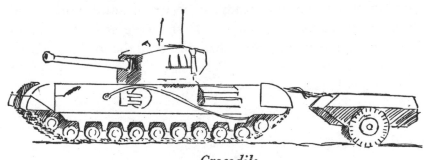

Crocodile

103

guard over it until I could get a breakdown vehicle sent along. After three-quarters of an hour he walked into Battalion H.Q., though it is only fair to say that he acted under the influence of an older man. He had deliberately disobeyed a direct order, and I sacked him on the spot.

I knew that I should never forgive myself if this section were to be overwhelmed, so I was back with them to see the dawn break next morning.

They had all had a quiet and uneventful night. But the company had been ordered to send out a patrol some hours before, and Corporal Taylor, M.M. and bar, had been put in charge of two men for the purpose. They were shot up and Taylor was missing. If I had been the Colonel I would have broken the company commander for choosing him. He could not have thought at all: sending out an N.C.O. who had done so much already when there were half a dozen others in the company who could well have profited by the experience.

We spent the afternoon trying to catch up with administrative jobs, which had been somewhat shelved since we left the woods near St. Oedenrode on October 19th. When Alec took over C Company David Martin became Adjutant, and when he was wounded forty-eight hours later, Harry appointed Jack Johnston, who was now trying to get to grips with things. David Scott-Moncrieff had become Intelligence Officer. Harry was busy writing citations. We were very fed up that our ration was only one decoration for the last three months on the 'periodical' list, i.e. for steady bravery and good work rather than specific acts of gallantry. There were at least a dozen N.C.O.s and men who more than deserved the Military Medal.

5

On November 2nd the law of averages claimed its own at last. For I was wounded, though only very slightly.

It happened in this way. The Brigadier gave us the rough outline of a plan to clean up the enemy north-west of 'S-Hertogenbosch. I was sent to choose a concentration area in some woods, but before doing so I had to be sure that there was a good track forward for vehicles. I noticed that there were sandbags on the floor of the jeep on my side, but none on the driver's. I asked Macdonald why this was so, and he replied that he had taken them out to clean the car. 'You drivers always have a good excuse for having no sandbags, but one day you may well be sorry,' I growled.

The Derbyshire Yeomanry had been through all these woods. We started to drive down a ride and I told Macdonald to stick to the tracks of the armoured cars. A few minutes later there was a blinding yellow flash with a deafening bang, and I found myself sitting on my bottom in the middle of the sandy track, a jeep's length behind. I was still clutching my map. I glanced quickly at my feet and was glad to see that they were both still there.

I shouted, 'Are you all right?' and was relieved when Macdonald answered 'Yes,' after a whimper or two. I got slowly on to my legs and hobbled over to the jeep, to satisfy myself that he had no limb missing, though he had obviously broken something as he was in pain and could not move. The whole of the front of the jeep was wrecked. In half an hour it would be dark, and I was now terrified of being benighted in the woods.

In my dazed condition it seemed as if life itself depended upon getting 500 yards to a main cross-track. I felt sick and there was a horrid acrid smell of the powder exploding charge in my nostrils, ears and hair. But worst of all was the stiffness in my legs; my trousers were torn and blood-stained and I felt as if somebody had slashed me across the shins with a crowbar.

When I came in sight of the corner I saw a jeep and shouted. Roddy Sinclair, the Brigadier, was in it, and never have I been more pleased to see anybody. At that moment some Derbyshire Yeomanry arrived, and we sent them down the track to rescue Macdonald. By the time we reached the klooster my legs had stiffened up considerably and I had to be carried down the steps to the Aid Post in the cellar. I was annoyed to find that I had a few small punctures in the front of each shin, a few inches below the knee.

The drive in the ambulance seemed to last a long time, and when I was carried out on the stretcher I was astonished to find that I had progressed no further than the Brigade Casualty Clearing Point, only a few hundred yards away. Four doctors looked at my legs and the verdict was, 'a fortnight, unless the bone is chipped'.

I submitted with good will to an anti-tetanus injection and five M. and B. tablets, but made an awful fuss when they insisted on taking off my boots. I had heard some dreadful stories about wounded being robbed and I was wearing my best pair; finally we compromised by having them tied to the stretcher.

Back in the ambulance I fell a prey to gloom. The chances of bits of metal going into my shin without chipping the bone seemed remote, and I pictured myself being away for weeks and somebody else taking my place in 1st Gordons. Again we stopped and once again I was carried out into a room. This time it was the Divisional Advance Dressing Station. Two doctors satisfied themselves that I was in fit condition to stand the strain, and on we went again.

This time it was a longer trip. I noticed how bad the springing was, and thought how painful it must be for the seriously wounded. I wondered why we were so prodigal with some types of expenditure, yet so skimpy with others. A 'victor' target was every gun within range and cost God knows what each time, and quite rightly when it came to a fire programme no commander ever thought about the tax-payers' money. Yet the Army tried to save by making us use wick lamps instead of Tilleys or Aladdins, and by rotten, cheap springing in ambulances.

After about an hour we reached the Casualty Clearing Station, outside Eindhoven. For the third time I was carried out of the ambulance and inside a school, and once again an orderly brought me a mug of hot, sweet tea as I lay there on my stretcher on the floor. At the Dressing Station they had told me that David Martin was here and going on well, and immediately I asked the duty N.C.O. for news of him. 'He died on the 31st,' was the reply I got.

I simply could not grasp this and continued to ask futile questions. I saw the sergeant making obvious efforts to be patient. He clearly thought I was not quite normal, suffering from shock perhaps. It was an awful blow to me. Later on I spoke to the surgeon. David had had a large piece of metal taken out of him and did well for two days, when he had a relapse necessitating another operation, which he had not the strength to survive. Dear, beloved David!

This was the sort of tragedy which was liable to shake one's nerve far more than personal experiences or near misses.

I did not get much sleep that night as, though I had no pain at all, my legs were very uncomfortable in any position. The X-rays showed only a very slight chip in one shin. But there was a lot of fluid in my knee which would take a few days to go down. It was not surprising, since I was catapulted out of the jeep by the force against the sandbags below my feet, so there must have been a considerable strain on the knee joints.

I was more worried as to whether I had cracked an eardrum as I had sharp earache when I got some water into it washing. I dared not say a word about this to anyone.

Macdonald was flown to England. He had two bones broken in one foot. He amused the orderlies by swearing that never again would he drive a car without sandbags. It was lucky that the mine was under my wheel and not his, or he would certainly have been killed.

I was the only battle casualty in this ward. It was a converted class-room and the other occupants were eleven soldiers, with pneumonia, bronchitis, bladder trouble, rash, food poisoning, and one Sten-gun face accident (a suppurating wound and a beastly sight). There was one nurse, a young, pretty and flirtatious but capable brunette, and two orderlies, both excellent fellows.

For a day or two I felt bilious and miserable. For I have never learnt the art of relaxing on a bedpan. It takes me all my time not to roll off.

On the day that the Division was due to attack, I fretted a lot, hoping that all would go well with 1st Gordons.

As I feared, a lot of casualties from the Highland Division were brought in during the night. The door would open, there would be a shuffle of feet, and a bundle tied up like a cocoon and reeking of chloroform would be carried in on a stretcher and put on a bed. I thought most of them were dying by the fearful groans they made, but several whom I had given up came to life and in due course sat up in bed. Most of them were Seaforths, and all agreed that the attack had been a great success; enemy small-arms fire was negligible, they said, and the only trouble was long-range shelling and mortaring. By 10 a.m. they were all away, the lightly wounded being flown to Brussels and the more serious cases direct to the United Kingdom.

I was very impressed by the two doctors who looked after me. Indeed I had heard nothing but praise of the medical services in the campaign. They told me that more than half the wounds they treated were from mortar fragmentation, and that the next highest proportion was mine injuries. One morning we had a sapper brought in who had been blown up on a mine. He had lost a foot and four fingers, had an arm broken and chest and shoulder injuries and was blind, poor chap.

My scratches healed up well and Wilson, the Australian surgeon, agreed to my going back after only four days there, though he said I must rest my knee while there was still fluid in it. I had a long chat with him. After talking about Burma we came to the conclusion that this campaign was cushy, and that most people did not appreciate how lucky they were: a quick mail and newspaper service, speedy evacuation to the United Kingdom if wounded, a good climate, friendly inhabitants, even fresh fruit and vegetables!

When I came to leave, I found I could not walk a step and had to be carried to the car, consumed with anxiety that we should meet Wilson on the way and that he would send me straight back to bed.

I rejoined the battalion in a nice country house outside 'S-Hertogenbosch. It was delightful to be back again with Harry and Co. and to hear all the news.

The next move was to Heeze, seven miles south-east of Eindhoven. We gathered that the coming operation was to clear up eastwards to the Maas, and as this would bring us almost to the German frontier, opposition was expected to be considerable. We found a nice house for the command post. The owner, Mr. Evers, had a factory which made ribbons, embroidered badges and 'galloons' – whatever they may be.

Our host was most interesting about the invasion and occupation of Holland. He told us that it was mainly treachery and the Fifth Column which defeated them. Before the war Germany offered 25,000 domestics who were gladly accepted, many of whom were spies, he said. Holland was full of German technicians; he had seven and sacked them all in 1937, which led to trouble with his Government. The Army was inefficient. Men were made to take commissions for no other reason than that they had a secondary school education; troops were considered trained after six weeks. It was the duty of one high-ranking officer to flood the Peel – the low country west of the Maas – when the invasion of Holland started. He came back to Heeze and said that it had been done and that no German could pass.

'Then why are your boots so clean?' said Mr. Evers. 'Make a record of it, Mr. Burgomaster. I charge this officer with failing to do his duty.'

Next day he went to fetch some wounded and found no difference in the Peel. Little of Holland's famous waterline was flooded. Everywhere there was incompetence or worse. The Dutch Navy, on the other hand, was excellent, and 'never was there a day in Rotterdam during the occupation without ten or twenty Germans being killed'.

We made great friends with that charming Dutch family. There were ten children, and families of this size are not at all uncommon in Holland.

Evers also told us about the bombing of Philips, the great Eindhoven firm which made wireless equipment and much else. Mosquitoes attacked it most accurately on December 6th, 1942, and very little harm was done to the rest of the town. A week later he himself was lunching in a restaurant at the next table to a Luftwaffe commission which had been sent to inspect the damage. He heard a senior German officer say: 'A masterpiece of bombing! You pilots can learn a lot from it.'

Like the Contesse de Hauteclocque, with whom we stopped for our last night on French soil, he told us how much the American stratosphere bombing was dreaded: how the Fortresses came time after time and hit Amsterdam instead of its airfield, 'then the R.A.F. bombed it so good that it did not have to be bombed no more.' In fact, they much preferred to be bombed by the R.A.F.!

The plot began to unfold. We were to do a daylight crossing of the Wessem Canal near Weert in about a week's time, in assault boats. 5-7th Gordons and two battalions of 152 Brigade were to do the same thing further to the left, so eight companies would be crossing at the same time. Zero Hour was to be 4.30 p.m., though I would have preferred it to have been after dark. A good deal of shelling and mortaring was expected. A German warrant officer who had deserted said that 394 Assault Gun Regiment with twenty-seven self-propelled guns had just arrived in the area.

We had a rehearsal of the canal crossing.

The plan was for tanks to dominate the far bank while the two leading companies advanced with the flat-bottomed, collapsible assault boats on the top of Bren-carriers. They would stop short of the canal and the boats would be taken off and 'built', i.e. pulled out to their full size and the wooden props bolted in. Then each boat would be carried forward and launched by the ten men who were to cross in it. The first crossing would be made by paddling, but after that the boats would be pulled from one side to the other by rope. The rehearsal went very well, as was to be expected with nobody shooting at us.

At this time most training instructions were about mines, which appeared to be becoming an increasingly important weapon. Almost every day there was a note about some new mine, either metal, wooden or plastic, or some new variation in the method of laying them.

The latest one was the schu-mine, a small wooden box about six inches by three inches, the lid of which was slightly raised when it was set. Being so small, it was easy to place under dead leaves or a piece of turf, and its effect was usually to blow off

111

the foot of the person who trod on it. We were to have more casualties from this schu-mine than all the other mines together.

My knee was improving, but I was far from well. I seemed to get headaches and felt tired and below par, which was a bore with a battle coming off.

The attack took place on November 14th.

Everything went pretty well, except that we unfortunately had about fifty casualties, including three officers wounded: Chappell, Barbrooke and Wood; a high proportion considering that the enemy did not stop to fight and the only opposition came from long-range mortars.

We left Heeze at 10.30 p.m. for an assembly area south of Weert: just a few farmhouses round which the companies clustered. I watched headquarters draw their dinners: three slabs of bully, hot potatoes and peas, hot prunes and custard, and tea, all cooked at Heeze and brought up in thermos containers. Harry and I established a small H.Q. in a farm: in a stone floor kitchen, with the usual sour smell of urine coming through from the cows and sows in the room next door. There was some hectic last-minute planning to do, while the Dutch family ate or stood about, taking it all as a matter of course.

Just before Zero Hour I went outside and watched the companies moving forward. Each man was as usual very heavily loaded, carrying arms, ammunition, small pack and pick or shovel. They were always very quiet and solemn when going into action: intense, approaching the grim. Those were the real heroes of war, I thought to myself as they filed past me, the men who actually went right up to the enemy position and through the doorway, they and the officers who led them. At one time in the 1914–18 war the average life of a platoon commander was ten days. Now it was about a month. There was not very much difference.

At Zero Hour the guns all round us opened up. I stood there for a time to see if I could hear anything coming back, but our artillery was making too much noise. Then the buffaloes, those great big black amphibious carriers containing our jeeps and anti-tank guns, churned past us on their way down to the water.

After a little I went forward to the cellar of a small farmhouse which had been badly knocked about. There I was told that the two leading companies were already over, and Harry, the Battery Commander and the Intelligence Officer, with their wireless sets in handcarts, were about to cross behind the two reserve companies.

Then the wounded began to come back. I found that they were all in B and C Companies, i.e. from the right-hand crossing; they said that two large mortar bombs had landed amongst them, when they were rather bunched up carrying the boats forward.

Meanwhile the two brothers Morrison, who were trying to launch a raft on which some anti-tank guns and jeeps could be towed across, and the buffaloes were in trouble owing to the steepness of the canal bank. I got them a bulldozer from the sappers, but this did not appear to make much difference. The buffalo boys made every effort and had a number of casualties from mortar fire while out on foot trying to find a better place to cross; but in the end, with one buffalo swimming up and down unable to get out on either bank, the attempt was given up. So now we had to wait until the sappers had built a pontoon bridge before starting to get vehicles over.

It was very crowded in the little cellar, the occupants of which were the adjutant, the battery captain, a medium artillery representative, three signallers, my servant, the R.S.M. and two Jocks whose precise duties were unknown. Also two Dutchmen and a girl of about seventeen; one of the Jocks snored, with his head in her lap. There were a few mattresses and some sacks, and with a small oil stove we were very comfortable.

I could hear on my wireless set that all the companies of the four battalions reported being on their objectives, though one said that it was under fire from Craven. (The jargon code names for this operation were hunts, thus 1st Gordons H.Q. was now at Grafton and the companies were at Blazers, Garth, Fernie and Quorn, while our two crossing places were North Berkeley and South Berkeley. Who was the fox-hunter at Brigade H.Q.? I wondered.)

The sappers had the bridge built soon after midnight but we had to wait until 5th Black Watch and 5-7th Gordons had got their fighting vehicles over before it came to our turn.

I found Harry and Battalion H.Q. in a very cold and draughty farmhouse, all the glass of which had been blown out. After breakfast the General paid us a visit. He told us that 154 Brigade had had a fair number of casualties from mines, chiefly the new wooden schu-mine.

I got a letter from Joyce that afternoon. Within an hour of being wounded I had written to tell her how trifling it was. This was just as well, as the War Office telegram five days later referred to '...*nine* leg injuries'. I eagerly awaited the letter which it said was to follow, as I was sure it would be a masterpiece.

We drove into Roggel without any trouble.

The church tower was blown down by the Germans before they withdrew in the night, so that we could not use it as an observation post. We picked a modern house with a modern woman inside it for our H.Q., and thought 'how nice this will be.' But no sooner had we finished lunch than orders were received for us to occupy ground covering the Zig Canal four miles away. The only buildings in the whole area were what was prominently marked on the map as 'California Farm'. I begged Harry to keep away from this as it was such an obvious target to shell; emphasis was given to this by somebody adding that the Brigade mortar platoon had fifteen casualties the night before from two direct hits upon the house they were occupying. So Harry said that he would put the minimum possible H.Q. in it, and the rest were to stay well back.

The companies moved out into positions between California Farm and the canal, and began to dig in. This brought down

114

heavy shellfire, but it was so inaccurate that it only caused three casualties. A lot of enemy activity could be seen beyond the far bank.

Soon after dark a Liaison Officer arrived from Brigade to say that Division required us to cross the canal that night, so that a bridge could be built for 154 Brigade to be pushed through tomorrow. We did not care for this idea at all, as the crossing was obviously well-defended and by this time it was too dark for reconnaissance. Harry went off to Brigade bristling with objections, but by the time he got there they, too, had realised that it was not a good idea.

While he was away we heard that one of our subalterns, Charles Morley, was killed while inspecting the canal. Apparently there was a possible crossing place along the top of a lock gate. He was just about to go over when he was hit in many places by a Spandau firing at him from twenty yards away across the water. His platoon, who thought the world of him, recovered his body after dark. He was a fine chap and always cheerful, an ex-London policeman with a huge jaw. His characteristic wave of the arm whenever he went into action was not to be forgotten. Only the day before Harry was saying how brave he was and that he hoped he would not go and get himself killed. He left a young wife and small son.

We were now reduced to only two officer rifle platoon commanders, instead of the twelve we should have had. Of course, this spoke very highly for our subalterns, who became casualties because they were always at the forefront of the battle. And it spoke equally badly for the replacement system. I remarked at the time that this battalion could do *anything* if it had officers, and nothing without them.

Alex Lumsden reported that his company had been very shaken by the shelling, in spite of the fact that they had had only three casualties. He said they just sat in their slit-trenches and would not even eat. So Harry had a long talk to the Brigadier about the shortage of officers.

There was a lot of enemy shelling a thousand yards away to our right. A sporting young girl came through it to tell us that there were twenty Germans in British uniforms in a village a mile away, and that they were rounding up all the Dutchmen. British or American uniforms? She was not certain, but khaki.

After lunch next day the Brigadier spoke to Harry on the telephone. He said that two companies of 5th Camerons had crossed on the left and were being fiercely counter-attacked. So, in order to create a diversion, we were required to make another crossing that evening. Harry said, 'Oh, my God!' in a voice of despair. The Brigadier was very apologetic and Harry replied: 'Well, you know my views. However, I will do my best.' While the company commanders were being sent for, Harry and I had a real good grouse about our being rushed into an operation in this way. He remarked that our only previous failure, at Colombelles, was due to the same factors that would be operative this time: tired troops having to attack from out of slit-trenches.

The Brigadier (none of this was his fault) came round and tried to get Harry to fix the time of attack for 5 p.m., or even 7 p.m. Harry said '9 p.m. at the earliest,' and I tried to support him by arguing that it could not be done before 11 p.m. Harry clinched the matter by saying that we had had five days to plan the last crossing, and now we barely had five hours, so Zero Hour was set for 9 p.m.

Though Harry was extremely anxious about the outcome of this operation, he behaved very calmly and sensibly. By 4.30 p.m. the company and supporting arms commanders had been given the broad outline of the plan and went off to look at the routes to the two crossing places before it was dark. Harry had had to choose these from the map as there was no time for him to go and look at the ground. By this time it was raining hard.

At 5.30 p.m. we all met again, in the kitchen of California House. The atmosphere was very cheerful as Harry gave out his orders, due to the jokes he made and the tone he set. The morale of the assembled officers, sitting on a few chairs but mostly on the floor, the window-sill and the kitchen stove, looking at their maps or taking notes, had never been higher.

I was very impressed and so was Lieut.-Col. Eden. He was a gunner friend of Harry's and on a few days' leave. He used to teach assault river crossings at the Senior Officers' School, though he had never actually taken part in one. Now he was going to cross with the infantry, to see if his pre-war teaching had been correct: a sportsman, if ever there was one.

The conference broke up at 6.30 p.m., leaving two hours for sub-unit commanders to give out their orders, feed and prepare for action, in so far as this could be done in the open in pouring rain. Most company commanders brought their N.C.O.s back into California House and gave up all hope of briefing the men.

Bert walked round with a large earthenware jar and everybody got well rummed-up, the first time that I had seen this happen. They left in a state bordering upon hilarity. As soon as peace reigned in California, I checked through the timings of the fire plan which had been so hurriedly prepared and made a couple of corrections, lifting two phases of it five minutes earlier for the greater safety of our forward platoons.

Then, once again, I stood in the doorway and tried to read the battle. I could see the tracer of our tanks on the canal bank and the jets of flame from the crocodiles. I could see a lot of shells bursting well this side of the water, clearly not the Government's. Later I heard that the bulk of the enemy fire came down in the gap between the two companies, since Harry had wisely chosen to cross on a front of eight hundred yards. A few shells, which landed closer, buried themselves so deep in soft mud before exploding that not much harm was done. Incredible as it is to relate, we had only two casualties.

About twenty prisoners were marched back and I listened to Likvornik examining them. They said that their company had twenty-two casualties from our shellfire that afternoon. They

117

also said that their commander was Lieutenant Fockt. Somebody remarked that it was to be expected that he would be.

Soon we got the news that all the companies were on their objectives and the sappers began to build their bridges. This time we were not attempting to get supporting arms over until the bridges were up, as the canal was too narrow and the sides too steep to have any chance of getting buffaloes or rafts across.

Theoretically the chief risk in these operations was that of being counter-attacked with armour before the anti-tank guns were in position. So medium artillery was always deployed against any such threat. These guns fired a 100-lb. shell and therefore had four times the destructive power of the 25-pounder, which itself was ineffective against tanks. Their officer told me that near Caen his regiment brewed-up two Tiger tanks and knocked over a third with their first salvo of the campaign.

We were all very relieved when the night's operation was safely and successfully over.

I think we were all secretly dreading that there might be some sort of fiasco if there were casualties among officers, since each company now had only two instead of five. Actually the margin between success and failure was perhaps narrower than one might imagine with tired troops, and war-weary N.C.O.s who did not feel up to taking the responsibilities of officers. Of course, it is easy for a man to avoid taking part in an attack in the dark; he can say he fell asleep at a pause or that he lost his way. I talked to Ewen, our Padre, who always of his own choice went into battle with one of the companies. He said what a small degree there was between sticking it and breaking down, when going forward under fire; how it only needed one man to shout, 'This is murder, I'm getting out,' and he would take half a dozen with him.

There was a lot of shelling in the next two days, mostly round the bridge area, and a couple hit California House. One broke the fanlight over the front door and a few small pieces

1. D-Day, Omaha Beach. Several landing craft foundered before they reached the shore.

2. A section advancing in Normandy.

3. Approaching the Reichswald Forest.

4. A German soldier passes a blazing American half-track in the Ardennes.

5. The 1st Gordons enter Goch.

6. The Prime Minister watches Retreat near Goch.

7. Gordon Highlanders resting in Holland.

8. Major General Thomas Rennie, Divisional Commander from Normandy to the Rhine, with his A.D.C., Lieutenant Douglas Tweedie.

9. Field Marshal Montgomery inspects a Gordon Quarter-Guard.

10. A rudimentary American advanced aid station.

11. Queuing up at a field kitchen.

12. 5/7th Gordons cross the frontier into Germany.

13. Amphibious vehicles crossing the Rhine.

14. Victory March Past at Bremerhaven, 12 May, 1945. General Horrocks takes
the salute.

15. Unveiling of the 51st Divisional Memorial at St. Valery, June, 1950.

went down the passage and into the kitchen, but without hitting any of the twenty people inside.

A lot of transport passed through to the left of us, for we ourselves were in an impassable morass, and so had become more or less non-operational. But unfortunately there were no buildings into which we could move. I paid C Company a visit. They had good deep sandy dug-outs, lined with straw, but they scarcely kept the rain out. As Alec said, it was miserable when you had to sit crouched under a groundsheet and could not even write a letter in comfort.

Alec's personal dug-out looked particularly uninviting. He was a member of the Stock Exchange and had no military ambitions whatever. When Harry offered him a company he only accepted because he felt that it was his duty to take a greater share of the risk and discomfort than that which normally fell to the lot of the adjutant.

Soon we had pushed the enemy back across the whole length of the Maas.

There was talk of the Division moving, though we did not know either where to or with what objective. As far as we could see we were not, like Caesar, going into winter quarters. The strategy of the Higher Command appeared to be to drive right ahead, without a pause, and try to finish off the war. Bert's theory was that some good troops would be wanted in the Reichswald, which from all accounts was an unpleasant place. I hoped he might be proved wrong.

On November 22nd we heard that the Division was to move in a couple of days to what was known as 'the island'. It was, in fact, an island, between the Waal and the Lower Rhine, though we were only in possession of part of the eastern end of it, between Nijmegen and Arnhem. It was too flooded for any major activity, so we hoped that it would be a pretty quiet area.

Harry was sent for by the General and returned with the startling news that he had been appointed Commander of 44 Infantry Brigade, in 15th Scottish Division. Further, the

General had made a strong application for me to be promoted to command in his place. I felt sure that he would not succeed in this, as the same signal that promoted Harry designated one Grant Peterkin, Camerons, to take his place. It was said that he was a superman to whom Army wanted to give a few months' experience of commanding a battalion (he had had a reconnaissance regiment for nearly two years) before he went on to command a brigade.

Everybody was terribly sorry that Harry was leaving, and I was very sad that our happy little family at Battalion H.Q. was being broken up. Anyway, it meant that he was no longer so likely to become a casualty. During battle, when I had been further back and Harry up with the companies, I had dreaded that a voice would come on the air on a forward wireless set and say, 'The Colonel has been hit.'

I was busy arranging a farewell dinner for Harry when word came for me to meet the Brigadier at Zetten before dark, with a view to spending the night with the American battalion whose sector 1st Gordons were to take over. My blown-up jeep had not yet been replaced so I had to take another, and before we had driven ten miles a big-end went.

From then on it was a question of hopping lifts. Two R.E.M.E. officers took me to Eindhoven, where I was picked up by a civil affairs major who put me down at 'S-Hertogenbosch, then a Canadian ambulance took me to Nijmegen, by which time it was dark and raining. The driver of the latter told me that the Hun still bombed and shelled the famous Nijmegen bridge which, four hundred yards long, was so much in the news when the airborne army landed. Indeed from the A.A. and flares it looked as if the Hun were having another go at that moment.

Nijmegen, with its 50,000 inhabitants, was a larger town than I expected, and I soon got lost looking for the Canadian Military Police. However, when I found them, the Orderly Corporal made no trouble about turning out a jeep to take me on my way, and I wondered if a British N.C.O. would have been allowed so much authority.

The nearer we got to the bridge, the more damage there was to be seen. It gave me an eerie feeling as we began to cross, with the moonlight struggling through the clouds and a rattle of musketry from time to time. The defence of this bridge was an interesting problem as it was in sight of the enemy on the next bend of the river. Not only did they shell it and try to bomb it, but they also floated mines down towards it, so our men on the banks, and in armoured cars on the bridge itself, shot at anything drifting downstream.

Safely over the bridge, we drove straight ahead and through the blinding rain. I had only a small-scale map and soon lost confidence in my reading of it. We came to a dead village. Houses were shattered, branches stricken down, and dead cattle lay about the main street. So many people had driven straight through our lines to the enemy, and many more had driven on to mines.

I decided to turn round. Returning, I remarked on the smell of death to my driver, and felt rather foolish when this turned out to be the brake linings. We stopped at the first house we came to and, as so often happened, the daughter of the house, who learnt English at the High School, interpreted for us. They put us on our way, and without further incident we arrived an hour later at the American Regimental H.Q. at Zetten.

After an excellent supper the Executive Officer (which corresponds to our second-in-command) of the 3rd American Airborne Battalion, from whom we were to take over, drove me across to them. Their command post was in the outhouses of a large baronial house, of which I had so far seen only the vague outline in the moonlight.

I slept like a log in my clothes in a cellar, under a communal quilt on one of the communal palliasses.

Next morning the Executive officer led me across to one of the estate cottages, where we had a wash and shave in the kitchen sink. Breakfast over, we drove forward a mile to the huge Rhine dyke, arriving there just as it was beginning to get light. The Major then sent the jeep back, explaining that all vehicles moving in front of Battalion H.Q. could be seen from the high ground on the far side of the river, and usually drew fire. So from then onwards we walked.

I had not previously soldiered with Americans. This officer, with his kindly, rugged face, his dry sense of humour, his clipped speech, his business-like efficiency, his pudding-bowl steel helmet, his short coat and tight-fitting 'pants' showing a broad expanse of buttock, might have come straight out of the pages of *Life*. Though we plodded through deep mud for hours I was sorry when our trip came to an end. I thought that if all American units were as good as this one, it was not surprising that their armies had done so well.

We had to hold about a square mile of flat country with two small villages each side of it, Randwijk and Opheusden. The latter was a horrible place, our allies said, for it was full of schu-mines which had blown off six American feet. The whole area was flat ground, broken up by a few farmhouses and avenues of trees, and overlooked from beyond the Rhine except right under the dyke. Beyond this there were two or three hundred yards of bare ground leading to the river, which was now very swollen; it looked to be nearly a mile wide. They said that one could expect about thirty shells a day in the battalion area.

Later in the morning I went to see the Brigadier, with many good reasons why the Black Watch area should include Opheusden. To this he consented, provided I took in Randwijk, to which I was quite ready to agree. So there I went next, and found that we could hold it with only one platoon in the village itself, with two posts on the dyke. I wanted to hold our area with the minimum number of troops, so as to rest as many as possible. With all this flood-water about, the risk of being attacked seemed to be nil.

The battalion arrived very late, and somewhat tired, having

marched all the way from Nijmegen as troop-carriers were not allowed over the bridge. I was sorry when the time came for my American friends to leave.

It seemed that this place was going to be exhausting for the battalion commander, who always had to get up very early in order to go round the area before daylight or while the morning mist was still hanging over the ground. Walking back across the fields for 10 a.m. breakfast, I saw some pinkfoot flighting very high. It reminded me of wild-fowling in Lincolnshire before the war, with the Humber instead of the Rhine.

We had church parade in the Baron's private chapel, which apparently was sufficiently Low Church for Ewen. I read the Lesson, Isaiah, Ch. 53, which was no doubt as incomprehensible to the congregation as it was to me. Walking back across the park after the service reminded me of an English country house week-end. The moated house was certainly a lovely place. The burgomaster of Zetten told us that the estate had been a thousand years in the family of Baron Van Lynden, who at that moment was in occupied territory. When the Americans were there the big house was full of refugees, but they left that morning. So in the afternoon we all moved across. We were certainly more comfortable there. There were a few shells in the night and I was not at all happy at the thought of more than fifty men of Battalion H.Q. sleeping on the top floor in the outhouses.

The Brigadier walked round with me early one morning. He told me that the Huns might well flood us out of this position. They had only to breach the dykes to the east to flood everything to a depth of three feet in twelve hours. In that case we should have a rush to get off the island, and of course the enemy would stonk the bridge while we were doing so; with one or two trucks brewing-up on it, it could well become a death-trap. A scheme for a withdrawal (Operation Noah) was being prepared, and orders were coming out for all transport that was not essential to be sent off the island.

My policy here was to live and let live, so that we could get a good rest. We did not shoot at the enemy unless they shot at us. But I said that every shell or machine-gun burst they sent over the river was to be returned threefold.

I tried to catch up with the office work in the evenings: citations for the last canal crossing, recommendations of N.C.O.s for commissions, a letter from the General about enemy mines, a new medical pamphlet, an instruction on the disposal of men below a certain medical category, another about misuse of Army equipment, and so on. Reading through the citations file I learnt that Harry had recommended me for a D.S.O., which was later downgraded to a Mention in Despatches.

One company had a platoon post rather far out, and one night they rang up to say that they could hear a lot of firing in that direction and their line to them was cut. It sounded like an enemy raid and I sweated a bit at the thought of it. However, two men of a ration party walked into Company H.Q., having just returned from that post, and said that the firing had all been coming from the direction of the Black Watch.

There was a conference about schu-mines at Brigade. To get back to it quickly from the morning round I took a chance and had my jeep meet me at C Company. This was inexcusable as it brought down an accurate mortar shoot on them. Alec said that he was hit by a piece of brick on his way to the cellar, and the C.S.M., who was having his breakfast, got some plaster in his mess tin. Luckily there were no casualties.

Everybody was very interested in the water level on the island. We had to check it three times a day and report to Brigade.

We were very glad not to be holding Opheusden. The Black Watch were having a lot of bother there. They lost an officer and a sergeant on schu-mines. They also lost a company commander, taken prisoner while on reconnaissance. Some of the many wild animals that were roaming around stampeded and started blowing themselves up on anti-personnel mines, with the result that the Huns in front of Opheusden thought that they were being attacked and opened fire.

There were only three Dutch in the whole battalion area. The Americans told them that they might get shot; they replied that they were too old to be frightened of that and their only dread was of being moved. The area must have been evacuated very suddenly, for in Randwijk the joints were still hanging in the butcher's shop. The village had been badly looted by the Americans. Of one formation it was said that they used bazookas to open a safe, and that their Colonel remarked that he did not object to this, but when it came to using an anti-tank gun . . . Not that British troops can talk about looting, I am afraid. Many of the ground-floor rooms were now occupied by tame rabbits, pigs and cattle. I heard that the General said 'Good morning' to what proved to be a goat looking out of a bedroom window.

Then one lunch-time the Brigadier rang up and said 'Did Harry tell you that there was a possibility of Grant Peterkin coming to take over the Battalion? Well, he's arrived. He's on his way round to you now.'

I took the new Colonel all round early next morning, and had to admit that he seemed to be a pretty good chap. It was the usual waddle through the mud after a dawn start, returning in the mist about 9.30 a.m. There was more firing from the other

Buffalo

side than usual, single shots and short bursts: the Hun doing the scruffy soldier's trick of cleaning the rust out of his barrel by firing. Afterwards I heard an odd tap-tapping and thought that it must be a machine-gun a long way off, though indeed the 'bursts' did not sound quite as one would expect. Then I looked up and saw that I had been listening to a woodpecker.

There was a rise of two and a half feet in the level of the Rhine in twelve hours, but still no change on the island.

One night I had a realistic dream: that I was standing on a bridge, that the enemy started to shell it and that I jumped very quickly into a slit-trench. I woke up to find myself lying on the floor, with shells landing outside in the park. We were shelled a little every night. Luckily the enemy did not repeat this in the daytime, or we should certainly have had casualties among people moving about. I could only imagine that the Hun thought that we had a lot of transport bringing up rations and supplies during the night.

Just after dark a private of 11th Parachute Battalion, who had been lying up on the other side since Arnhem, crossed the Rhine in a boat and walked into A Company. It was a very stout effort and I was sorry I missed seeing him.

Douglas Renny, commanding 5-7th Gordons, and I were told we could go on three days' leave to Brussels. There had been no further rise in the water level, but most people seemed to think that the island might well be flooded before we got back. If this were so I knew I should be sorry. I had grown quite attached to this spot: to the view across the Rhine from the dyke, to the long avenues of poplars and the wild-fowl flighting overhead, to the flooded fields and ditches and the morning shoulders of mist, to the pigs in the parlours of Randwijk, and to the baronial hall, the most comfortable H.Q. we had so far had.

We got away soon after lunch, in Douglas's big staff-car.

I felt very carefree. At Louvain we stopped for a haircut and shampoo, and I ate a pound of luscious grapes during the process. After supper we went to a night-club. The girls were as pretty as birds. The saxophones gulped and shivered, retched and heaved. But Douglas and I soon felt more than ready for bed. Both of us were too tired to enjoy ourselves, drink or no drink.

That night for the first time for a month I did not have to sleep in my socks to keep warm. Oh, the joy of central heating and a private bathroom!

The Plaza was very comfortable. Joyce and I had stayed there before the war, and the dressing-table looked very bare without her things on it. It was now being run by N.A.A.F.I. as an officers' leave hotel and was very popular, not least because they had a stock of captured German liquor which was being sold off at such prices as three francs for a gin or brandy, about one-twentieth of the price outside. Sensible people stoked up well before going out for the evening, though, as Douglas said, this practice did smack somewhat of organisation.

Since all the restaurants were closed, we lunched at the Officers' Club in rue d'Arlon. On the way there we were stopped in the street by an old man, small, dark and ferrety; his front teeth were all gold and his clothes as black as his market. He wanted us to change some notes for him. Trafficking in currencies was of course a court-martial offence and we sent him about his business.

After lunch we went to the races: two on the flat, two over hurdles and two 'chases. There were a few British officers riding, presumably from 21 Army Group H.Q. in Brussels. It was one of those tricky figure-of-eight courses, like Bournemouth where I threw away a race in 1927 by getting lost.

By dinner-time Douglas had become attached to a Belgian count, so I teamed up with two of the 15-19th Hussars. They told me that they never had any trouble over deserters. This was perhaps not surprising as tank crews were all very good types, whereas infantry had to take the bad along with the good. On the other hand, they were faced with an increasingly large number who said that they could never again fight in a tank:

127

usually men who had escaped from one that was on fire, with perhaps unpleasant results to the others in their crew. We had a grouse against the ground staff of the R.A.F., so many of whom seemed to be stationed in Brussels. Of course this was most unreasonable for we could not win the war without them. But one hoped they realised how lucky they were compared with the rank and file of the infantry.

After dinner we went the rounds. By chance we found ourselves in one of the bars where the young Belgian *maquis* had brought me early in September. The *patron* was miserable and looking ten years older. His wife's arm had been amputated. She was accidentally shot by one of the young resistance youths on a self-appointed patrol. In a nightclub I ran into David Scott-Moncrieff, on his way through to France to buy some wine for the Mess. As far as I could make out, he was talking art to a tart.

'And how many Rubens have you in the Beaux Arts?' I heard him ask.

The blondie blinked at him goggle-eyed.

Next morning I bought a lot of Christmas presents, mostly toys for the children.

Douglas and I lunched together again and he was very interesting about 5-7th Gordons' last action beyond the Zig Canal. he was with a forward company when it was counter-attacked. Over the wireless he called for the artillery, but the Battery Commander queried it as he considered it too close. Douglas sprinted all the way back to his H.Q. and ordered it down a hundred yards beyond his leading position. He said that he felt most uncomfortable about running lest that should give a bad impression, but he considered that if he had not done so the company would have been overrun.

During this action he saw a Jock sitting on top of the earth excavated from his slit-trench, firing a Bren, rifle and piat in turn into the mist, and shouting out abuse at the enemy, in Gaelic!

After lunch we went to the Waterloo Golf Club and played eight holes, with vigour but no great degree of skill. On the way back I paid a duty call on a Belgian cousin by marriage. I had a vague idea that I had seen her some years before, at a family wedding in London. My impression was of a rather plain and disagreeable girl, so I had put off this visit until near the end of my last day. Never did I make a greater mistake, for Livia is charming. She spoke perfect English, and produced her two boys for me to see if there was a trace of likeness to mine.

Later she took me out to dinner at the house of a Belgian diplomat. I tried to steer the talk round to conditions under the occupation, no easy task as everybody only wanted to forget it.

However, Livia did say feelingly how awful it was to wonder each morning what bad news the day would bring forth: usually that some friend had to be hidden, or had been shot or imprisoned or deported to Germany, or had disappeared without a trace. Our host said that he loved England, but he *did* wish we could have had just fifteen days of occupation by the Germans, so that we could understand what it was like.

I think he was right when he implied that we English did not, could not, understand. I was astonished when they told me that until now there had been no dancing in Belgium since 1940. I pointed out that during our darkest days we danced in England. They replied that there was hardly a woman in Belgium who had not either a father, husband, brother or lover who was not either dead, prisoner of war, or in hiding. As Livia put it, 'We have had no cause at all to dance, and even now we only do so to entertain our liberators.'

On my third and last day I lunched with Livia, to meet her mother, who was Lady-in-Waiting to the Belgian Queen Mother. The Baroness told me that, though they had an English mother, she and her brother were brought up in her father's nationality, Italian. She said that his family was now dying out for the only young male was killed at El Alamein. I thought to myself that he might well have been

129

killed by the Highland Division, and how absurd this all was.

Before starting back we heard that the Brigade had left the island, so we drove straight to its new location south-east of 'S-Hertogenbosch. I gathered that Noah did not function too well when the floods came, and that it was a bit of a scramble getting away, though there were no casualties and no great loss of equipment. The Hun crossed the Rhine in boats and sniped at us as we were withdrawing. Only 49th Division was now left on the island, holding a small perimeter round the Nijmegen bridgehead.

I felt immensely better as the result of my leave. For the last month I had been getting very tired and irritable and, worst of all, increasingly jumpy.

Jim Cassels, who commanded 152 Brigade, had supper with us and gave us an explanation as to why our last canal crossing was mounted in such a hurry.

Melville, who commanded a company in 5th Camerons, was told only to cross if there were no opposition. He was a superb, natural leader, and decided that the Germans holding the far bank did not amount to 'opposition'. So his company attacked them, killed six and took thirty prisoners, and the rest ran away.

Another company was pushed across at once, and all next day they were shelled or counter-attacked, but the position was held and that night two more battalions were put across. At the same time our Brigade advanced on the right, and the result was that the Division on our left was not called upon. Melville was given a well-deserved D.S.O. and sent off on forty-eight hours' leave to Antwerp. He was last heard of driving a tram, and Jim was awaiting a plaintive letter from the Town Major.

We were now in Berlicum, a small village six miles from 'S-Hertogenbosch. As nobody knew how long we should be out of the line, I started a cadre to train junior N.C.O.s.

The young lads were very keen. Perhaps we all enjoyed the discussions most. The first was about our war aims, and I found them surprisingly well able to express what we were all fighting for.

The next subject was 'Why I will (not) choose the Army as a post-war career.' All thirty said they would not stay on after the war, and the reason given was the same in each case, that they wanted the greater freedom of civvy street after the factory hooter had blown. They all agreed that they had been happy and well cared for while in the Army, but they wanted a life where there would be no discipline after 5 p.m., no night exercises, no dress regulations, no orderly sergeant to shout 'Lights out' and turn them out of bed at Reveille. Marriage was regarded as an unequivocal disqualification for Army life. This was only to be expected, since there was no marriage allowance below the age of thirty before the war and men were many years on the waiting-list before being allotted a married quarter.

I had a comfortable room in the local constable's house. There was a small, frightened boy of thirteen in the family who had had a large piece of shell through his shoulder; but luckily it was healing up well, with no loss of movement to his arm. The policeman told me that ten people round there, including some children, had been blown up on boche mines, and that one of them was killed trying to bury a German corpse that had been booby-trapped.

Ewen began to run a battalion rest centre at 'S-Hertogenbosch, in a hotel which we had taken over and temporarily renamed the Bydand Arms. There was no lack of girls willing to wait, and two dance bands which were only too anxious to play for an evening for a hundred cigarettes. The men's Christmas dinner was to take place here, so I hoped that no unforeseen move would occur.

We had two M.E. 109's very low overhead one day. It was only the third time that I had seen enemy aircraft since I landed on the beaches.

While we were at Berlicum a letter arrived from Beardwell, a young officer who had greatly distinguished himself leading patrols before being badly wounded at Lisieux.

He wrote: 'The surgeon had to remove one of my kidneys and also sliced off some liver . . . I was sorry to learn the sad news of David Martin's death. He saved my life by plugging up the hole in my back with a shell dressing and so stopped some of the blood getting away, while under rifle fire. He was a damn brave man.'

Of course David had never mentioned this.

I ran down to Antwerp one night and arrived a few minutes after a V1 had landed on a cinema and the adjoining N.A.A.F.I. restaurant. There must have been several hundred casualties to soldiers on leave. A lot of damage had been caused by flying bombs, and after this disaster the Divisional Rest Camp was closed down.

David Scott-Moncrieff returned from his mission, after many adventures. On reaching Reims he was told that he had to obtain special authority from the Paris director of Heidsieck if he wished to buy more than six bottles. On arriving in Paris he was promptly arrested by the Assistant Provost Marshal, since the city was out of bounds and his 'on duty' pass signed by the Colonel was inadmissible according to the regulations. David bitterly resented this as Paris was an old friend of his, and he now describes the A.P.M. as 'the worst kind of Englishman – the Englishman abroad!' He was given half an hour to get out.

On the way back he came to an overturned Army lorry, full of champagne and deserted by its driver. Some civilians were beginning to loot it. He cursed them in his fluent, faultless French for stealing wine belonging to the British Government. They helped him transfer it all to his truck and David drove on, at full speed!

We heard that 5th Black Watch and 5-7th Gordons had each had an officer away buying wine which ended far less satisfactorily. Wilding of the 5-7th spent three days in a Paris prison cell while they checked up on his statement. The Black Watch officer fared even worse, having £200 in Belgian francs stolen from his sporran in a night-club.

Montgomery held an Investiture, at which officers and men of the Division who had been awarded decorations were presented with the ribbon. Afterwards he made a speech in which he said that the German Army was on its knees and, having no petrol, would never again be able to mount an offensive.

Next day we heard that the Divisional Commander had been to a conference at Corps H.Q. This was a bad sign. I hoped they would not move us, as most elaborate arrangements had been made for the men's Christmas dinners.

Grant Peterkin was proving a tremendous success as commanding officer. He had personality, brains and charm, but above all, drive and enthusiasm. He was a tall, well-built man with sharp features and very blue eyes, clean-shaven, and fair hair brushed nearly straight back.

December 18th opened with a conference of commanders at Brigade, and in due course Grant Peterkin returned with a lot of secret stuff for my ear alone. We were to make a non-operational move eastwards to Beers next day, for the purpose of getting into position to attack through the Reichswald and up to the Rhine early in the New Year. As this concentration had to be kept hidden from the enemy, the move was to take place after dark.

So off I went to reconnoitre Beers. It looked like being rather a squash, with Brigade H.Q. taking the biggest and best buildings, none of which was large enough for the Christmas dinners.

When the Battalion left for Beers, I stopped behind at Berlicum to finish off the last three days of the cadre. It seemed very quiet with only myself and Murray, my servant, alone in the house.

I studied the maps. The Reichswald lay beyond the German frontier. It would be good to be fighting on enemy soil at last.

After all these years I found it hard to realise that we should so soon be invading Germany.

Then I heard that, in spite of what Montgomery had said a few days before, the Huns had attacked in the Ardennes. The report said they had penetrated some distance, though this was obviously untrue. It could hardly amount to much.

Mortar

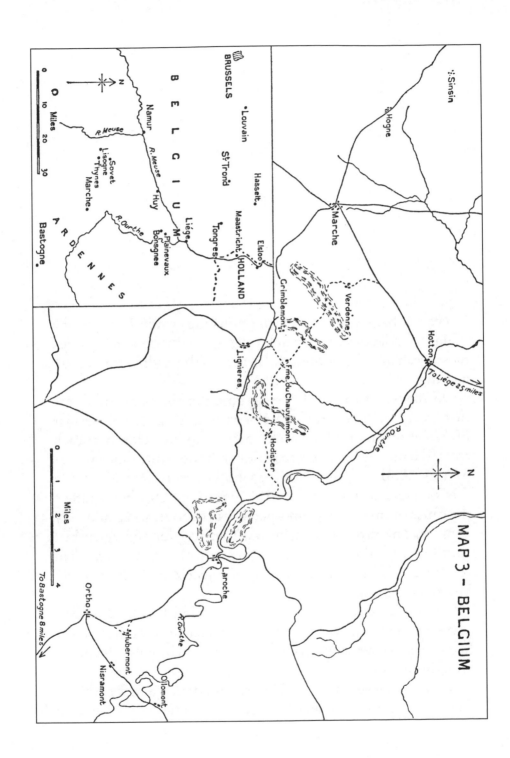

MAP 3 - BELGIUM

Part Three

Belgium

6

However, half-way through the morning, while I was in the middle of a lecture, a despatch rider arrived with a mysterious message from the Adjutant: 'Bring in the cadre, for we are moving far.'

On the way to Beers I passed, going in the opposite direction, forty or fifty jeeps and 15-cwt. trucks with the familiar HD in crimson on a blue background. I looked closely at each and it did not take me long to realise that they were unit advance parties. And all going south, whereas only last night the Division had been moving north! I asked myself what could be the cause of this sudden, unexpected turnabout, and could only come to one possible conclusion: that we were being rushed south to stop the new German thrust in the Ardennes. I had reinstated young Ackers when my new jeep arrived. Now I told him to step on it.

I found Battalion H.Q. eating a hurried lunch. 'Advance parties to Hasselt' was the only information they had so far been given, so we seized some bully beef and biscuits and drove straight off again.

It was a long run down to Hasselt and dark when we arrived. I could see no sign of any Brigade representatives, so went to

Corps H.Q. in the Royal Imperial Girls School. Here there was chaos. The schoolyard was hopelessly jammed with all kinds of transport, to the confusion of several cussing, honking drivers. There were no lights or signs, and the dark passages within were thronged with soldiery who did not belong to the H.Q. With difficulty I found my way to the map-room. Here, if there was not precisely a flap on, they were certainly taking a keen interest in the German break-through. G Branch had no idea where the Highland Division was to be found and had never heard of 153 Brigade. 'But you must have some communications to a Division under your command,' I expostulated. Well, perhaps if I returned an hour later they might have.

Another Highland officer, now part of this H.Q., took me downstairs to look for food. In a large class-room we found a cook ladling out stew. Worried-looking staff officers were in the queue with clerks and orderlies and the crews of the Guards' tanks which were blocking the yard outside.

We borrowed two mess tins and mugs from the kitchen, and found a table in a corner. I asked at once for details of the battle. My friend told me that it started on December 16th. The Germans attacked with twenty-two divisions, including a high proportion of armour, on a frontage of twenty-five miles and where the Americans were numerically rather weak. Hitler himself addressed representatives of each formation before it started. They had now reached a point thirty-five miles south-west of Liége.

It came as a complete surprise to the Allies. In this connection the Field Marshal's remarks a day or two before it began – 'The enemy can never again mount a major attack' – should be remembered; not to sneer at a very great general but to show the fallibility of our Intelligence Service, which failed to give warning of other German coups, such as the invasion of Norway.

Still nobody could tell me where the Division was, but this time they did at least know the general area it had been allotted.

I drove there and soon picked up the little green 87 lights which led me to Brigade H.Q. in Bourg-Léopold.

There I had a chat with the Brigadier, who had a bottle of brandy. We agreed that this German thrust was an excellent move, and I don't think the cognac was responsible for our reasoning. We considered that it would be easier to destroy the enemy out here on our own ground and away from his wire and minefields, his concrete emplacements, his carefully sited lines of fire and his ammunition dumps: the formidable defences of the Siegfried Line. Roddy Sinclair was a splendid man and I was sorry when it was time to leave.

The battalion had been allotted Tessenderloo, an attractive little old market-town, at least so it looked in the dark. In the square I met the signal sergeant, who pointed out the house chosen for our H.Q. I rang the bell and was surprised to be greeted in French; somehow I had overlooked the fact that we were in Belgium once more. I made a note to remember to carry my shell dressing and morphia capsule again, if we really were going to fight once more.

The first event of the morning was a conference at Brigade, which the Colonel and I both attended.

Somewhat unsuccessfully we tried to find out more about the general situation. The Brigadier had not been able to discover what reserves the Americans still had in hand. As far as I could make out from the map, there was nothing to stop the German spearhead except the Household Cavalry Regiment on the line of the Meuse. Then came the thunderbolt: the Highland Division was to take up a defensive position round Louvain, which is only fifteen miles from Brussels itself! One realised that the situation was considered serious.

Soon we found ourselves in a little straggling agricultural village about three miles south-east of Louvain. On the way there I had a word with Jerry Sheil,[1] who commanded the

---

[1]   Killed in action on April 29th, 1945, the last casualty in the Division.

Divisional artillery, and was one of its best-known figures. He was of the same opinion as the Brigadier: that it was better to fight the Hun out in the open, rather than back among his defences.

But John Frary did not agree with these commanders. He mistrusted all this talk to the effect that it was a good thing to be attacked by twenty-two divisions, for it reminded him of the general attitude after the fall of France: 'So the Germans have overrun another country. Now we know where we stand. Jolly good show!' We called John the doormouse because he liked his bed so much, but he did not sleep when signal lines had to be run out.

The wireless emphasised the gravity of the situation. It began by quoting from the German radio, which claimed that they had taken 20,000 prisoners, destroyed or captured 179 tanks and fifty guns, etc. It gave news of parachutists being dropped in American uniforms (of which we had been officially warned). It spoke of flying bombs being used to support the attack. And finally: 'All correspondents are agreed that the attack is not likely to be halted before Christmas.'

I wondered what the form was in Brussels. No doubt it was much the same in the Plaza and the night-clubs, but I wondered what the more responsible people were thinking? One hoped there would be no premature digging of trenches and loopholing of walls round there, or the civilians would certainly get the wind up.

On December 22nd, after what had been the fourth move in four days, we had arrived at Esloo, a little village seven miles north of Maastrict, at which I was told to meet a representative of Brigade at midday.

The rendezvous was at American Corps H.Q., and there was some confusion as it was split into two, Forward and Rear, and Rear was more forward than Forward. Outside was a jeep with the following inscription below the windscreen: 'Dedicated to the men who died in the jeeps from which this jeep was built.'

While waiting for the others to appear I went inside to study the situation map. The two main panzer thrusts were apparently being held, as their leading elements were no further forward than they had been two days before. 101 U.S. Airborne Division, our friends from the island, were completely surrounded at Bastogne, though according to my informant they said they were not and only needed more ammunition. Identifications of panzer and panzer grenadier divisions had been obtained to the north of what was now termed the Bulge, suggesting that a thrust might well be coming from that direction. So we had been moved across into a convenient reserve position.

Battalion H.Q. was in the usual klooster, but rather more interesting than most, as it was a nice country house built round the ruin of a thirteenth-century castle, complete with moat. We had trouble at first with the Father Superior's representative, a superior young abbot of about my own age. He had obviously plenty of accommodation but said that he could only give us one or two rooms and not till next day. After we had taken possession he was to be seen flitting down the passages like a lost spirit, muttering about 'Hitler methods'.

Our rôle of being in reserve gave us hope that we might be there for a few days, so I went round the companies to see how they would be placed for their Christmas dinner. They would not fare too badly: A Company in a hall, B in a couple of pubs, C in two large farmhouses, and so on. In one of the pubs I found Bob dancing the tango with a waitress at 10 a.m. Total war!

The Hun was still using paratroops. They were said to have dropped two hundred behind our lines in the night, and that they were driving round the countryside in American uniforms. So our jeep was carefully examined as we drove into Maastricht.

The more I saw of the Americans, the more I liked them. I took Jack Johnston to their hospital to have three teeth out, and they could not possibly have been kinder. They seemed to have so much more pep about all their activities. One could take welfare, for instance, and contrast the dreary British dental waiting-room, where you would be lucky if you were given a ration box to sit on, with the one we went into, decorated with a Christmas tree, pin-up girls, paper decorations, carnival lanterns, crystallised fruit, etc. And one could look at Maastricht: practically a front-line town, corresponding, say, to Nijmegen in our sector, yet with plenty of entertainment and several first-class American clubs for both officers and other ranks. And when the Americans ran a club they put in charge of it the most sophisticated and attractive married women they could find. The British, on the other hand, usually staffed it with the type of spinster who looked as if she were in need of welfare herself.

We were still there on December 24th, and hoping that the gastronomic orgies of the morrow would not be interrupted.

But on Christmas Day a series of warning orders arrived during the morning, each one slightly increasing in tempo.

So we put forward the men's dinners from 5 p.m. to 2 p.m., though without any great degree of confidence. At 12.30 p.m. orders arrived for us to move at 2.15 p.m. Nobody knew where we were going, nor why. The G2 at Division looked in to wish us a merry Christmas. 'I only know that we are moving south in a hurry, so it must be rather serious,' he said.

As usual, I rushed on ahead with company representatives to allot accommodation in the new area. Outside American Army H.Q. at Tongres the Brigade staff captain told us that the Division was moving to just south of Liége. He then gave each of us our unit area. As we drove through the city there was a dog-fight going on overhead. For the German Air Force to be up in strength in daylight was something altogether new.

Liége is a huge place and it looked very derelict. Few houses seemed to have any glass, yet the damage was less than that in London in 1940–41. Leaving the town and climbing out of the

Meuse valley on to the wooded high ground to the south, we found ourselves mixed up with part of our gunners' column, some cars of Division H.Q. and a few odd trucks and ambulances, all hopelessly lost. None of us had better than 1-100,000 maps, so frequently we jumped out of our cars to shout at each other: 'Happy Christmas. Where the hell are we?'

Perhaps Christmas had a little to do with it. Yet few formations have done anything so creditable as that move at short notice on Christmas Day. The sappers said that every one of their drivers was drunk, but never before had they completed a move without a single vehicle breaking down. There were certainly a few comic sights, such as a sergeant of 5-7th Gordons riding in the front of a carrier, wearing neither hat nor coat, in fact scarcely anything except a very happy smile, and frantically waving a small red flag. Liége was said to be one of the most communist towns in Europe. At any rate, this spectacle drove the population almost into a frenzy and largely accounted for the warmth of our welcome.

The country round Bonsgnée is very steep, but most attractive. Just to the south of us there were several lovely wooded valleys and a river in spate. It reminded me in places of the Speyside, of parts of Derbyshire, of an approach to the Alpes Maritimes, even of the way through the hills to Kashmir.

But as a billeting area for a battalion it appalled me. There was one modern house and two or three farms on the top of a ridge. I stood on a precipice and gazed at the panorama below me. It was certainly beautiful, but there was an almost total lack of houses. So a hurried visit to Brigade H.Q. was necessary, as the result of which we were given accommodation in Plainevaux, which had hitherto been allotted entirely to the Black Watch.

When I got back to the house on the top of the hill, after going round the companies, it was to find that Battalion H.Q. had fallen on its feet for Christmas Day. Our host, M. Lalou, was a director of various companies in Liége and he and his wife were a charming couple. They said at once: 'But of course you will dine with us tonight.' So in the end, and so very unexpectedly, we had a most enjoyable Christmas dinner party.

Afterwards we lit the tree in the oak-panelled hall. I went down to the cellar and brought up Michel, aged four. The servant also fetched her daughter, and somebody had the wit to make these two small children kneel down together to say their prayers in front of the little crib by the side of the Christmas tree. Of course they looked perfectly adorable! The flickering light of the candles was reflected on their bowed heads, and on the lined and weather-beaten faces of the six or eight officers forming circle round them. Their childish prayers were in shrill falsetto against the deep bass of the R/T earphones still crackling and burbling away in a corner.

From time to time we all went out on to the terrace, to listen to the flying bombs speeding overhead and to look down at the lovely, moonlit panorama of the snow-covered valley below us. We were all delighted to find ourselves in such beautiful country.

December 26th was another clear, cold, frosty day and the ice was bearing on the garden pond. We awoke to the song of the guns far away to the south. The Hun still seemed to be making some progress, in spite of the R.A.F. who flew 7,000 sorties on Christmas Eve and dropped 10,000 tons of bombs upon their lines of communication. But they had still not quite reached the Meuse, along which we now had 6th Airborne Division, who were rushed out in a hurry a few days before.

We were to spend a week with that charming Belgian family. Fortunately we were able to return their hospitality with a few of the things they could not procure, such as a greater range of food and a little coal (three sandbags-full, to be precise). The defaulters cut firewood and the Pioneers boarded up the panes that had been blown out by flying bombs. These missiles flew over on their way to Liége at an average rate of one every forty-five minutes. Many landed close enough to rattle the windows.

We could get very little news as to what was happening in the Bulge, in fact only what was given on the wireless.

By December 28th it seemed clear that the German thrust was now completely halted. For some time they had failed to turn up northwards and only succeeded in extending further to the west. Had they been able to keep up the momentum of the early days and to turn up northwards and cross the Meuse in force, Brussels would have been close and they would soon have been astride our lines of communication. But I cannot believe they ever had any real chance of getting so far and achieving such results.

For the first week the weather, though cold, was foggy and the Air Forces were unable to do much. But they certainly made up for it afterwards, causing tremendous havoc to the enemy supplies and communications.

There was a good deal of argument amongst ourselves as to whether we were likely to be used, for the Americans might have considered it a point of honour to clear it all up without using British troops. But we felt sure that of all our divisions we had the best chance.

Few battalions used to take their pipers into battle, since it was impossible to replace them if they became casualties. I thought this policy was right, though I was never very comfortable about it, since it was so contrary to the traditions of a Highland regiment. Ours had been piping and dancing reels in Brussels for over a month, and the Colonel sent me to look them up.

There seemed to have been some panic among the civilians, who were afraid that the enemy would reach Brussels and then proceed to take it out of them for their jubilation at being liberated.

I got back in time to hear the 9 p.m. news, in which the Germans were reported to have admitted that they had begun to retire. Moreover, they even said that their withdrawal in the centre was due to the fact that they were fighting 'the famous

51st Highland Division'. This explained an odd remark of
Livia's when I had telephoned to her. She was very surprised to
hear that I was in Brussels, and said: 'But aren't you fighting?'
to which I replied: 'Not today.'

An account of German activities in American uniforms was
circulated.

They had been organised in jeep parties of three or four
with missions of sabotage or intelligence. The three whom the
Americans announced shooting a few days before, a cadet
officer and two N.C.O.s, were provided with all the necessary
papers and equipment, and were even coached about formations so that they could answer questions. This party was
ordered to report upon the bridges over the Meuse by wireless,
but they had been behind our lines only half an hour when they
were asked for the password and, not knowing it, were arrested.

There was a good story about Burnett, who commanded the
Field Regiment that supported us. He, too, did not know
the password, nor had he his identity card on him, so the
doughboys insisted upon taking down his trousers to see
whether he was wearing German pants.

It had been a quiet and pleasant week, except for the V1's
flying over to the tune of about fifty a day. Liége was said to
have had no less than eighty-eight during the hours of darkness
one night. Brigade H.Q. had one in the garden of their château
and several people were cut by glass, though fortunately none
seriously.

On the afternoon of December 31st we were discussing the
advisability of starting some training, when a warning order
arrived to the effect that we should probably move next day.
No particulars were given and there was much speculation as to
whether it would be to the north and back to Holland, or south-
wards to fight.

Half-way through dinner a message giving our destination
arrived. It was sent out for the Intelligence Section to decode,
and after a quarter of an hour Sergeant Childs came in and

handed the Intelligence Officer a piece of paper. Military security precluded us from telling our host and hostess where we were moving, so we were unable to satisfy our curiosity until Madame rose from the table. Then David whispered: 'South,' and a great thrill ran through us all.

Afterwards we sat round the huge log fire and played old-fashioned games with pencil and paper until the moment came to see the New Year in, which was done in the traditional manner. Then, and for the last time, we went out on to the terrace to look down at that lovely, frostbound, moonlit valley. Far away below us a light twinkled where one of the companies was having its own carousal.

I wondered how many of our little company would see this brave new year to its close.

We bade an almost tearful farewell to M. and Mme Lalou; to Christian, the girl of fourteen; and to little Michel, a rather backward child in consequence of a double mastoid, whom we had seen putting on weight and increasing in colour and liveliness each day, as the result of our good rations. We felt sorry to be leaving them behind in their fly-bomb area.

Whatever we may have thought when we received the signal, our new area seemed to be as peaceful and far removed from war as the previous one.

Sovet looked all right on the map when I was given it as a billeting area that morning, but when I got there I found that the S.S. boys had preceded me and burnt most of the houses down in reprisal for maquis activity. No other unit seemed to be interested in Thynes and Lisogne, so we went there instead: two very nice little villages in an agricultural countryside.

To our surprise we were now told that we might be there a fortnight, so we proposed to start training in earnest. It was all rather an anti-climax, though indeed we might have been in many worse places.

Immense interest was being taken in home leave which started about now. We asked ourselves once again why A

Branch was always so incompetent. The latest General Routine Order was to the effect that the fighting troops vacancies for February and March would be greatly cut down *as it had been found that leave allocations for Line of Communication formations had been under-estimated.* Nobody blamed them for having made a miscalculation, but why publish such a tactless explanation?

The adjutant showed me the figures of the four rifle companies' casualties since D-Day. They were appalling. Their combined officer strength was 20; their casualties had been 9 killed and 30 wounded. Their combined Other Ranks' strength was 500; their casualties had been 149 killed and 351 wounded, a total of exactly 500.

And this with half the fighting still to take place!

McHaggis got himself into the news once again.

He joined the battalion during the three weeks we were holding the line near St. Oedenrode, an old, plausible soldier amongst a draft of youngsters. He spun Harry a glib yarn about the lengths to which he had gone in order to get himself posted to us, on the strength of which, and especially because of his name, Harry appointed him his personal orderly. But there was never room in Harry's jeep or carrier for McHaggis, as well as the necessary signallers, so before long he was sent to a rifle company.

That same night he went absent. A few days later his conduct sheets arrived and showed him to be a thoroughly bad character who had already deserted several times. That had been over two months ago, and since then a batch of military police charges against him had reached us at least once a week, the last one on each sheet being invariably 'escaping from custody'. At last he had been brought back to us under escort, but that morning he had again escaped, driving off in the truck containing the pipes and drums and the pipers' kilts. Of course, this was a disaster of first magnitude and one which looked like making us the laughing stock of the Division.

For a change I was the last to leave Lisogne when we moved on January 5th.

But not before a deputation, headed by the village *curé*, arrived about the looting and vandalism of our predecessors. I listened patiently to two old villagers, each with a long list of their stolen or damaged property. Then I accompanied the *curé* on a tour for inspection. Each house we entered had been sacked: ransacked from top to bottom with the contents of each drawer and cupboard strewn upon the floor.

I knew to which division they belonged, and perhaps I was not very surprised when I was told which Regiment it was. For this battalion had been in the next barracks to mine a year before. They stole our N.A.A.F.I. safe and a lot of kit out of the Quartermaster stores. They rifled the officers' bedrooms while we were all out watching a boxing competition. Finally they got our P.R.I. cash-box. I remember being asked at a dance what their regimental crest was, and my partner's peal of laughter when I replied that it should be a couple of jemmies and a broken lock.

We none of us thought much of the new location. Battalion H.Q. and one company was at Hogne, in a huge derelict house that had been empty for five years. Three companies were at Sinsin, two miles away, and the remainder were spread round the country in farms. The main road between Sinsin and Hogne was usually blocked by a long column of stationary traffic, for all the roads were badly iced-up at this time.

We were certainly very much closer to the battle, for Marche, only three miles away, was under occasional shellfire. The front line ran along the high ground just beyond it and was held by 53rd Welsh Division. 51st Highland, 53rd Welsh and 6th Airborne were the only British divisions down there.

On January 7th I walked into the Orderly Room to ask Grant Peterkin a question about a demonstration he had told me to arrange.

'You needn't think any more about it,' he said. 'Look at this.'

He handed me a signal from Brigade, which read: 'TOP SECRET WARNING ORDER REMAINDER OF DIV WILL CONCENTRATE 8 JAN 153 BDE GROUP WILL ATTACK 9 JAN'.

Everybody then began to laugh, at seeing me beaming all over. Nobody else wanted to go up into the snow-covered mountains to fight, at least that was their pose. It was a question of temperament. I regarded boredom as the greatest evil and was prepared to put up with any amount of discomfort, or a reasonable measure of anxiety, to avoid it. Nor was I alone in this, for John Frary said to me later in the day: 'This news has raised my morale no end. I hate running telephone lines out to companies all day long in a place like this.'

While we were still discussing the news, the Colonel was called to the telephone to be told to go on leave next day, a queer state of affairs. As he said to me: 'I am sent here to get practice in commanding a battalion in battle. I am not allowed to go on leave for six weeks while nothing happens. Then the day before an operation starts, I am sent on leave!'

I replied that I quite saw his point, but he could hardly expect me to sympathise as he knew I liked commanding the battalion, and especially in battle.

That afternoon we were put into the picture at Brigade H.Q. 1st Gordons were to open the innings by seizing some high ground. It was to start two days later; we should all have liked longer to make preparations, but now that the Boche was on the run we had to keep cracking him.

We had not been in action since the last canal crossing six weeks before.

First thing next morning I went to see the Royal Welch Fusiliers, who were then in reserve in Marche. They had been campaigning in the snow for a week or two and I wanted to ask their Colonel a few questions. He told me that in his experience a battalion could function up there for four days, after which the men were not very much use.

He emphasised the importance of all the obvious points, such as a constant supply of dry socks and hot tea. We had heard of another R.W.F. battalion being badly mauled in a counter-attack, and I asked him about this. He said they had not sufficient screen out in front to give warning and were surprised before they were dug in. Two hundred young Nazis full of brandy attacked them, supported by tanks. The battalion had three companies overrun and one hundred and sixty casualties.

I then went up into the woods, to see another battalion through which we were going to attack next day, and was horrified to find that none of them had shaved for four or five days. The forward right-hand company belonged to a different regiment, the Royal Welch Fusiliers, and was commanded by a splendid type of officer. He was stout and grey and elderly; a connoisseur of port, I did not doubt, for he looked as if his spiritual home was in clubland rather than on that snowclad hillside. He was wearing a pre-war great-coat with brass buttons up to the shoulder. I noticed that they had been polished that morning and that he and all his men had shaved. It was obvious that he was father and mother to the young lads under him.

Just in front of his company area and on the forward slope was an isolated farm called du Chauvaimont. When I arrived he had just returned from a small raid on it, in which he had captured five enemy and rescued a wounded British soldier. Now he led me down to just behind it, so that I could see the valley below, and the high ground on the far side which was our objective. The farm was quite visible to any enemy holding the ridge opposite. And had they been holding it they surely must have seen the Welshmen enter the farm, so the fact that they did not then mortar or shell it gave me reason to hope that they had gone back some distance, and that our advance would be unopposed.

The General's conference was not until 2 p.m., so I went to it full of hope that the operation had been postponed twenty-four hours, as at one time had been contemplated. My face fell a mile when I heard that there was no change, for I knew what a fearful rush it would mean. The General talked till 3.30 p.m. By the time the Brigade Commander had finished and I had given the artillery my fire tasks it was 5 p.m., with my own Order Group summoned for six.

It then took three-quarters of an hour to drive the two miles to Sinsin, along that icebound, traffic-blocked road. I rushed into C Company's billets and asked for a room, where I jotted down a few headings for my orders while the lamp kept going out. The electricity had also failed in the village hall, and few were able either to take notes or to see the large map that had been specially drawn for this briefing. So only the Company Commanders had a proper grasp of what it was all about.

I hoped I should never again have to lay on an operation in too short time with a battalion spread over five miles, with telephone lines cut and impassable roads.

We were due to start from Hogne at 5 a.m.

Corporal Robb, who had never failed us yet, produced tea and boiled eggs at 4.30 a.m., but my servant and driver were not ready for me with the jeep at 4.45 a.m., as ordered, and I flew into a blinding, undignified rage.

At ten to five I was on the main road, staring through the darkness in the direction of Sinsin and wondering in what sort of muddle were the three companies due from there in five minutes' time. Judge, therefore, my astonishment when they arrived punctually, complete and in the right order. We drove five miles through Marche to the small hamlet of Verdenne, where we had breakfast at the roadside, the men sitting in the troop-carriers for warmth. With the artificial moonlight of the searchlights reflected on the snow, it was a light as well as cold and frosty morning.

At seven we left the village and started up the hill. It was a long, long walk up a narrow, winding track, through snow-covered birches and firs. Slowly the stars set and the searchlights one by one went out as dawn came in the east. The rising sun tinged all the snow pink. Gradually its rays gained strength until they were reflected on the crystals of frost, so that the forest was soon shot with a million twinkling gems. It was a lovely, unforgettable sight, and there were we going to war: Frank Philip the Battery Commander, and I, walking together up that slope as if it were leading us to a ski hut.

Out of sight ahead was C company with its troop of tanks. Behind us were two jeeps with the wireless sets. Sometimes we overtook a few men towing a sledge, home-made, of corrugated iron, and hitched it on to the back of a jeep. After two hours the trees petered out and we found ourselves on a plateau.

Up to this point the snow had been cleared by a bulldozer. But from here forward no work had been done on the track although we had been assured that it was a R.E. priority task. So now we had to find a way across hard, frozen fields where the snow was thin, avoiding the sunken lanes where it had drifted to a depth of several feet. In this way we reached the top, just behind the R.W.F. company I had visited the day before.

A Company was now sent forward and took up position around the Ferme du Chauvaimont, to be a firm base halfway down the hill. As soon as they got there Bert Brown and his Aid Post moved into the farm buildings, and C Company crossed the valley: a long, straggling line of black dots against the snow, their tanks bigger black blobs amongst them. I stood behind a large pile of logs in the farmyard, watching their progress and ready to launch D as soon as C were safely across. Up the slope they went and disappeared into the scrub at the top, and not a shot was fired. The only trouble was due to the depth of snow at the bottom of the valley, and the tanks had to tow the two jeeps moving with the company.

Followed by the next two companies, D and B, my H.Q. moved across the valley. Now the trouble started. The head of C Company was held up by mines just inside the woods at the top of the ridge. This slowed up everything for about two hours. Repeatedly the sapper section with them would clear the track and they would all start off again, only to come to another lot of mines fifty yards further on: they were trip-wires and linked Teller mines, very unpleasant.

While we were thus held up, the enemy started ranging on the Ferme du Chauvaimont. Shells landed on either side, an obvious bracket, and Bert, who was standing in the yard talking to Denis Aldridge, in command of A Company, shouted:

'We had better take cover!'

As he moved away a shell struck the gable end of the farmhouse. He was hit in the head, stomach and arm. His orderlies dragged him inside at once, bandaged him up and rushed him back to Hotton. But when they reached there he was dead. I was desperately cut-up about this, and knew that I should miss him perhaps more than anyone. We had begun a friendship which would have lasted through the years.

After shelling the farm the enemy turned their attention to the track leading through it, down which we had come and along which the last company was then strung out. They also stonked the edge of the wood behind C Company. Until they could get forward we were all held up; we could only sit there and watch the enemy artillery practice and wonder where they would decide to shoot next. There would be half a dozen loud cracks and everybody would crane their necks to see the smoke drifting away from six dirty marks on the snow. Luckily enemy observation did not extend much below du Chauvaimont and we on the next reverse slope were not visible. Meanwhile our tanks were hauling everything up the hill for us.

Owing to the mines, it took two hours to move five hundred yards. But after that we got forward quickly and soon occupied our objective: various copses astride the track which had been chosen from air-photos. It was one of those very strong natural positions which one so seldom found: all the companies had excellent fields of fire and our tanks could cover the front hull-down. So when twelve enemy tanks were reported a mile away I fervently wished we would be counter-attacked.

In due course 5th Black Watch and 5-7th Gordons passed through us and down the track to Hodister. Food and blankets were brought up while we sought what comfort we could in the deep snow under the fir trees. I had one 160-lb. tent and a Tilley lamp brought for the command post, in order to have light and shelter to study maps and air-photos for planning any subsequent operation. Under this four of us were quite comfortable, but I knew that everyone else would have a pretty miserable night.

In the morning we received orders to occupy Lignieres.

Again we were held up by mines. Gordon, the subaltern in command of the R.E. section, decided to explode them in case they were fitted with anti-handling devices. There followed a series of loud bangs, each of which sent a cloud of dust and smoke into the air, which brought back a few enemy shells.

After half a mile an insignificant path petered out. Though the tanks could crash through the young fir trees, the jeeps with the wireless could go no further. I followed the company on foot till I saw that they were entering Lignieres, then ran back five hundred yards to my wireless set to tell the companies to come this way and the transport to go round. Once I grovelled in the mud on hearing the whistle of a shell which landed pretty close.

The next event was a mortar concentration on the company just as they were starting to dig in, though fortunately no casualties resulted. Later we heard that this came from 9th Parachute Battalion at Grimblemont, who had not been informed of our movements, although I had expressly asked that they should be.

Gordon was very energetic on arrival here, looking for mines and booby-traps. I now noticed that he was pale and limping, and discovered that he had a nasty flesh-wound in the thigh from one of the shells which landed near the track through the woods. He had merely put on a shell-dressing and carried on, saying nothing to anybody. Later I was able to get him a M.C. for those two days' work.

Lignieres (nobody could quite get the name so it was known to us as Lingerie) is a nice little agricultural village. Our command post in the largest farmhouse was rather unsatisfactory. Owing to the size of the family we had only two small rooms. Unfortunately harmony was marred from the start by their discovery that two pairs of hair-clippers were stolen after our arrival; there was no doubt that they were there, as David Scott-Moncrieff saw them on the dressing-table. I had every man's kit searched, but all to no purpose.

There followed two quiet and peaceful days.

I strafed the platoon commanders because one or two men had trench-feet as the result of standing about a long time in wet boots. Prevention of it was a question of drying socks, and those men who were out manning defensive positions had to have theirs dried for them under platoon arrangements.

January 13th was an unlucky, unpleasant day.

At 5 a.m. we were ordered to start at 6.30. I jeeped on ahead of the battalion, with David Scott-Moncrieff and the two signallers in the back. Bob Secretan, our tank squadron commander, was following me in his scout-car. We stopped at Brigade H.Q. in Laroche, where I was given orders to go through Hubermont and occupy Nisramont as quickly as possible. '5th Black Watch are just about in Hubermont now,' the Brigade Major said. So we continued down the road into what soon became very open, snow-covered country.

After three miles I came to the reserve company of the Black Watch, occupying a large isolated farm on the left of the road. I enquired of the Company Commander whether his battalion was in Hubermont and received a reassuring answer, so asked him to send the company commanders straight on when they arrived. We soon came to where there was a turning to the left which led to the north end of Hubermont a quarter of a mile away. The south end of this small village was close to the main road, five hundred yards ahead, and I could see the Black Watch there.

We turned left and drove into the village, passing a German armoured half-track in front of a house. I assumed it had broken down or run out of petrol. Fifty yards further on we passed another, garaged in a barn. I swung the jeep round, off the road and between two buildings, and Bob lost no time in following me. An old Belgian peasant came out of a house and told us that there were about twenty Huns still in the village and on both sides of our little party, which consisted of three officers, one driver and two signallers. I told Bob to talk to Brigade on his R/T and ask them to tell the Black Watch to hurry up and send a company here.

While he was doing so, what did I see but a procession of five jeeps: the four company commanders and the signal officer all driving gaily towards us. We hurriedly pulled them into where we were, which increased our strength by another five officers.

Soon we heard one of the German half-tracks coming down the lane towards us. As it passed the side-turning where we stood I put down a stonk with my pistol and everybody else fired madly. We had the satisfaction of knocking off three men who were riding on top of a trailer behind, but the vehicle itself turned left, across an open field and on over the snow towards Nisramont.

Soon afterwards the other was driven off in that direction also. Meanwhile the Black Watch were firing wildly at both of them, so wildly in fact that David was shot through the shoulder and in due course departed towards the rear on a stretcher strapped to the top of a jeep.

The country between Hubermont and Nisramont was open and devoid of cover – 'Quite like the desert,' Hastings, my signaller, remarked. I did not like the look of it one bit.

I chose a building for a command post, and told the company commanders to study the ground while I went back to fetch the battalion. As quickly as possible I led them into the village, very worried that they would get shelled on the way in, for the whole of Hubermont is overlooked by Nisramont and the ridge which it stands on. Fortunately the haze, which we had noticed every morning between about 8 a.m. and 11 a.m., was still fairly thick. Nevertheless the last company was spotted and a few shells landed.

Then those of our tanks and S.P. guns which had been able to ascend an icebound hill a mile back started to arrive. Almost before we knew what was happening we had lost three Shermans and one S.P., with an officer (he was going to have been a parson) and two or three men killed and half a dozen wounded. They had been knocked out by Panther or Tiger tanks, shooting from the opposite ridge two thousand yards away.

Ackers, my young driver, showed the greatest gallantry pulling wounded up through the turret of one of these tanks while they were still under fire.

From now till 7.15 p.m. we had a steady stream of shells and mortar bombs upon the village. It was quite obvious that no attack could be launched from it in daylight, especially since artillery smoke does not work in snow, which has the effect of extinguishing the chemical.

About this time the Brigadier arrived at the Black Watch H.Q. at the far end of the village. I sprinted three hundred yards down the lane and sat on some straw beside him. At that moment a shell landed somewhere very close outside. 'This is perfectly bloody,' he said, and I agreed.

He told me to push on directly it was dark. I ran all the way back and spent the next two or three hours planning the operation. Meanwhile, from our command post window, we could see the stuff continually crashing down on the village, and I was glad that the sandbags which we always carried for just such an emergency were banked across the window-sill.

The wireless set was in the jeep outside, with the lead to the microphone coming through the window into the room. While I was speaking on it I heard a sickening crash of glass and wood, but could not look round as the extension was only just long enough to pass under the sandbags. It was a lengthy conversation. When I put down the microphone and earphones and looked round, I was astonished to see Frank Philip, the Battery Commander, as green as an olive, sitting in a chair with his head and arm bandaged up. He had been hit by pieces of shrapnel which had come through the front door and down the passage. Twice more that afternoon did we have shrapnel flying round inside that room, large pieces which had cut through the single layer of sandbags, and how we had only the one casualty from these three shells was incomprehensible.

Bill MacMillan arrived to say that there had been a direct hit upon his farm across the road. His company had had a dozen casualties from it and were in a pretty poor state. We sat there and talked things over. I thought what a grand chap he was: Bill, in a grey polo sweater above his battledress trousers, with strength of character radiating from him and not a suspicion of excitement or anxiety, although much depended upon him as leading company commander in the forthcoming attack.

From time to time our artillery shot up the woods on the ridge in front of us. At 5.20 p.m. the enemy was still there and sniping at a company of the Black Watch. It was dark by 6 p.m., and soon afterwards George Morrison brought some transport over the hill with a hot meal which did everybody good. The last shelling was at 7.15 p.m., and at 8 p.m. our advance started.

As I stood in the snow at the corner of the lane, watching the two leading companies start, I heard the rumble of tracks moving through our objective, which in fact was the Boche pulling out. So, though we did so slowly and with caution, we all moved into Nisramont without any more shooting taking place.

Next morning, from my bedroom window, I looked out across the snowfields to Hubermont, and realised once again how hopeless an attack from there would have been in daylight. The day before there were two hundred Germans with nine tanks in this village, or so the Belgians said.

We were told to send out strong patrols in various directions to collect any German stragglers. One of these was led by Danny Reid, the second-in-command of D Company, who went off with a platoon. Danny was one of the great characters of the battalion. Of all our officers he was probably the finest individual fighter and the greatest natural leader. But he liked to pose as being wild and irresponsible. I had told him to go as far as a river two miles away. He left at 9.30 a.m. When he was not back by 3 p.m. I began to be worried and sent two armoured cars to look for him. Almost at once the patrol returned, riding on the top of them.

His explanation was that there were no stragglers to be captured by the river, so they crossed it and cleared Ollomont on the far side. Now he had returned with some prisoners and a certificate signed by the burgomaster to the effect that British troops had been the first to enter the village. He thought this was a good exercise for the young soldiers in the platoon. Of course it was a foolish thing to do as Ollomont was an American objective and they might well have put an artillery concentration on it just as Danny and Co. were entering.

From this hill we had had a grandstand view of the American attack: first a bombing programme by waves of Fortresses, then an artillery barrage followed by the advance of their infantry.

One of the Fortresses was shot down from a great height. We could see it turning over and over like a falling leaf. Technical-Sergeant Sewell landed by parachute in the battalion area. An hour or two before he had been at Great Yeldham in Essex, and I gave him a note to take back to friends of mine, whose house overlooked the airfield.

That night we heard that the American divisions attacking from north and south had linked up. So the Battle of the Bulge was over.

General Rennie came to see us next morning. It was one of his many engaging characteristics always to visit his battalions after a battle. He told us that the adjutant of the Divisional Reconnaissance Regiment was killed in the night by one of those small, aerial anti-personnel bombs which, by the worst possible luck, landed on a window-sill.

In the afternoon I followed the German tank tracks over the snow, to see the positions from which they fired at us. I also examined the hits which had been scored upon the Shermans in Hubermont, while a tank corps officer explained to me in detail how inferior was our design to that of the Germans': in armament, armour, periscope design and magnification. The Sherman tank won the battle of El Alamein but became obsolete upon the appearance of the Tiger before the end of that campaign. I cannot understand why the service chiefs and politicians could not openly admit this instead of issuing reassuring, soothing statements.

We had a party with Bob Secretan and his officers. It was a sad occasion for they were giving up their Sherman tanks, to be converted into an amphibious regiment. We had had this squadron supporting us on most of our operations since Normandy, and could not have wished for a better. They looked on themselves as being almost Gordon Highlanders.

I went for a walk in the woods and came upon one of our sergeants lighting a wood fire underneath a dead and frozen Hun strung up to the branch of a tree. He was trying to thaw him out, in order to take off his boots. Personally, I found the Army boots quite adequate, but most people seemed to think that the German type which went almost up to the knee was warmer.

Whatever controversy there might be about boots, there were no two opinions as to the unsuitability of the kilt for war. Proud as we always were to wear one when 'walking out', we were thankful that we nowadays fought in trousers. No garment could be more uncomfortable than a kilt for a wet slit-trench in winter.

There was nothing to do for three days and everybody was very happy resting.

I greatly missed David Scott-Moncrieff and Bert Brown. David, so charming, so dreamy and artistic, would, as in other slack moments, almost certainly have been turning over his postcard collection of old masters or the pages of *The Connoisseur*.

There was much speculation as to our next destination, and everybody was hoping that it would be in Belgium and not Holland. Then we heard that it was to be Turnhout, in Belgium and not far from Antwerp.

We moved on January 18th. John Frary and I dodged the column and had lunch with Madame Lalou, Christian and Michel on the way. We gathered that life had been very dull there since the Gay Gordons left.

It was a long journey and the battalion did not arrive until well after dark. Everybody was delighted to be in Turnhout, as for the first time we were in a place where the men could go to a cinema or variety show merely by boarding a tram. As Brussels was only about 40 miles away, I went there one evening for a bath and a haircut, and took Livia to a night club. She said that a few pompous officers in 21 Army Group H.Q. had their legs badly pulled when the German threat was at its height. They were told that the underground movement was making preparations to hide them. When they replied that everything was well in hand, the answer they got was: 'That is precisely what you said in 1940, and you left us next day!'

Three parts of the campaign were over: France, Holland and Belgium. And now we were approaching the last and the greatest – Germany!

161

Part Four

Germany

7

I was very sorry when we left Belgium on January 23rd and moved up to Oisterwijk in Holland. It was, incidentally, the first time in the course of our wanderings that we had returned to a previous location. But we were not going to be here very long. We understood that this was only a staging area on the way to Germany, and that in about a fortnight there was to be a big attack and we were to break through the Siegfried Line.

For the first time since Veules-les-Roses, and only the second during the campaign, we had a battalion mess instead of the usual company messes, in a very attractive modern road-house which was much more like a small country club. That night we had a dance, the partners being nurses from a neighbouring Canadian hospital. They all smelt very nicely of Brussels. It is odd how one just accepts scent at home and hardly notices it. Unfortunately one of the drivers got drunk and wrapped his truck round a tree on the way back from the dance, but nobody was hurt. Corporal Robb said he knew the man well as they both came from Turriff, and he would never have let him have a drink if he could have helped it.

The Corps Commander, General Horrocks, visited us and said how pleased he was to have the Highland Division under his command for the forthcoming operation. He was a great man who had just recovered from a serious wound which he received in Sicily. He told us about a Jock in 52nd Division who robbed a German field cashier on Walcheren Island of the equivalent of £1,100. This German complained very indignantly, and said that the man in question could be identified as he had given a signed receipt. He produced a grubby bit of paper on which was written: 'This bastard had 11,000 guilders. He hasn't got it now.'

Alec returned from home leave and was full of amusing stories about it. He was riding in the usual leave party three-tonner and just before getting to Bourg Léopold, the railhead, there was a great screeching of horns, and Montgomery, preceded by several outriders, passed them. Then someone stopped him and said that the Commander-in-Chief wished to speak to him. He went forward, expecting to collect an imperial raspberry for not having pulled into the side of the road more quickly.

'Is that a leave party from the Highland Division?' said the great man. 'From the Highland Division? Very well, then I'd like to give them some cigarettes.' But the donor had never been thanked for them, for when they opened the parcel they found her letter inside.

We learnt that Brigadier Sinclair, who was home on sick leave, would not be back in time for the battle, so Grant Peterkin would be acting Brigade Commander and I should be commanding the battalion. In that capacity I went to the Divisional Commander's briefing. It was followed by a most sumptuous, really quite pre-war, lunch. This was a feature of all the General's final conferences before an important operation, and it was always known as the Last Supper.

I visited the Canadian battalion which we were to pass through when we attacked, and I had a good look at the ground through my glasses. Except for a few farms and hamlets, it was very flat and open as far as the Reichswald (State forest). The

German frontier runs along the western edge of it. This side of it was Holland, but I was told that all the Dutch near the border were pro-German. The only difference between them and the Germans was that you could not treat them as such; it seemed that they were vermin, but protected by the game laws.

We borrowed a charming little summer-house for a map-room. Here we could spread out all the maps, drawings and air-photos for the operation, and in privacy for of course secrecy before so important an operation was essential, and with most of the battalion sharing houses with the local people, things might well have leaked out. I had a daily conference in it with the Company Commanders and other key officers, and as a member of the Intelligence Section was always on guard, they could come in at any time to study the air-photos.

It was in the grounds of a charming Dutch family and I only

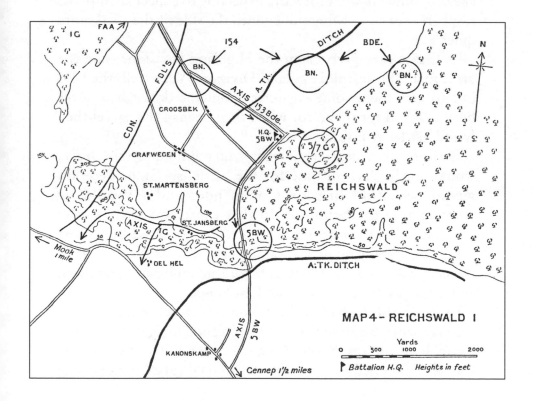

MAP 4 – REICHSWALD I

wished I had met them sooner. It was such a joy to meet people with the same tastes as myself: travelling, books, golf, bridge and so on. They spoke perfect English, French and German, and knew these countries well.

I liked the Canadians so much that I was always glad of an excuse to visit them, and I went over to the Cameron Highlanders of Canada. They were astride the Mook-Gennep road (*Map 4*) and our job was to take from the rear the Hun positions facing them. They told me that these were very strong as the enemy had had a long time to prepare them. They were therefore so deeply dug-in that no amount of mortar or shell-fire affected them, and there was a good deal of wire and anti-personnel mines. Many of their positions covering this road were dug horizontally into the side of the wooded ridge and so were peculiarly hard to get at. We knew that we would find it a tough nut to crack.

Our last day at Oisterwijk passed quickly in giving out final orders and in briefing all ranks of the battalion. Perhaps this is badly expressed for I suppose I did not really give out any orders at all, and this was merely the last of a series of daily conferences during which each phase of the forthcoming battle had been most informally, and perhaps somewhat facetiously, discussed. Thus I might say: 'Next, C Company, if they're not by this time bomb-happy, will pass through A and occupy so and so. How does this suit you, Alec? O.K. That's settled, then.'

I am certain that the atmosphere in which battle orders are given out has a great effect upon morale and that the commander should be at pains, by little jokes and a profusion of Christian names, to keep it as light and informal as possible. In the past I had heard commanders say sternly, 'Now, gentlemen, I am going to give out my orders,' while looking at the same time the very personification of grimness, with the result that everybody left saying to himself: 'God, how bloody this is going to be!'

This was something which I had learned from the Divisional Commander. Thus the General, at a meeting of his commanders before an important operation, would perhaps get up and say: 'A lot of tripe has been issued in connection with this party which some people will read and some will not. I, myself, have tried to read it but I haven't understood it all, so perhaps I shall not make myself very clear.'

So, when I briefed the battalion, in two halves in the local cinema, while ensuring that the wall-maps were as good as they could be and that everybody thoroughly understood the narrative, I tried to keep the men amused so that they would leave the hall in high spirits. We were lucky in that we had had ten days to prepare this operation and, as they had also been briefed at least once by their company and platoon commanders, they should have known all about it. In fact, I did not think we had ever been launched into battle so favourably.

The operation was to begin at 1 p.m. on February 8th, and the Division was on the right of 30 Corps. The object was to break into Germany through that part of the Siegfried Line which was based on the Reichswald. 154 Brigade would move at Zero Hour and had to get a footing on the edge of the Reichswald. Our Brigade's task was to pass through them and then turn south and south-west and clear the Mook-Gennep road which, owing to flooding in the north, would probably be the only main road available for a Corps axis. 5th Black Watch were to get the high ground at the south-west corner of the Reichswald. When they were there we were to pass through them and then turn west, clear the enemy from the wooded plateau backwards towards the Canadians and then cut the Mook-Gennep road.

We reached Groot Linden, quite a small place, without incident during the afternoon before the battle started. The German wireless announced that British forces were about to cross the Maas and attack the Reichswald!

I was very strung up that night, wondering what the morrow

would bring forth. I have often wondered what exactly influences the state of one's nerves. Sometimes before riding in a steeplechase or making a parachute drop or a speech, I have been very much on edge, without actually feeling precisely frightened; at other times, for no apparent reason, I just have not cared a damn. Perhaps it is something to do with one's liver! Anyway, I felt very restless on this occasion.

There were over a thousand guns taking part in the opening barrage and most of them were in our garden. Or so it seemed. At any rate there was a deafening crash at eight o'clock that morning and the jangle of falling glass. I thought: 'Heavens, the house has had a direct hit; I wonder who has been wounded.' But it was one of the heavies or super-heavies in the garden just in front of us, and every time it fired great sheets of window-pane came tumbling down. From then on there were times when it was almost impossible to carry on a conversation, so

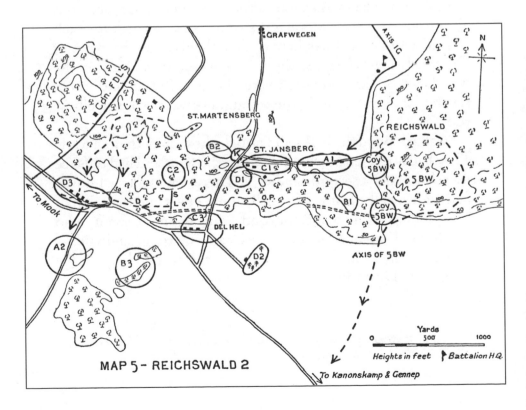

MAP 5 – REICHSWALD 2

fierce was the gunfire. We had a new weapon called a flying mattress supporting us for the first time. It fired 1,000 rockets into 400 square yards or 400 rockets into 1,000 square yards, I was not sure which.

We left Groot Linden at 10 a.m. It was a nice morning and I hoped it would remain so. We had a two-mile march to the Mook bridge and were held up by traffic for the best part of two hours 200 yards short of it. I didn't much care for this as I thought the Hun was bound to shell the bridge, the only one within miles, but nothing happened. For a time the confusion was considerable. However, we got moving at last and over the Bailey bridge across the Maas we went, five yards between men and 100 yards between vehicles. I think we all lengthened our stride and crossed our fingers while going over, but all was peace and quiet.

It was another two miles to our assembly area in a wood behind the Canadians. As soon as the companies got spaced out either side of the track down the centre of it, a truck for each arrived with a meal. I would have liked them to have been better dispersed as one or two shells passed overhead and burst in the wood two or three hundred yards behind. But as there were several other battalions in the wood there was not much elbow room.

I walked round the Jocks and noticed how quiet they all were. They had not eaten much. I felt much the same and had to force myself to take a second sandwich. There was the usual noise, half whine, half whistle, of a shell coming over and the crash of it exploding in the woods beyond. Murray,[1] my servant, who had been off-colour for some days, came up to me and said:

'Please, sir, I can't stand it any longer. Can I go back to the transport? I just can't stand it.'

---

[1]   In one or two instances, of which this is one, the name has been changed in order to conceal an identity.

'Blast you! To hell with you!' I raved at him. 'I can't stand it either, but I'm going to. Get back to your position.'

Later in the afternoon the doctor told me that he was definitely a medical case and that he had evacuated him.

I could see that things were going rather slowly, as there was a long delay over launching the Argylls, who were next to us in the wood. So I pottered over to Brigade H.Q., which was a few hundred yards away and dug in next to that of 154 Brigade. They told me that 154 had got most of their objectives and 5-7th Gordons had just started, that there was a bit of stuff coming down on the road which was to be our axis, and some trouble from Groosbek to the right of it in the form of one Spandau still firing, in spite of the pasting that place had already had. Grant Peterkin was in tremendous form and I thought to myself what a grand brigadier he would make.

I returned to the battalion and told them what I had heard: that everything was going well but slowly. It was getting on for 4 p.m. and we had been there for about three hours already. It is not pleasant hanging about waiting to move forward into battle, especially when the road you will have to pass down is being shelled. Then the Black Watch were started. At 4.45 p.m. we were told to be ready to start at 5.30, so it was time to put on our pads.

I was nervous that we should be launched too early and have to hang about on the way forward under fire, while the battalion in front of us was held up. I mentioned it to Grant Peterkin, yet this is precisely what happened, though it is easy to understand his position with the Divisional Commander at his elbow pressing him to get on and capture the Reichswald. So when we had gone about a mile we came to the tail of the Black Watch, still 800 yards short of the wood.

I felt very miserable. There was quite a bit of shelling and hardly cover for a rat, since there was no ditch alongside this third-class road and the few houses had been reduced to little more than rubble. And thus we remained for some four hours, when we might well have stayed where we had spent the afternoon and have had the evening meal as well.

I walked forward a little way and saw rear companies of both the Black Watch and 5-7th Gordons on the roadside. When I got back it was to find that Frank Philip, the Battery Commander, had established our Tac H.Q. in a small room used for keeping hay and cattle food. Two candles were guttering away on a manger. I told someone to walk back and find the carrier with the 500 self-heating tins of soup and have them issued out. Then, with Ian Edgar, I went forward again.

By this time it was dark. There still seemed to be a good deal of rifle, Bren and Spandau fire about a thousand yards in front, just inside the Reichswald. We walked up the middle of the road, passing the dark forms of many waiting fighting men, sitting or sprawling at the roadside; many were fast asleep. I heard an officer talking and asked him what the trouble was, but as usual nobody at the back had any notion. All they could tell me was that the formation just in front of them had stopped. So on we went, till a lamp sign just short of the forest bade us turn to the right and soon we came to the Tac H.Q. of 5th Black Watch.

George Dunn was commanding and told me that they had met little resistance, all the shooting being on 5-7th Gordons' front further to the left. His difficulty was that all tracks through the forest were hopelessly blocked by trees, felled both by enemy demolitions and our own shellfire; he had not been able to get a single vehicle into the Reichswald. But the companies were all getting into their positions without any bother. So I decided to go across the open along the edge of the forest; there was nothing to be gained by going round through the Reichswald now that it was too dark to be shot at from afar.

Followed by A and B Company Commanders and a small party to lay white tape along the route, I went on to have a look. We walked along a very muddy track, with the forest looking black and sinister on our left. By this time the moon was up, and with all the searchlights groping in the sky we felt rather exposed, strolling along there in the open. To the right of us was an open field, completely devoid of cover. We saw dead cattle 300 yards away, and I wondered whether any not so dead Huns might not see us. Our direction was parallel to the frontier. We were ten yards inside Germany. At the far end (*Map 5*) we found the two Black Watch companies digging-in just inside the Reichswald, and they confirmed that all was quiet.

George Morrison and Dennis Aldridge went back, met their companies and led them forward into their positions (*A1 and B1 – see Map 5*) without incident. B Company's patrol soon brought back a few prisoners from the re-entrant in front of them. Before very long all the companies had reached their objectives along the track leading from St. Jansberg to St. Martensberg (*A1 to B2*) and no enemy had been met. It was very dark inside the forest, so we decided to go no further that night and to make the best of it for the three or four hours that were left before dawn. Danny Reid reported that there were a lot of enemy just in front of D Company (*at D1*).

The first problem next morning was breakfast, complicated by the fact that none of the vehicles could get through the mud and over two Hun trenches to reach us. Two companies eventually went back a mile and fed in the next house to the Black Watch H.Q. A few tanks, which succeeded in reaching us about 9 a.m., carried on top of them cooked breakfasts for the remainder of us. There was a shortage of water and, for the first time in any operation, I did not get a shave.

As soon as they were ready I pushed off the first two companies: B with the dismounted carrier platoon mopping up St. Martensberg and all the enemy positions north and north-east of it as far as Grafwegen, and D to clean up the valley just west of their position. B soon started rolling up the prisoners; they got about 150 in all during their little jaunt. But D got into difficulties, for the Huns were entrenched in the valley, and they came back with the leading platoon commander, Fraser, and one or two men missing. We found their bodies later.

So I put down a sharp shoot (Scale 5 from the regiment of 24 guns: 120 rounds) after registration, and then, with a troop of the tanks firing from the ridge, Danny and D Company had no difficulty in completing the job and collecting some prisoners. Some of our stonks fell rather near B Company, working away on the right. It was necessary to take this slowly, as if too many companies were milling about at the same time one could not use the artillery.

The next company to go was C, and after we had fired the guns on the centre of a network of trenches (C2) across the valley, they went over and occupied them. There was no difficulty about this; it only took time. C and D Companies, both in excellent spirits, were now parallel to each other and facing south, and their next phase was a two-company attack off the high ground and down on to the plain below, C to take Del Hel and D the copse just east of it (D2).

I watched this attack from a wonderful observation post on the hill in front of D Company's first position. Danny Reid had reported that he'd seen about sixty Huns going into it, in addition to those previously there, and all were starting to dig hard. There were no less than nine of us there to witness the slaughter when we turned the 25-pounders and 4.2 mortars on to them before the attack.

It was a wonderful sight to see D Company race across the open ground and on to their objective, with enemy mortar fire coming down just too late behind them. From the observation post we could see the Huns streaming back in little packets into a wood beyond. It was a gunner's dream, but unfortunately there was so much traffic over the air at the time that we could not get through to the guns.

Having seen D Company take their objective, I walked back to the command post in the houses 300 yards behind. There I found a note from the Brigade Commander: 'I am sure you are doing everything you can to open the Mook-Gennep road as soon as possible, as it is required for the Corps axis. We want the sappers to be able to work on it as soon as it is dark.'

Meanwhile I was beginning to worry about C Company as I had heard a lot of firing, and especially when some stretcher-bearers began to come in with wounded and said that things were not going very well. I was just starting off down the hill when Alec came up on the air to say he had got Del Hel, but that it had been a bit sticky and he'd had some casualties.

When I joined Alec Lumsden down at the bottom he told me that a young officer of nineteen, whom we had been rather worried about, had been splendid: he'd apparently made up his mind that he had no chance and might as well die bravely – at any rate, in the face of intense fire and with one or two wounded shrieking with pain, he ran forward, leading his platoon until they had charged in and taken the position. By now our bag of P.O.W. was nearly 300. So far everything had gone according to plan and all the companies to the objectives which had been allotted in the summer-house a week before. But I might have guessed that the luck was soon to break.

Before C and D Companies started their attack, I had sent A Company round right-handed to clean up the enemy strong-point (*D3*) astride the main road immediately in front of the Cameron Highlanders of Canada. They were allowed two and a half hours for this, and then, at 4.30 p.m., were to cross the road and establish themselves in the copse (*A2*) just south of it. Simultaneously B Company were to pass through Del Hel and occupy two small woods (*B3*). A Company had not been in touch with Battalion H.Q. by wireless since D-Day, so I fixed the time for A and B Companies to cross the road before A left. I also sent a field-telephone and line party with A Company.

B Company were delayed and did not put in their attack till 5 p.m. As they entered the north end of their objective, after crossing the road, they came under mortar fire. A few moments

173

later I heard a loud cheer as the company charged through the wood with fixed bayonets.

Almost immediately afterwards Chamberlain said: 'A Company through by line, sir.' I had had no news of them for nearly three hours and hoped that they had mopped up that strong point and were now in their final position. So judge my dismay when Dennis said that his company had failed to take it, that it was very strongly held and protected by mines which had caused him several casualties, and that they had been finally stopped by at least three well-sited Spandaus.

This gave me a very nasty jolt and I had to do some rapid thinking. I told him that I would attack with another company from due east, along the ridge, as soon as it was dark. Then the line went dead.

I did not like it at all. But the position simply had to be taken. I remembered the message I had received an hour before. I knew that both the Divisional and Corps Commanders were waiting for the news that 1st Gordons had opened up the road. Failure was unthinkable.

Although D Company had already made three attacks that day, I decided to use them again, with the dismounted carrier platoon in reserve. It seemed to me that the responsibility for this attack was altogether too great for a company commander – even Danny Reid – so I decided to take personal command of it. I told Alec to take over the rest of the battalion. By this time the Black Watch were down in Kanonskamp, so the general situation was good.

Danny Reid and I talked it over and decided to take a start-line (*see Map 5*) running northwards from a German command post which had already been cleared. So we marched round towards it in single file, along a narrow path at the foot of the very steep ride, with trees on either side of us: Macpherson's platoon in the lead, then Danny and I, then the remainder of the company, followed by Moir and his carrier platoon.

Just as we got there we were ambushed. There was a burst of

Schmeisser in front, and the sharp explosions of one or two German grenades. Immediately five or six Germans came to life in trenches on either side of the path. They must have been asleep, for one-third of us had already passed them. There was an instaneous crash of automatic fire from the column and every one of them fell, riddled with bullets. It was all over in about two seconds, and our only casualty was Macpherson, slightly wounded in the leg. Actually it was a most efficient performance on our part, but all I thought at the time was: 'God, how bloody! Ambushed before we've even started, this is going to be the bloodiest show that's ever been.'

We climbed up the face of this steep ridge and the four platoons deployed, two in front with two behind them, facing west and behind the imaginary start-line. But the wood was jungle, so many branches and trees having been felled by our shelling. We might well have been in darkest Africa.

Every hundred yards took us about fifteen minutes, and the confusion was indescribable. I found myself scrambling along with Porter, at the head of his platoon, he in front with an automatic very much at the ready, and me close up, keeping direction with a compass. I knew that Sergeant Matthews' platoon was just behind us; but as to where Danny and Macpherson and the rest of the company was, I hadn't a clue. All we could do was to push on slowly, climbing over tree trunks and branches or crawling under them. 'What an awful balls up of this I've made,' I thought to myself, having lost all control. 'It's going to be a ghastly failure.'

Then we heard some shooting in front, and soon came upon Danny and Macpherson in a clearing. They had taken the first position and had some prisoners. Danny said that the enemy were dug-in round the houses a hundred yards ahead of us. We went forward a little way to see the form. Several Spandaus were firing vaguely in our direction and a light mortar was crashing its stuff down on the main road fifty yards to our left.

It was fearfully dark among the trees in spite of many flares behind the Canadian lines. Much red tracer was also going up beyond, and a fine display of fireworks and distant explosions told me that an air-raid on Mook was taking place. It was a lovely sight, a real Brock's benefit, and for an instant I thought of the Fourth of June and the Eton Boating Song, and wished I could forget all about the job in hand.

Danny pointed out to me the dark shape which was the nearest house, and it was obvious that the Huns were holding it. I could see the flame from an automatic firing from just below it. Danny, who feared neither God nor man, said:

'It's much too dark. Can't we wait till daylight, when we shall see what we are doing?'

'No, Danny,' I said, 'it's got to be done now.'

'Very good, sir,' he said. 'But it's going to be a horrible show.'

'I don't care a bit,' I replied. 'We've got to take this position now, cost what it may. Get all the Bren-guns up in line. Fire rapid for one minute and make as much noise as possible. I don't believe the sods will put up much of a show, once they realise we are right behind them. As soon as the Brens stop firing we'll rush the place.'

I leaned against a tree and listened to Danny running the show. The same light mortar kept slamming down close to us on our left. Everybody was a bit frightened, except perhaps Danny. I heard him moving from platoon to platoon, full of confidence, putting them in position and giving orders. Then the leading platoon moved forward. 'Get on, you bastards, what the hell are you doing hanging back on the right?' I heard his loud voice shout.

There was a cheer and bursts of Sten and a wild surge forward, and in a moment a shout of 'Kamerad!' and a column of Huns, seventy-one in number, came running out with their hands up. They said there were no more of them, but I told Danny we must go right through the position as far as the Canadians.

The front platoon fanned out and we went forward in the

moonlight, climbing over broken walls and piles of rubble interlaced with a honeycomb of trenches. I was afraid that some enthusiast in front might shoot at us, so I passed the word back to the two pipers with Company H.Q. to play the regimental march, and before long we heard the distant strain of 'Cock o' the North'. I feared that our friends would not hear it, so we went forward shouting 'Canadians!' at the top of our voices.

It was obvious that there were no more enemy, and soon there was no attempt at military formations or precautions: just a score of men scrambling over the obstacles, in high spirits that the job had been done and a little elated, as everybody always is by bright moonlight on a perfect night.

Danny and Porter were in the lead, walking side by side, and I was perhaps ten yards behind them. We heard the pipers of the Camerons of Canada and knew that we had not far to go. Then there was a loud bang and Danny fell down with a groan.

'Everybody stand still exactly where you are,' I shouted, for it was obviously a schu-mine. 'Danny, how bad is it?'

I knew it was either a broken ankle or the whole foot blown off – what the doctors call traumatic amputation. Danny's language and Porter, who at great personal risk stepped two or three paces over to him and applied a first field-dressing, told me that it was not too bad.

We shouted at the top of our voices to the Canadians for pioneers with mine-prodders and stretcher-bearers. I looked around and realised now that we were in a narrow no-man's land, only fifty yards wide, between the German and Canadian positions. Danny, Porter and I were in the middle of a mine-field, but fortunately those behind us were still in the old German diggings so I told them to go back.

A Canadian company commander came forward to a wire fence in front and said that the stretcher-bearers would not be long. He told us how pleased he was to see us as they had had seven men killed by snipers during the last week, from the position which we had just cleaned up. Danny was getting restive

177

lying there on the ground, and his language progressively worse.

'Never mind, Danny,' I shouted. 'The moonlight's lovely and I'll get you a bar to your M.C. for this day's work, you mark my words.'

But I, too, was becoming impatient for all this time I was standing on one leg – literally, and for about three-quarters of an hour – not daring to put the other to the ground. I don't think I've ever felt quite so foolish in my life. Then the Canadians came bustling up with two or three officers and four or five stretcher-bearers.

I thought there was altogether too much bustle. 'For God's sake . . .' I shouted, and there was another loud bang and one of them fell down, badly injured. It now took a long time to get out the two wounded men, with every footstep being prodded first. Danny had ceased to be talkative, and I learned that he had received a lot of wood splinters in the back of the head, as Porter had in the face. When the stretcher party had left, the Canadian pioneer sergeant prodded his way up to me and led me safely out of the minefield by my planting my feet precisely in his footsteps.

By this time Macpherson, who had carried on in spite of his leg wound, had been evacuated, so D had lost all its four officers in the course of the day. I formed up the company and marched them back. I was dead-tired, and felt none of the elation to which I was entitled when I reported to Brigade that the road was now clear.

8

The Siegfried Line battle was probably one of the most important in the long, proud history of the Gordon Highlanders.

We took more than 350 prisoners. Our casualties were one officer killed and three wounded, four other ranks killed and seventeen wounded. We had got off very lightly. We owed a great deal to our battery of artillery which fired 830 rounds per gun in the day in support of us.

There were no enemy left in this part of the world. All the companies were now in buildings and we looked forward to a good long sleep.

Next night the Black Watch crossed the River Niers in assault boats, the bridge having been blown, and entered Gennep from the north-west in the early hours of the morning (*see Map 6*). The site for the crossing was well chosen, being a mile from the town itself, so a large measure of surprise was achieved. We were told to cross in the same place and pass through them, in order to clear and occupy the southern part of the town.

About 10 a.m. I went forward and found Bill Bradford at his H.Q. about 100 yards beyond the bridge in Gennep. Two of his companies were clearing streets just beyond his H.Q., and Bill summed up the situation as 'the enemy are fighting well until they are shot at.' The third and fourth companies were still between the town and the crossing place in a long trench which had been most conveniently dug by the Huns. On the way back I met a poor whimpering lad who looked no more than sixteen

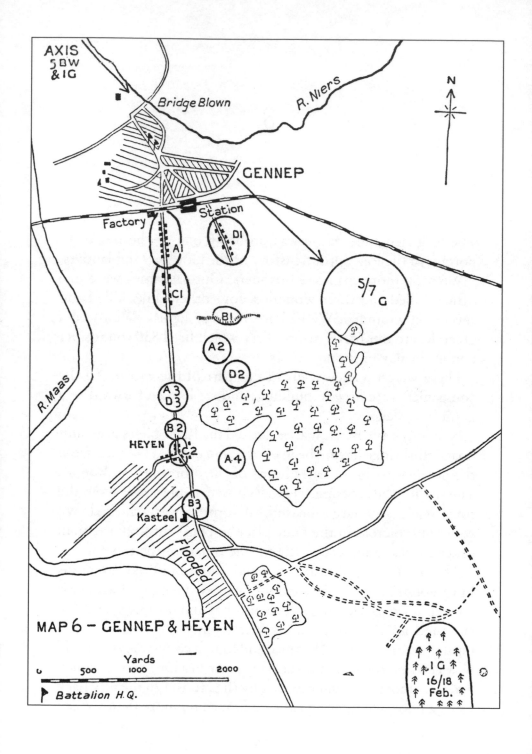

AXIS
5 BW
& 1G

Bridge Blown

R. Niers

N

GENNEP

Station

Factory

DI

AI

CI

5/7 G

BI

A2

D2

R. Maas

A3
D3

B2

HEYEN

C2

A4

B3

Kasteel

Flooded

1G
16/18
Feb.

MAP 6 — GENNEP & HEYEN

Yards

0   500   1000   2000

Battalion H.Q.

and told me between his sobs in broad Scots that he c'dna stan' it nae mair. So we walked back together with my hand on his shoulder, at least metaphorically speaking.

Our first two companies went through in due course and I established a H.Q. next door to Bill's, which by this time was on the main street further on in the town. There was a good deal of shelling, particularly on the bridge site, and I felt sorry for the sappers who were trying to build a new one.

Then Bill walked into my house, looking very disgusted and indignant, to say that he had just had a direct hit on his H.Q. which had killed his signaller and jeep driver. He also told me that his left-hand company was having trouble and had received about twenty casualties from small-arms fire – Spandaus and snipers.

I heard our two companies doing a lot of shooting so I ran up to see what it was all about, dodging from back garden to back garden, and in that way up the street. The leading platoon was crossing the gaps between houses under cover of smoke grenades.

Alec Lumsden was very cool and keeping excellent control of his company, never moving more than one platoon at a time. With him he had the commanders of the two following platoons, so that he could show them just where the platoon in front was working and from what point they were required to take on. I was also impressed with the coolness of one or two N.C.O.s who could tell me exactly where it was not safe to loiter and from which houses the shooting was coming.

After talking to Alec and George Morrison, and having judged the strength of the opposition, I decided to take strictly limited objectives astride the main road as far as the level-crossing and to get the four rifle companies firm there; then, after that, to strike outwards and clear up the whole area north of the railway before going further.

So we got ourselves into position there, holding tightly the main street and blocks on either side of it; but there were odd

181

Spandau parties roving about in most of the rest of the town and they were in the large factory just across the railway line. C Company was occupying a big yellow milk factory about seventy yards this side of it and they had duels, piat *versus* bazooka, which broke a lot of glass but did not seem to hurt anybody.

Ian Edgar came in and broke the dreadful news that John Frary, our signal officer, was missing. Apparently they were going to look for one of the companies, John to get a line laid to it and Ian, as Intelligence Officer, to find out the situation. They took a wrong turning and saw two men standing in the doorway whom they took to be ours. There was a shout of 'Hands up!' and a burst of Schmeisser as Ian dodged round the corner. He swore it was aimed at him and not at John and he was confident that he was a prisoner. I thought this was likely as John's reactions were slow and, taken off his guard, he would not think quickly enough to do anything but put up his hands. His poor wife, Anne, would, I knew, be very worried as they wrote to each other every day. I was very fond of him and would miss him and his sleepy manner and dry sense of humour. He would be a great loss to the battalion as he was a most efficient signal officer, and the quiet, brave type. I had the street carefully searched in the morning and there was no sign of John's body, so I was even more confident that he was a P.O.W., as later proved to be the case.

C.S.M. Morrice made a magnificent remark that morning. When C Company heard that they were going to do an attack, one man said he wished to report sick as he was short-sighted. 'That will be all right,' said the C.S.M. 'In future you will always go into action fifty yards ahead of your section so that you will be able to see the enemy.'

In the middle of the night I got orders to prepare to take the high ground north-east and east of Heyen, a mile south of Gennep, and 5-7th Gordons were to attack at the same time on our left and secure the remaining features which overlooked the

182

town. It was quite a complicated little operation and I spent the five remaining hours of the night in my cellar Command Post planning it and the fire programme, and how to get the best inter-communication. 'Inter-com.' is the key to every battle for when it fails all control ceases, and it was particularly difficult since the companies' wireless sets were not good enough.

We spent most of the morning messing about, cleaning up the station and odd houses which overlooked the railway embankment, our start-line for this attack, with the result that I gave out my orders very late. Then the good Corporal Robb brought in some food which Frank Philip, the Battery Commander, and I proceeded to sit down and eat, although we both knew better. The result was that, by the time we had finished lunch, the fire programme had started, and now we had to make our way to our H.Q. for the start of the battle.

We had hardly got outside the door when a shell hit the house above us. I felt the blast on my neck and Frank said: 'That's a near one.' In the half-mile we had to go we dodged at least twenty more. We just sprinted like hell for fifty yards, then nipped into a house to regain our breath, and so on. I was very annoyed, firstly with myself for having been so stupid, and secondly with our own medium artillery which, as well as the Germans, was shelling us.

We started off with a two-company attack, A and D, to take the two rows of houses immediately beyond the railway line. They had the benefit of a smoke-screen which shielded them from the high ground further south, but also made it difficult to watch their progress, and to some extent hindered the troop of Churchill tanks supporting them. Neither company had any great difficulty, but D lost Frank Hopkins, their second-in-command, on a schu-mine crossing the railway, and Ronald Davies was wounded by wood splinters in his hand at the same time, though he pluckily carried on for the rest of the day.

Then C and B passed through them (*to C1 and B1, see Map 6*). B Company was directed on to a small sandy ridge covered with diggings, which they proceeded to charge in their now familiar style and for which they were well supported by the tanks. They claimed to have killed twenty Huns and that several more went away wounded and shrieking with pain. So far so easy, and I moved my headquarters up to C Company. I now had to send A, and then D, forward (*to A2 and D2*). Then I found that I couldn't get any orders through to D as their wireless was not working. Finally I sent a tank across to them with a written message.

A and D reached their objectives without any trouble. By this time it was getting dark and raining hard. One gun was shelling the road between us and the level-crossing, but otherwise all was quiet. C Company stopped just at the north edge of Heyen. They were held up by a Spandau which Alec thought was in the ruined church, but it was too dark to be sure and I told him not to get involved in a battle. So they made themselves firm round a few houses at the roadside. I put B Company just behind them and sent them some mortars and anti-tank guns.

We were on all our objectives except one, the hillock (*A4*) east of Heyen, and A Company was told to get there at first light. It was only of value to the enemy in daylight, since it over-looked Gennep.

Just as I had begun to roll myself up in my blankets upon the one bed in the cellar Command Post, Alec Lumsden rang up to say that his Company was being attacked from the direction of Heyen.

'Right,' I said, 'I'll bring down the artillery at once.'

Frank was already at his set and needed no telling. In some field three or four miles behind us the eight guns of his battery were already loaded and laid on this fire task. Eight sleepy sentries were standing there, one in each gunpit, their greatcoat collars turned up, their shoulders rounded, their thoughts far away, but each one ready instantly to pull the lanyard which would fire the shell if the Tannoy loudspeaker crackled and spoke. Similarly at the battery command post, and at the two troop headquarters, sleepy duty officers were sitting there, sipping tea, pumping up the Tilley lamp, reading, writing letters, doing their post-war planning, awaiting any sudden call.

'Charlie, peter, queen, one, to charlie, peter, queen, over,' said Frank into the microphone.

'Charlie O.K., over,' came the instantaneous answer.

'Charlie one to Charlie, sunray here, fire sugar oboe sugar, over,' said Frank.

'Charlie, wilco, out,' came the reply, so quickly, so quietly, so confidently.

I once saw a film about a submarine. I remember a shot of the commander just before he fired his torpedoes at a German battleship, his nerves and body tense and driving his brain for all he was worth. I suppose I was something like him as I crouched on the edge of a chair, staring at the layout on the map, gnawing my nails and, like a cat about to pounce, watching Frank at his set. I snapped out a few orders. To Thomson, who had taken over Signal Officer that morning: 'Tell all stations to open up at once' (in case the telephone went). 'Then tell the exchange to clear the line as soon as C Company wants to speak.'

To the Adjutant: 'Tell B Company to stand to and inform A and D what's happening.'

To the I.O.: 'Wake Neil, Hastings and Chamberlain and tell them to get into my jeep and open up their sets.'

As soon as I heard the battery wilco, which means 'your order understood and will be complied with', I ran up the stairs, out of the door, and stood in the open under the stars, listening for the shoot.

'Oh, let it come down,' I almost shouted aloud, 'let it come down.'

Immediately, and less than a minute after Alec had telephoned, I heard away in the distance a faint pop, pop, pop as the guns fired, then nothing at all for five or six seconds, then a faint drone, becoming louder as the first eight shells approached and passed overhead, followed by the bouncing bangs as they came crashing down just beyond the threatened company.

I ran down the stairs and into the cellar and noticed how tense was the atmosphere. Frank was speaking on the telephone to his forward observation officer, enquiring whether he could, with safety, bring the line of fire closer to the company. Everybody else was silent.

Then there was a clatter in the passage and in shambled a breathless corporal.

'No.-14-Platoon-is-surrounded-sir,' he said, as if it were all one word.

He did not quite know why he had run a thousand yards non-stop back to the Battalion Command Post, instead of going to his company H.Q. Somebody, he was rather vague as to who, had told him to fetch help.

I supposed that one must expect this sort of thing to happen occasionally, even in the best battalions.

Then Alec asked for me on the telephone.

'I think it's all now in hand,' he said; 'it was only a cheeky fighting patrol which fired some sort of phosphorus grenade at the thatch of one of our houses, and then shot at the men when they ran out silhouetted against the flame.'

In the morning he told us that one German stood in the road shouting: 'Come out, you English swine!' The platoon commander's servant shot him, and he was found to be an officer. The paybook in his breast pocket was drilled neatly through. After this raid the companies all had a somewhat anxious night, a higher proportion than before standing-to in the slit-trenches and in the rain.

In the morning we moved B Company and our command post into Heyen and the position was strengthened with a platoon of machine guns and a section of 17-pounder anti-tank guns. Our patrols reported that there were no enemy in the large wood just east of A Company, but that they were entrenched 300 yards south of the village.

After lunch the acting Brigade Commander came up on the air and told me to come back to a house near the level-crossing where I could talk to him on the telephone. When I got through to him he told me to be ready to move further south. I pointed out that the troops were very tired, having had only one good night's sleep in the last four. He then suggested a rather more limited operation and said that it might not come off, but that I should make plans for it. So I stayed on there to work it out. Shortly afterwards Alec spoke to me by R/T and said that an enemy tank had appeared at the edge of the wood about 500 yards from A and B Companies. I replied:

'That's all right, if it comes any further our guns will shoot at it. But I'll get some of our Churchill tanks down.'

I then spoke to Grant Peterkin, who ordered a troop forward, and I went out and stood in the road to brief the troop leader as he passed. Perhaps he had a stomach-ache or had received bad news from home, for the performance of his tanks was the windiest and wettest imaginable. It took them thirty minutes to get jacked up and come five hundred yards to us. I said:

'Go straight down the road. There's plenty of cover. Stop when you reach Heyen, then get out and have a look on foot.' There followed fifteen minutes R/T conversation with his squadron-leader, who was trying to command the troop from back at Brigade H.Q. It then took the troop twenty minutes to reach Heyen (one mile away) by some circuitous route, by which time it was dark and they had to come home.

Just after the Churchills had started, Alec came up on the air again to say that a second and perhaps a third tank or S.P. gun had appeared near the first and that there was some infantry with them. This, of course, altered the whole situation and astonished me. It seemed unthinkable that the enemy should try to retake Heyen after they had allowed us to walk into it. Moreover, the battalion had not been counter-attacked since we were in the woods near Escoville last June. I said:

'Right, keep on firing the guns. I will bring forward D

Company to C Company's position and also the dismounted carrier platoon.' Alec said that there were indications that the enemy were trying to get round our right, so I told him to move one or two platoons of C Company to counter any such threat. Meanwhile the infantry came in with great determination and a few succeeded in getting into an old castle on the right of B Company and only 200 yards from Battalion H.Q. Unfortunately the armour kept their distance and did not enter the field of fire of any of our anti-tank guns, but Neville Smith, the anti-tank platoon commander, and a crew manhandled a six-pounder into a new position and, with Neville laying the gun, fired four rounds at the nearest S.P. It was not easy to aim at as it kept jinking about behind a haystack, and another spotted the gun's position and fired back. Not until the six-pounder had been knocked out and a large splinter of metal had gone through his tam o' shanter did Neville stop trying.

I found everybody very much on the *qui vive* at Battalion H.Q. In fact, a rifle pointing through the letter-box, of all places, greeted me at the front door. By this time it was getting quieter, though this was because B Company had temporarily run out of ammunition, as I discovered later. But our mortars were still firing. Between the four of them they fired over 600 rounds, and I think it was their fire more than anything else which broke up the attack and caused the enemy to withdraw. B Company had borne the brunt of the attack, and it was largely due to their company commander, George Morrison, that they put up such an excellent showing.

Sergeant Dunlop and his brother-in-law, Dickson, were both killed during this attack, by a direct hit from a tank shell on their dug-out. It was very sad as they were both fine chaps, especially Dunlop. He got a M.M. in the desert and deserved a bar to it as he had commanded a platoon for many actions when we had been short of officers. To add to the sadness he was due to go home on leave next day.

Only once before had we been so short of officers. We started the Siegfried Line battle nine under strength, and casualties since then (one killed, one missing, seven wounded) had now reduced us to seventeen. But I was told that 152 Brigade were worse off, as they had had some very stiff fighting in the Reichswald against parachute troops.

We took over some ground two miles south-east of Heyen to make more elbow room for 52nd (Lowland) Division, who were to pass through us next day. There was nothing difficult about it, and we were soon dug in among some spruce firs on nice, sandy soil like Camberley Heath. We were now rather counter-attack conscious and registered our fire tasks, both artillery and mortars. For some months we had been inclined to pay mere lip service to our defensive arrangements.

Five new officers arrived that evening. Two of them were brothers, Howitt by name. We now had two MacPhersons and also two Thomsons. They were all Scots and all excellent fellows who had been kept at home training others, incredible considering how many lightly wounded officers were available for this. I was particularly pleased to see Arthur Thomson as his brother was a great friend of mine and was exceedingly gallant in 1940, until he was killed; in fact, those with him said that he deserved a V.C.

52nd Division went through us. They were a magnificent formation with a fine tradition from the first war, but inexperienced, as one could see by the amount of transport they took into battle. First they were a mountain division, then reorganised to be landed by air, and finally brought out here as ordinary infantry some months after the rest of us. C.S.M. Morrice made another good remark, telling his company to get cleaned up before 'this new division' came through.

We had now become non-operational, and Cornish, my new servant, put out my pyjamas, though perhaps they looked a little out of place in a command post. He was Danny Reid's old batman and therefore pretty well guaranteed not to go bomb-happy. We managed to get three companies back into

Gennep, which was a bit of luck as it was now raining hard.

We heard that four thousand reinforcements had been flown out in Dakotas. At any rate seven more new officers, making twelve in two days, reported in the evening. One was only eighteen. I felt dreadfully sorry for them all.

February 18th was spent in preparing for the next day's operation – the capture of Goch.

The plan was fairly simple.

Goch was to be attacked from the north-west (*see Map 7*). 15th Scottish were to go for the far side of the river and 153 Brigade the near side. Of 153, 5th Black Watch were to start by taking all the main parts of the town south of the river, up to and including the big square. Then 5-7th Gordons were to pass through them and take on from beyond the square as far as the railway. Our objective was the area just south of the 5th Black Watch – 5-7th boundary. This included the beginning of the

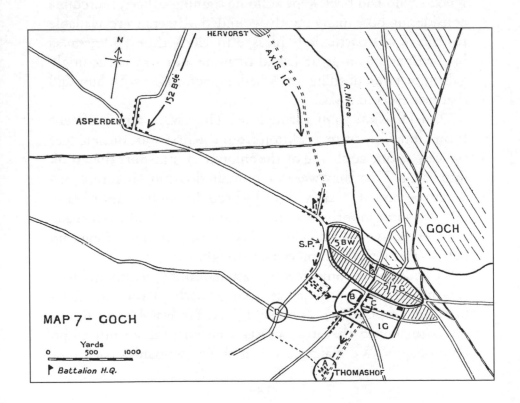

MAP 7 - GOCH

main road leading out of the town to the south-west, with two road junctions, and there was a school, a factory and several largish buildings in the area. Air-photos showed that the town had been very badly bombed and most of the streets were cratered or choked with rubble.

I spent that night at Brigade H.Q., in a big schloss named Grafenthal, and slept in what must once have been a coachman's room above the stables. The day started with a Brigade Liaison officer waking me up pretty early to say that 5th B.W. had got into the town without any difficulty, that 5-7th Gordons had been committed, and that my battalion had been called forward from Gennep and should reach me about 9 a.m. This they duly did and the companies and transport were dispersed in the areas we had chosen for them the morning before.

The first two companies in the batting order were A and D, and after about an hour I set off with their Company Commanders, Arthur Thomson and Casey Petrie, and Kenneth McDonald who had just taken over I.O. There was a lot of mortaring and shelling on the road into Goch and we twice stopped and took cover. There did not seem to be any great hurry, as one could see that the 5th-7th were not getting on very well from the number of their fighting vehicles which were held up at the roadside. We found the Black Watch H.Q. just inside the town and established our own near it. Ackers and Neil were sent out at once to fill sandbags and put them on the sills of the two windows.

Bill Bradford told me that they had had no difficulty in getting into the town and occupying the area astride the main road as all the Huns were asleep at the time in cellars. But when they tried to clean up a larger area in daylight, they soon found themselves in difficulties with snipers and Spandaus. Companies of 5-7th Gordons were now fighting in what was nominally the 5th B.W. area and had scarcely entered their own objective. It was painfully obvious that first impressions were wrong and the enemy had every intention of defending the town.

The rest of the day was perfectly bloody. It just could not have been more unpleasant. As soon as the area of the square had been cleared, I decided to try to clean up the main street running south from it. It was obvious that the other two battalions were fully committed and could not do this, although it was really the boundary between them and should have been done before we arrived.

This street was the main one leading into our objective and A Company got to work. Almost at once their commander, Arthur Thomson, was killed, shot through the head by a sniper in the first few minutes of his first action, while standing in a doorway talking to Bill Kyle, his second-in-command.

Kyle took over and did very well, and the company made a certain amount of progress, but resistance stiffened and it was clear that no further advance could be made in that direction without heavy casualties. The street was badly cratered by debris so we could not use tanks or crocodiles, and my sortie by the bulldozer was met by aimed small-arms fire from snipers.

Meanwhile O.C. D Company, with his platoon commanders, tried to find a way across the rubble and fallen houses towards his company's objective – the big building in the north-east corner of the battalion area. He soon came up against snipers, and one of his officers, Harrison, the eighteen-year-old who joined us only two days before, was hit in the head, though fortunately it was only a graze. While this was taking place the troop of tanks was trying to find a side-turning which would take them up to D Company's objective. The leading tank, while still on the main street 100 yards beyond the square, was hit by a bazooka and all the crew became casualties.

It was clear that we couldn't make much progress towards our objective from the direction of the square, so I thought that my best plan was to attack with the other two companies, C and B, through the housing estate to the west. At this time C Company was under cover in the row of houses 200 yards north of the first Battalion H.Q., and D Company was in houses off the main street. Both companies were therefore close to the road junction which was chosen as their start-point.

It took one and a half hours to mount this attack, as in addition to the time required for reconnaissance a troop of tanks and a troop of crocodiles were to support it and a smoke-screen had to be laid on to defilade the right flank of the two attacking companies.

The attack was completely successful. C Company first occupied the housing estate, then B passed through them to their objective, the school and buildings round the main road junctions. C Company then went through to the buildings beyond. The tanks and flame-throwers gave excellent support to this two-company attack; one flame-thrower went up on a mine at the road junction in B Company's objective. B Company reported that as far as they were concerned, the smoke-screen was most successful, but it did not prevent a very heavy mortar stonk on the housing estate just after they had left it and while C Company were still in possession.

C.S.M. Morrice said that it was in his opinion the heaviest single concentration the battalion had encountered since El Alamein. Nevertheless, the company had no casualties owing to the good cellars of all these houses. Shelling and mortaring was very heavy both on this day and the following one, and certainly the heaviest shelling the battalion had had since D-Day, and only the excellent cellars, which seemed to be a feature of all those German houses, saved us from having very heavy casualties.

While this attack was taking place, Brigadier Sinclair, who by this time was back from sick leave and had resumed command, told me that he wanted us to send a company to the cross-roads (D) south-west of the housing estate, and another to Thomashof, a very large farm with many out-buildings. I said that I would do so before first light next morning; we both agreed that, with that heavy mortaring, it was necessary to get across the open ground under cover of darkness.

With that extra commitment, it was obviously not feasible to take all the buildings within the battalion's original objective, so I told George Morrison and Alec Lumsden that B and C were to hold only the main street down to the road junction and such houses just east as could be conveniently occupied.

D Company hadn't done much, so I told Casey Petrie that they would have to go to the cross-roads. I had no worries about this, as old Casey was a thoroughly experienced officer and the Divisional Recce Regiment had been almost as far in the afternoon and reported that they thought the area was unoccupied.

I could not take B or C for Thomashof as they had borne the brunt all day, and Alec Lumsden and George Morrison had both done so much already. That left only A Company. But I wasn't at all happy about sending A Company off into the blue on this night attack. Bill Kyle was a stout-hearted lad, but not very experienced. That morning he had had the unnerving experience of seeing his company commander killed while talking to him. There was only one other officer left in the company, Charlie Howitt, whose first action it had been. And one of the three platoons was commanded by only a corporal.

I gave a lot of thought to it during the evening and finally decided to command the company myself. I asked Kyle if he minded, and he seemed quite pleased. In a way I was rather glad to have this opportunity, which I regarded as an act of self-discipline. Of late I had been finding it increasingly difficult to leave the nice, safe Command Post when there was shelling.

Nothing was known about Thomashof except what I could learn from the air-photos. From these I saw that our objective consisted of one very large building with five biggish outhouses round it. In addition there were two smaller houses detached from and about a hundred yards our side of the main group. Several enemy trenches could be seen.

I made the simplest plan possible. The medium artillery

194

would shell Thomashof during the night, scale five from sixteen guns – eighty rounds, each 100 lb. We would take the shortest route from the cemetery just in front of B Company, who would be responsible for patrolling this area to secure our start-point. The I.O. would lay out white tape for the first 200 yards, after which it was 1,100 yards by compass across open country. Corporal Henderson's platoon would take the first two houses, then Howitt's platoon would go for the main building, and Sergeant Cleveland's platoon and Company H.Q. for the two nearest outhouses.

Zero Hour was set for 4.45 a.m., but I afterwards postponed it till 5.45, which I thought would get us across the open ground in darkness but give us the benefit of first light to clear the somewhat alarmingly large buildings. I had the two officers and all the N.C.O.s in the Battalion Command Post cellar and took great trouble in briefing them, and they all had a good look at the air-photos.

I sent a note to the Brigade Commander explaining the short-age of officers and N.C.O.s in A Company, and that for this reason I felt I should take command of this company night attack, and therefore could Grant Peterkin come up during the night and take over his battalion. Later the Brigade Intelligence Officer came up and said that he was in bed with a chill, so I told Alec to come and take charge from 4 a.m.

It had been arranged that I should join A Company at 5.40. About half an hour before that I came up from our cellar and stood on the pile of rubble outside, to take stock of the night: the brightness of the moonlight; the effectiveness of the search-lights: the strength and direction of the wind; the amount of enemy shelling and mortaring (still considerable), etc. I heard a lot of heavy stuff crumping down in the direction of Thomashof, so I told our medium representative to stop his guns firing. Just before I left the Command Post he told me that they had not fired since 4 a.m.

I went round the corner and joined A Company just as it was

falling in. But the same heavy-calibre shells could still be heard crashing down ahead, and in the stillness of the night the loud, resounding bangs were undeniably frightening. I walked a few yards ahead to a clearing, and then took a compass bearing on where I heard the guns firing. When I plotted it on my map I saw that it was from the south-east corner of the Reichswald, just where I knew the Scottish Horse, the Divisional Medium Regiment, was in action.

So I told Kyle to get the company back under cover and ran up the street to B Company's H.Q. to speak to Alec on the telephone. I told him that there was no shadow of doubt that it was our guns firing, and I gave him the bearing I had just taken. Alec replied that he had just told the gunners that all the guns in Second Army were to cease fire! So I ran back to A Company. Hitherto there had been odd shells dropping about the place, all fairly close, but as I was on my way back, an imperial stonk came down all round. Cornish, my servant, and I dived into a house just in time.

A few minutes later, when all was quiet again, I emerged into the street, dusty and sweating, and began to look for Kyle. Then I heard those same guns crumping their stuff down once more along our route. Each explosion sounded like the crack of doom as it resounded and echoed all round in the darkness.

For an instant I considered cancelling the attack. Then I told Kyle to form up the Company. we had already lost a quarter of an hour, and it was about 6 a.m. when we moved off. After going about 200 yards there was a salvo of mortar bombs and the column checked. After half a minute I went forward and found nobody ahead of us, and cursed the leading men for not having followed those in front. Then we found McDonald, the I.O., very cool and confident, and he walked with me to where the tape ended.

It was a lovely clear night with visibility a good 200 yards – rather too much for the job in hand, I thought. It was pleasant to be in open country after the dirt, dust and shelling in ruined

Goch. Except for the column of silent men and a house burning away on my right, I might have been going to an early morning duck flight. Then there was another loud crump ahead, and I realised that although the guns in question were firing from the direction of the enemy, there was a remarkable echo coming back from the Reichswald, and this it was which had made me take a bearing to what appeared to be the position of our own artillery. Luckily that was a parting shot, and those particular guns fired no more.

All went well for a time, and the leading platoon had no difficulty in taking the right hand of the first two houses. I then ordered Howitt's and Sergeant Cleveland's platoons forward. It was just getting light, though it was too dark to distinguish friend from foe at twenty yards. One Spandau was firing from 200 yards away, but not apparently at us. We seemed to have achieved surprise.

With Kyle and Company H.Q. I followed Sergeant Cleveland's platoon through an orchard, across a stream and up to the two nearest of the main buildings. Sergeant Cleveland's platoon entered the left-hand one, and we the right. Ours consisted of a large cattle byre with about six smaller rooms leading off it. By now there was a certain amount of firing taking place, for in several directions the enemy appeared to have come to life. It was still pretty dark and I was afraid of us shooting each other. I paired off the men with us and posted two at each of the four doors of the byre.

Kyle went outside for a moment, and when he returned he was shot at by his servant at five yards' range, and missed. Then there was a burst of fire from one of the men in a doorway behind me.

'You bloody fool!' I shouted at him, as someone fell in the straw at his feet, gasping, groaning and choking his life away. But this time it was a full-blooded Hun, though unarmed and half-dressed.

I went to the window to read the battle. There now seemed to

197

be hardly any shooting taking place. It was clear that Howitt's platoon had not taken the main building for there was not a sound from there nor any sign of them in front.

I went across to Sergeant Cleveland's platoon next door. He told me that when anybody tried to cross to the next building they were fired on by two Spandaus from dug-in positions in the garden behind. It seemed to me that the Company was not in any particular danger as the buildings they were occupying were substantial and the enemy were not showing any aggressiveness. But it was obvious that more men would be necessary to clear the remaining buildings. We were not through to the battalion by either R/T or line so, after consulting Kyle, I decided to return and send up another company and some tanks.

On the way back I found that though Corporal Henderson's platoon had still got the first house, they were not yet in the second one, which was held by the enemy. Corporal Henderson was firing at it somewhat ineffectively. I told him to use his smoke and rush the house, and then take the whole platoon across and join up with Kyle.

Cornish and I then had a very nasty time getting back over the open ground, as it was light enough to be seen and two Spandaus fired at us. We ran like mad, taking it in short rushes from cover to cover. Luckily there were one or two small bomb craters in the largest field, without which I do not think we could have got across. As an additional insult somebody fired one shot from an anti-tank gun at us.

Unfortunately, for one reason or another, it took about two hours to get B Company off with some tanks. Just before they started one or two men from A Company came in to say that the company had been overwhelmed and they were the sole survivors.

Even with the armour to support them, B Company had quite a difficult time and some ten men killed in capturing Thomashof. They took about eighty prisoners. George

Morrison, as usual, was exceedingly brave in what was a very nasty attack, for which he later received the D.S.O. He was very sick about the support given him by the flame-throwing tanks, only one of which would cross the open ground with his company.

One of the new officers, Ventris, also did well, being wounded five times in the course of the battle and only giving up when George ordered him to do so. He had been with us only four days. 'It was fun while it lasted,' he said, as they took him away on a stretcher. I had made Alec and George toss up as to which company should do this attack. George lost, so Alec insisted in accompanying him to give him his moral support for the first part of the attack. What magnificent chaps those two were!

From one or two survivors and a stretcher-bearer who was taken prisoner and escaped, it seemed that Howitt's platoon reached the front of their building and saw one or two men in the doorway. Thinking (God knows why) that it might have been some of the rest of the company, they challenged them, and the reply was a burst of fire.

Howitt was killed – we found his body that night – then the rest of the platoon scattered. The enemy was very strong and shortly afterwards put in several attacks, and the company was overwhelmed through lack of leaders. No doubt parachute troops or commandos would have made short work of the Huns in Thomashof, but our experience was that once the leaders were hit, an attack petered out. But they fought well as we found eight or ten dead, and we guessed that a number of the forty-three that were missing were wounded.

I felt utterly exhausted that night and depressed beyond words, as I thought that this disaster was my fault. Firstly, I could have asked for Typhoon attack on Thomashof the day before, and secondly I should have insisted that the place was too big to attack with one company, which was all we had available while still having to hold part of Goch.

I was up very early in the morning and went round the companies, getting shot at for my pains by a Spandau merchant a hundred yards from the square, in a street which was clear the day before.

George Morrison and B Company were very tired. D was in much the same state; their little cross-roads was a shambles; most of the houses were burnt out, and two armoured cars and a carrier had blown up there on mines. The shelling and mortaring since we had been in Goch had been pretty well non-stop, and we had all had some near shaves. One landed very close to Cornish and me as we were on our way back to breakfast after visiting one of the companies. There was a great yellow flash, a powerful blast and smell of cordite, and we dived down the cellar of the house we were passing; not until some minutes later did I discover that I had a small splinter in my finger.

After breakfast Alec rang up to say that Ian Edgar and three of his platoon H.Q. had been killed and two more wounded, by a shell which landed on a cellar window-sill. Sergeant Coutts, the carrier-platoon sergeant since El Alamein, was also killed when standing in a doorway that evening.

We all had several more narrow shaves next day. They wore one down in the end. Six months before I had found them slightly exhilarating, just as when one has ridden in a number of steeplechases without a mishap it does one's nerve good to have a harmless fall. But now I had seen too much and had too great a respect for the law of averages. The shelling here was certainly prodigious. Two new officers got hit on their way up to join their companies. I had not met them and now I probably never should.

I spent the day with George at Thomashof, to give him a chance of resting. It was a beastly place. We were shelled all day, and the machine-gun platoon had had twelve casualties out of fifteen men, from one unlucky shell, though of course they should not all have been in one room. We had to lay on a proper little operation with a smoke-screen and artillery programme to get them back, as there was a Spandau which covered the road corner so that a vehicle could not come up there in daylight. It deliberately fired at an unmistakable ambulance which contained twelve wounded, which I was able to take quite philosophically as they were all Germans.

George told me about one of his sergeants, Strahan by name and a brave chap. They approached a dead German officer. 'Steady, sir,' said Strahan, 'he may be booby-trapped.' George instinctively took a pace back, whereupon Strahan removed the watch, fountain pen and Luger pistol. (Lugers were highly prized as they could be sold for £10 to Americans.) He had now been wounded and the doctor said that when he reached the Aid Post he could hardly feel his pulse for wrist-watches.

Ewen held a most dramatic burial service for those who were killed round Thomashof. There were two long graves, one full of Gordons and the other full of Germans, and Ewen stood on the mound of earth, silhouetted against a burning farmhouse, in battledress with a white padre's collar, and a steel helmet in his hand.

A small group of us stood in front, listening for the whistle of shells and ready to dart back inside the building at any moment. I was very upset that little Chamberlain, who had for so long been my signaller, was amongst those we buried. As I could not use my jeep he had been sent down with A Company's line party, and killed. He had always had a ready smile for me.

We stood-to at dusk and there was a rattle of musketry. I thought: heavens, we are being counter-attacked; but it was only a pig being killed. That night we had pike for supper, killed with a tommy-gun.

We were bombed once again by the R.A.F. in broad daylight and perfect visibility. The whole of one stick fell in Goch. The Colonel commanding the divisional sappers was hit in the head and was not expected to live, and the Argylls had about a dozen casualties. We were lucky to escape without any as one bomb fell in C Company's area and burnt out all their transport.

Whenever we were bombed by our own people we were furious and said that it was sheer carelessness. It may or may not have been, but at any rate there was no doubt at all about the deep debt of gratitude the Army owed the R.A.F. Throughout this campaign the enemy had had no Air Force to harass us and was often short of artillery and mortar ammunition. This was due to our bombing of their factories and supply lines, and it saved many, many soldiers' lives.

Our casualties for these four operations – Reichswald, Gennep, Heyen and Goch – were nearly half the Battalion's fighting strength:

	Killed	Wounded	Missing	Total
Officers	4	14	2	20
O.R.s	29	106	48	183
				203

While we were resting at Goch I took two days' leave in Brussels.

I shared a room at the Palace Hotel with Spens, Argylls, of 227 Brigade in 15th Scottish Division. He was full of praise for 6th Guards Tank Brigade which supported them, and said how they would go anywhere, even through woods by moonlight. I wished we had them with us. There was a check-up on every one in uniform in Brussels, to rope in the deserters. They even inspected the kits of all officers in transit, on the look-out for loot or black market. Unfortunately I had left my pass behind, but heard about the check-up in time and got another from a friend at S.H.A.E.F. H.Q.

I went to the Cerf in the evening, where champagne cocktails cost only fifty francs. There I met a squadron-leader in the R.A.F. 'So you are in the 51st Division,' he said, looking at HD on my arm. 'I hear you are not prepared to advance any further unless you are guaranteed *no* air support.'

We started a little training in Goch – street fighting, an exercise with the tanks, etc. We were still nearly all living in cellars as all rooms above ground had been so knocked about.

We had always read in the papers that the Germans were almost at starvation level and that most of their possessions were *ersatz*. There was certainly no evidence of this in Goch: on the contrary there was every sign of plenty. The cellars were full of bottled fruit and vegetables, literally hundreds of jars, and the farmyards showed no shortage of stock, poultry and feeding stuffs. The linen cupboards and pantries would have been the envy of any British housewife, and such Germans as were now beginning to appear had good clothing and shoes. In fact they seemed to be at least as well supplied with everything as our people were at home. The effect of all this on the troops was once more to undermine their confidence in the Press, the B.B.C. and any Government statement – all of which they would now be even more ready than before to dub as 'propaganda'.

On the subject of the Press it was very annoying that all the papers referred to these last battles as having been fought by the Canadian Army; no mention that in fact more than half the Second Army had been engaged, having been placed under the command of the Canadian Army for the operation. Of course this was not the fault of the journalists but of the Army Public Relations Department. But it annoyed the men, and no wonder. The stupidity of the Army over news censorship still passed belief. It was well-known how we left America to think that all the fighting in the Middle East was being done by Dominion troops and Indians – so little mention for so long of British formations. How much morale in the Army would have gone up if they had released unit names and how bucked our Jocks would have been to see '1st Gordons' in print once a month or so. They would have cut it out and kept the cuttings, and what a difference it would have made to a unit!

Meanwhile the Division was made up to strength again with

203

both officers and men, which showed that it was already known that there were more bloody battles ahead of us. These last reinforcements, coming so soon, had a significance which was apparent to everyone.

My new servant, Cornish, suited me admirably. Most men referred to the Germans half-affectionately as Jerry, and were only too ready to give them a cup of tea as soon as they surrendered. Not so Cornish, and I had seen him take a cigarette out of the mouth of one of them and stamp it underfoot. Like me he would have skinned them alive or boiled them in oil without any compunction whatever.

When I asked him whether he would like to be servant to me, he replied that he would but that he couldn't do any of this lady's–maiding (and, what's more, he wasn't going to, his voice implied). Nevertheless, when there were no women to do it he washed my underclothing and darned my socks as well as any of them. He told me that I was the fifth officer he had had during the campaign, the others all having been killed or wounded.

We had a visit from Churchill, and were very proud that we were the only Division he spoke to. He looked very well and as pugnacious as usual. Montgomery (in a green sniper's jacket) accompanied him, and all the big shots. He came to a Divisional Retreat, the massed Pipes and Drums. It started with the Last Post and 'Flowers of the Forest', that haunting piper's lament, in memory of those who had fallen since the start of the campaign. I thought of some of the Gordon officers: David Martin, Albert Brown, Murray Reekie, Johnnie Grant, Arthur Thomson, George Stewart, magnificent chaps every one of them, and what a loss to the nation!

I remembered officers in England saying how quickly in war you recover from the death of a comrade. I suppose this is true in a way, since though you may lose half the officers of a battalion in one day, others take their place and the machine still goes on. But I for one could never forget those good fellows.

Unfortunately Churchill arrived one and a half hours late and we were standing in a drizzle until then. We had been told to cheer when he left but there was not a murmur from the Jocks. They thought the world of Churchill but they are independent and undemonstrative at the best of times, and they just weren't feeling like cheering.

On March 6th we heard that we were 'going back for training'. I was glad to be seeing the last of our cellar in Goch and, for the moment, of Germany.

That morning I took a stroll up to the cemetery. The rapid deterioration of the German situation could be seen in their graves. Firstly, an elaborate stone memorial to the men of 190 Infantry Division who fell in 1940. Then well-made black and white wooden crosses for the dead of October, 1944. But for those who were killed after October the crosses became more and more crude; latterly there was neither paint nor crosses but just any old piece of wood sticking up in the ground with a name written on it in pencil. Finally, mass graves dug with a mechanical excavator and no identification at all.

The German crosses were Maltese in shape. On the upright below the cross was the man's name, then underneath it his rank and regiment, home town, date of birth and death, and below that sometimes where he was killed. Thus 'Gerhard Lorengen, Pionier 3 Pl, Ers Bte 20, aus Dresden, geb. 11-8-20, gef. 9-10-44'; or 'Wilhelm Locht, Gefr' 1-Füs t B 26, aus Leipzig, geb. 22-4-18, gef 21-10-44 bei Grafwegen'. Sometimes you saw the signs Y for born and λ for died.

I found the grave of a British officer who, I imagine, died of wounds in the Goch hospital. The cross said: 'Englander Lt. John Johnstone, geb 15-10-18, gef 5-2-45. E.M. Army – Nr 4273599 Recce R.A.C.' Beside him were buried two Canadians, 'Canadien Cpl Zak Zaharik' and 'Canadien Pte Pick'. As the dates on all three crosses were just before our last operation, I thought they must have been killed or wounded on patrols.

There were also the graves of a lot of civilians, mostly railway

and party officials and their families, no doubt killed in
the bombing. Thus: 'S.A. Rottenführer Valentin Freece',
'Zugwachtmstr Adolf Haarhaus geb 1883', 'Frau Stubs-
wachtmeister Oscar Hoffmeiss'. Likvornik told me afterwards
that the German railways had ranks and uniforms just as in the
Army.

9

We moved to Neeritter on the Belgian-Dutch border. Battalion H.Q. was in an old moated house, something between an extra big farm and a château. It was a stately looking house with lovely avenues leading to it; a moat and a bridge over it, and pigeons cooing in some big old beeches just behind it completed the picture. Though only 200 yards from Neeritter, it was just over the Belgian border. The difference between Holland and Belgium was noticeable, though perhaps across the breadth of only one field: in Holland are found well-built and scrupulously clean houses and usually dull, heavy women; in Belgium untidy and unattractive houses but the women were usually good-looking.

Two of our former officers returned to us here. Bruce Rae, who was wounded for the third time in November, with a nasty scar on his jaw, and Bill McFarlan. Bill's right hand was paralysed and he was also lame. He wangled his way out by getting posted to our Battle School at Louvain, but when he landed at Ostend they saw his medical category was B and said he could go no further. So he just hopped on a lorry and reported to us.

George Forbes arrived back from a signal course and Gray also came back, one of our few wounded officers to return to us. We could never make out why we so seldom seemed to get wounded officers and N.C.O.s back, and felt it must be another shortcoming in the Adjutant-General's department. Gray had grown a moustache; he said he had matured a lot.

We were now getting down in earnest to planning and training for the Rhine crossing. I had often wished I had taken part in the historic D-Day landings, but I suppose the odds were that if I had not missed the first month of the campaign I should not have got through till now, and this forthcoming operation promised to be the next most important and interesting. The initial assault crossing was to be made by the two Scottish divisions, ourselves and the 15th, and it was a great honour. Montgomery was supposed to have said that Scottish troops were best for assaulting.

We attended a lecture on the organisation for a big river crossing. It boiled down to one regiment (the Royals) controlling the whole thing. They were to have posts in the marshalling, loading and dispersal areas, on the near and far bank and so on, using the wireless in their armoured cars to call forward the infantry when there was room for them at each successive stage.

My job was to be in the loading area – to supervise the loading of the companies and later the vehicles into the buffaloes. (A buffalo is a big, tracked, amphibious vehicle about the size of a tank, which lets down at the back like the beach landing craft used on D-Day. It crawls down the bank and into the water and then its tracks drive it across to the far bank, where it noses its way out again.) I was not exactly looking forward to it. It was necessary to load vehicles from a hard road with a turn-round, so it meant hanging about at a road junction for many hours in presumably a good deal of shelling and mortaring. I felt that I would far rather cross with the companies and fight the battle on the other side.

We all felt we ought to be crossing now and not in a fortnight's time. No doubt there was a lot of community digging and mine-laying taking place on the other side, and to this extent every day that passed was a day lost. However, to mount an operation of this size was bound to take a lot of time. The ammunition build-up alone was a tremendous problem.

With the shortage of experienced platoon commanders and N.C.O.s our minor tactics were by now so minor as to be almost non-existent, so we had to have something to compensate, which, as usual, was overwhelming artillery support.

I was woken one night by a signaller with a message pad. I think I must have been dreaming that I was commanding the battalion in a battle, because I woke with the fixation that this was an order to attack at short notice. But instead it read: '30 Corps to 1 Gordons. Personal from General Horrocks to Major Lindsay. Congratulations on well-deserved award of D.S.O.'

Of course, I was astonished. It was ages since anything really nice had happened to me. In the next hour I turned on my torch several times just to make sure I had made no mistake. Then I gave up trying to sleep and got up and wrote and told Joyce all about it. In due course she replied that it had been a good week as Lindsay *ma* had got his football colours and I had received the D.S.O.

I felt badly in need of a bath and a haircut, so ran down to Brussels after lunch – seventy miles. I clicked for a party with Livia and some Belgians, where I dropped a monumental brick. Someone started talking about conditions in Germany and I was asked if I had seen any signs of food shortage. I told them all about the preserved fruit in the cellars in my fluent but execrable French and used, I do not know why, the word *préservatif* for *preserves*. Half those present started talking all together and the other half shook with laughter. Later I asked Livia what a *préservatif* was. '*Un petit manteau pour quand il pleut*,' was her reply.

We had a regimental reunion. It started with a football match and then Retreat played by the massed pipe bands of the 1st, 2nd and 5-7th Gordon battalions. All the special Gordon tunes: 'Marquess of Huntly', 'Captain Towse, V.C.', 'My Highland Home' and 'The Cradle Song'. 'Just the job for Unter den Linden,' as I heard a spectator from an English regiment remark. The pipe corporal of 2nd Gordons was pointed out to me as being the son of pipe-Major Lauder, a famous Gordon V.C. of the first war. As well as the officers of the three battalions, there were two Gordon Brigadiers there, Eddie Colville and Roddy Sinclair. After tea we danced reels, and the timbers of the old moated house shook till I feared they might give way.

I was president of a court martial all one morning. They were the usual cases of desertion from the field of battle. We gave two ten years, two five years and one twelve months. We knew that when we awarded a ten-year sentence it would be reduced to three or four and that the man would serve perhaps six months. So if we thought a man should get, say, two or three years, we passed a sentence of ten or fifteen.

We had our first rehearsal on March 15th. It was quite fun doing an operation without anybody shooting back, no bother at all. There was no tactical aspect to the exercise as the sappers had only had time to clear mines from a small part of the far bank, so we just sat down in one of the few fields which was clear, and awaited our turn to be ferried back again.

The Black Watch went past as we were sitting sunning ourselves, and there was some baa-baa-ing on the part of our Jocks. This was an allusion to an old scandal of a Black Watch N.C.O. who stole a sheep. To this the Black Watch replied with, 'What's for supper tonight, boys?' to which their answer was a chorus of 'Cheese!'

This referred to an incident in 1916 when a big round Dutch cheese rolled off the back of a ration truck in the dark and some jumpy Gordons riddled it with bullets. It was all very good-humoured stuff, this chaff, and there was a lot of laughter on both sides. But some of us stopped it as one never knows where these things end, and once a feud between two regiments starts, it may last, literally, for a hundred years. There was a terrible feud between the Black Watch and the Gordons in the first war which had fortunately quite died out, and the last thing one wanted was to see it start up again.

5-7th Gordons and 5th Camerons had stolen a march on us. The 5-7th had had their pre-war white spats and diced hose-tops sent out, and hairy white sporrans for the Pipe Band. But the Camerons had gone even better; they had kilts, bought privately, for every man in the battalion.

We read in a Divisional Intelligence Summary that the first assault crossing of the Rhine was that of Julius Caesar in 55 B.C. Apparently he deemed it unworthy of either himself or the Roman people to make the crossing by boat, so he built a wooden bridge from Gaul to Germany, between Andernach and Coblenz. Ten days after starting to bring up bridging material, Caesar's bridge was built and his army had begun to cross – a wonderful achievement for those or any other days in view of the depth of the water and strength of the current. He must have had some good sappers.

Now we heard that Grant Peterkin had got a bar to his D.S.O. Actually it should have been the original D.S.O. since it was a periodical award dated last September when he was in 15th Division, and his immediate award, which came through first the other day, should have been a bar to it, which just shows how absurd the current system was. But still no Military Medals had come through for the men, which made us very angry.

On March 18th we had our final briefing at Divisional H.Q. Even the provost notices had signs with 'Last Supper' on them, which some may think was not in the best of taste.

We left on the afternoon of the 21st, so as to arrive in our concentration area near the Rhine after dark. We were now at a place called Marienbaum, twenty miles inside the German border and about four from where we were to cross. It had been smashed up and most of the roof was off our H.Q. house. A gun tried to knock the place down a bit more in the morning, but stopped after firing some twenty rounds.

I jeeped up for a reconnaissance of the crossing area (*see Map 8*). There was a high dyke stretching along this bank, and no movement for half a mile this side of it could be seen from

211

beyond the Rhine. This stretch included a long straggling village which was being held by one or two companies of 1st Royal Ulster Rifles in 3rd Division. They had to be pretty alert at night as the Hun was sending over patrols to try to see if we had been dumping bridging material.

There had been occasional salvoes of shells and mortar bombs, and I noted that our chosen loading area had by no means escaped attention – it was at a cross-roads and an obvious target. I visited R.U.R. H.Q. and arranged for their three-inch mortars to help us with a smoke-screen which we should want at one stage of the night, and also got their nearest formation to agree to dig some slit-trenches for the company waiting area next door to the loading area. They said they would boil up some tea for the companies as they passed through. Although the enemy could not see anything immediately behind the dyke, he could see everything a bit further back where

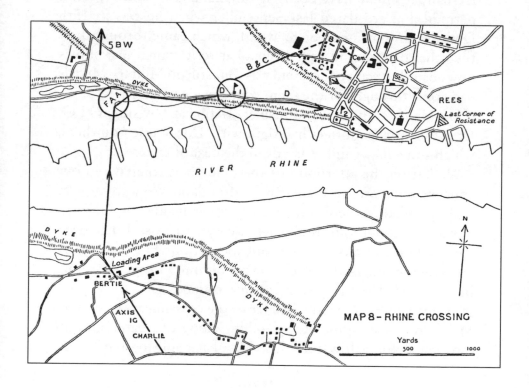

MAP 8 – RHINE CROSSING

the country was extremely open. So we had been keeping a constant smoke-screen during the hours of daylight, which extended some sixty miles along the river.

I saw many odd sights: Pioneer Corps companies with bridging material and the R.A.S.C. making dumps, both in the front line; our medium and heavy artillery deployed within enemy mortar range; some gun-crews stripped to the waist digging frantically for victory, while other soldiers wandered past them on bicycles and even on horseback (there was no shelling that day); odd men milking cows; thirty dead cows in a minefield; some ownerless and rather skinny pigs scavenging round; masses of tanks and lorries containing bridging material moving forward; many notices put up by 3rd Division asking us to minimise our dust, one of which was quite witty: on the first tree 'Ashes to Ashes', on the second 'Dust to Dust' and on the third 'Your Dust turns us into Ashes', with underneath a small picture of a grave with a cross on it. The Huns seemed to have been evacuated from here.

We were to cross to the left of Rees and then turn right-handed and capture the town, and to start at 9 p.m. after a four-hour fire programme. The guns would then switch round to the right to fire in support of 15th Scottish, who would start, about five miles upstream, five hours after us. As soon as we had captured Rees, the R.E. were to start building a large number of rafts and bridges of all sizes and kinds. Several thousand sappers were to be involved in these exploits; their vehicles alone numbered 940.

Of course nobody doubted that the whole party would be a cake-walk. The only thing that remained to be seen was who were going to be the unlucky chaps to get hit.

The fire programme started at 5 p.m. on March 23rd. There was a continuous ripple of slams and bangs as all our guns, stretching across so many fields behind, were firing, and it went on for four hours until the Black Watch began to cross at 9 p.m.

For a time I sat in a little cellar only eight feet by six feet just on the edge of the paddock where we were going to load up the buffaloes. We were about a hundred yards from the Rhine. Cornish, my batman, Ackers, my jeep driver, and Bowlby, a signaller, were with me. Ackers, just twenty, had a clean, shining, almost baby face and was always smiling. He had shown in the past that he was completely indifferent to shell-fire; Cornish was ten years older, tall and rather gaunt, and like Danny Reid, his previous master, he was a bit of a tough character. Bowlby was a new-comer to the regiment, from a disbanded Queen's battalion, and was a short little chap with a prematurely old face, rather like Mr. Punch. He reminded me of those drawings of little old men by Emmett.

Meanwhile quite a lot of stuff was beginning to come back from the other side, mostly medium and light mortar so far. One mortar in particular was dropping its bombs all round this house. I was glad we had got ourselves installed before the fire programme started. Cornish brewed up tea on a small paraffin pressure stove a foot away from me. Ackers wrote to his mother, and I told him to ask her to send us another of her excellent home-made cakes.

While sitting in that cellar on that of all occasions, I read a *Sunday Times* review of Lord Moran's 'Anatomy of Courage'. It quoted his theory that courage must be husbanded. 'Courage is will-power, whereof no man has an unlimited stock, and when in war it is used up, he is finished. A man's courage is his capital and he is always spending.'

How right he was! I could think of an officer with a M.C. and Bar and several N.C.O.s with M.M.s who bore this out. They were all decorated for fine leadership in North Africa and Sicily and presumably must have been the pick of the battalion. The officer was finished before he was killed and the N.C.O.s – the few that remained – were all pretty well useless by this time. They all had to carry on far too long. I could quote my own case too. Until a month or two before, though I hated being shelled, I used positively to look forward to the thrill of battle. Now, though I had not yet got to the stage of dreading an action, I got no pleasure out of it and looked forward only to the end of the war.

At 7.30 p.m. there was still one and a half hours to go. A tremendous rumble of guns behind us, their shells whistling overhead, and the nice sharp banging, bouncing sound of our 25-pounder shells landing on the far bank. But the same mortar was still smacking down right in the loading area, and one dreaded the thought of a mortar bomb landing in a buffalo with twenty-eight not-so-gay Gordons inside.

However, the battalion all got across the Rhine between 11.15 p.m. and 1 a.m., and without a single casualty – wonderful, wonderful luck. Such shelling as there was fortunately came down between the companies.

It was a lovely night with a three-quarter moon. I shall always remember the scene in the loading area: the massive bulk of the buffaloes; the long ghostly files of men marching up to them, their flickering shadows and those of a smashed farmhouse and the armoured car at the Royals' post; a few busy figures darting here and there in the moonlight directing people into this and that buffalo; a chink of light shining up from the slit entrance to the command post whence came a continual flow of R/T conversation in the usual jargon: 'Oboe five to baker four – oboe five over,' and so on. All this against the background of the guns firing with the steady rhythm of African drums.

War is full of odd contrasts, and just when the scene was looking its most macabre and sinister I saw something white scurry out of a hedge and dodge into a passing soldier. There was a clink of his shovel knocking against a rifle and an oath as he stumbled, and then I saw that it was a sheep and the first lamb of spring as they came trotting up the path towards me.

At 1 a.m. I was back in the cellar. We were not to load our carriers and jeeps into the buffaloes until after the Black Watch. Once again Cornish brewed up and we listened to the battle on our wireless. It appeared that D Company had had some

215

casualties, and C were held up as B, in front of them, were having trouble. The Colonel tried to get the two company commanders to their sets to talk to him. They seemed to be working perfectly and I could hear the companies talking quite plainly on the other side of the river. Once or twice they had difficulty in hearing each other and then our set, though much further away, came up on the air and passed a message.

At 5 a.m. I went outside, but the Black Watch vehicles were still loading, so I returned again to that grubby little cellar. The buffaloes were having trouble with their tracks as the result of the rough going, and there were long intervals between their reporting back for reloading. There was a recrudescence of shelling and mortaring, and one or two in the loading area, the first since Zero Hour, but the only casualties were two men of a Black Watch anti-tank guncrew, from long-range rifle fire coming over the dyke. The bullets were pretty well spent and they were not badly hurt, more amazed at being hit when they had heard nothing.

I thought of having a nap, then news from C Company, and not too good, began to come over the air. I started to get anxious so took over the earphones and told Bowlby to get some sleep. Ackers and Cornish had both been snoring loudly for some time. The first intimation of trouble was Alec asking the Colonel to send up his spare officer, who had been left on the far bank with the company greatcoats and some other kit which they had taken across and dumped. Then he was telling D Company in the farmhouse area to send up part of one of his platoons which had not crossed the dyke with the remainder. It was not hard to guess that this meant that the company had been shelled on its way forward, and that a platoon commander had been hit and some of the platoon had in consequence got lost or gone to ground.

Meanwhile B and C Companies were fighting in the housing estate and gardens on the far side of the dyke and meeting a good deal of resistance. A little later I heard Alec at the end of a conversation with the Colonel say, in a cheerful voice: 'Of course it will soon be light and the advantage will then change, I don't quite know in whose favour.' But it soon became apparent that it was in the enemy's, for C Company was still fighting in the orchards short of Rees when they came under fire from the Boche holding some of the houses at the outskirts of the town and by this time able to see well enough to shoot.

The next thing I heard was an acrimonious conversation between Alec (C Company) and George Morrison (B). Alec was telling George that he hadn't put a platoon where he said he was going to, and that the enemy had in consequence been able to get round his flank. He then spoke to the Colonel and said he was pinned down in the open with Huns on three sides of him and that he must withdraw on to B Company as he was getting casualties, could not get forward and his position was untenable. Having extracted a reluctant permission from the Colonel to withdraw, he decided to hold on for a little longer, and then began to feel his way forward once more.

About 8 a.m. I heard him report that he had reached the first row of houses in the town. Later on I heard B Company say they had passed through the cemetery and reached the edge of Rees, having taken about seventy prisoners. An hour or two after that Bowlby said he gathered that D Company had also reached the town, along the water's edge.

We had just started to load our vehicles at about 10 a.m., when General Rennie arrived. He told me that all was going very well and that the bridgehead was now about eight miles wide and two miles deep.

It was about 3 p.m. before I could cross with my jeep. As soon as we got through the dyke I was amazed to see the great throng of sappers that were working on the bank in full view of the enemy still holding Rees a mile up-river. An occasional shell came over and landed with a splash in the Rhine, sending up a tall column of water. I soon realised what an ideal place had been chosen for crossing, as on each bank the green meadows

217

sloped gently down to the water. I was struck by the breadth of the river – it is much broader than the Thames at Westminster Bridge – and by the speed of the current.

We reached the far side without incident, and the buffalo took us about 400 yards across the grass and up to the road, where there were guides for each unit. I saw one or two carriers which had blown up, and there was a good deal of white tape and Mines notices. It did not take long to reach the farm where Battalion H.Q. was established. It was badly knocked about. There were more Mines notices round the small garden immediately in front of the house, and a regimental policeman at the doorway told me that D Company had lost three men there on schu-mines when they reached it.

Inside I found the Brigadier in conference with Bill Bradford and the Colonel, planning the coming night's operations to continue the clearing of Rees and district. As soon as they had gone, the Colonel told me that General Rennie had been killed in his jeep by a mortar bomb when driving to 152 Brigade H.Q. It must have been quite soon after he left me.

This was a terrible blow. It was especially sad as he had gone so far with us and had now been killed on the last lap. He always set great, perhaps exaggerated, store by the personal bravery and example of officers, and so scorned to drive about in an armoured car like several brigadiers so sensibly did. His death was not so very surprising in view of the risks he took. You cannot dice against the law of averages and get away with it for ever. I remembered him standing at the start-line of the battalion attack on Secqueville-la-Campagne last summer when there was a good deal of mortar fire, and no doubt he had since watched many other battalions go into the attack. I also remembered that he was very narrowly missed by a sniper, who put a bullet through the window out of which he was looking, when making a reconnaissance before our first canal crossing.

He was a great man and great figure, one of the tallest men in the Division, and quite unmistakable to any Jock as he stood at the roadside and watched them moving up into battle. He always wore a naval duffle coat with the hood hanging down at the back, his hands in the two large front pockets, and on his head always a tam o' shanter with the red hackle of his old regiment, the Black Watch; I am quite sure he did not even possess the ordinary general's red hat. No wonder the Jocks loved him. He had undoubtedly made the Division what it was at that time, the best in Second Army.

At the Battalion Command Post I could now piece together the sequence of events on that side of the river. Enemy shelling was pretty heavy during the night and, as I feared, C Company had the worst of it, one salvo coming down in the middle of one of their platoons, killing Titterton, the platoon commander, and inflicting about twelve other casualties. Titterton was a tall, good-looking young officer who had joined us about a fortnight previously. I hardly knew him. Rodger, a Canadian subaltern in D Company, and his platoon sergeant, Matthews, had also been killed. They were in a Hun trench near the water's edge when it received a direct hit. Matthews was one of the few remaining sergeants who had commanded a platoon times without number when we had been short of officers.

The Intelligence Officer, Kenneth McDonald, had been wounded – shell splinters in the face – but he was said to be not too bad. A shell landed very close to him and the Colonel as they were walking up to the farmhouse. I had not seen Grant Peterkin under fire until the night before; he was one of the naturally cool and brave sort. Gray had also been wounded for the second time, but the doctor said he was not bad either, multiple small wounds in the arm and shoulder. So it had cost us some fifty casualties, including four officers, to reach the outskirts of Rees after crossing the Rhine. And there was no doubt that we had been let off lightly. I could not get over the fact that we got the whole battalion across the water without a single casualty.

219

During the evening the enemy put some very heavy and accurate concentrations on the south bank in front of Rees, and one feared that the sappers and pioneers must be having many casualties. The enemy had obviously got an artillery Observation Post in the east side of the town, and the sooner we cleaned it up the better.

At nine o'clock we listened to the news and, for the first time, they released the names of units and formations. The Second Army had crossed the Rhine in five places, with the famous 51st Highland Division in the lead. This Division, which had fought all the way from El Alamein, etc. They were followed five hours later by 15th Scottish and two hours after that by the American 9th Army. A battalion of K.O.S.B had joined up with 6th Airborne Division, and so on.

Meanwhile we were supposed to be capturing Rees and, for the moment, were not doing very much about it. Apart from the fact that we were all tired, having had no sleep the night before, everyone who actually has to do it knows that street fighting at night is not possible. So the Colonel appealed to the Brigade Commander to allow us to start again at first light, which was now about 5.30 a.m. It was referred to the Corps Commander, but we were told to go straight on as the importance of clearing Rees, so that the sappers could build their bridges unhindered, was paramount.

So Grant Peterkin gave out orders for us to start again at nine that night (not that we had stopped all day, except for a pause of about two hours in the evening for food). Then we discovered that the Black Watch, who were clearing the station and surrounding buildings in the northern part of the town, were doing a wide encircling movement and were not likely to reach the station area before first light.

This altered the whole situation and the Colonel immediately put off our start until midnight. But we did not dare tell Brigade this. They thought we had started at nine and more than once asked us for a report. It was a little tricky trying to give periodical progress reports about an operation which was not taking place, and I had to temporise with 'going slowly according to plan', etc. We were really only taking very limited objectives that night, to get us into a good jumping-off position for the morrow.

Those of us who were able to turn in for a few hours during the night slept rather unevenly as the artillery, just across the river, were going great guns all night. In fact I dreamed that a huge demon of a gunner was lashing the crews with a gigantic whip, crying 'Faster, you so-and-so's, faster!'

By breakfast time the companies had all taken their limited objectives of the night before, and D and C Companies had reached the church and cleaned up all the waterline as far as that, but the enemy were still resisting fiercely in what was still rather more than one-third of the town. After breakfast Grant Peterkin decided to move our command post down to a large cellar in a house in the nearest street in Rees, half a mile from us. He went on with the wireless set and one or two officers, leaving me to bring on the remainder of the men and vehicles in my own time. Soon after they had left, two or three salvoes of fairly heavy shells came down between us and the new H.Q., and I hoped they had been able to reach it in time. I put off our departure for about twenty minutes, by which time peace reigned again.

When I reached the cellar I was greeted by: 'The Colonel has been hit,' and there he was, sitting in a chair, saying he was quite all right but looking pretty green. I sent for our doctor, who said he had a small fragment in the ribs, and that of course he ought really to go back, but he didn't think it had penetrated, in which case he would be all right. I said:

'For God's sake go back, for you will only cramp my style if you are going to sit at my elbow while I command the battalion,' which perhaps was not very well put. He replied, 'No, you go down and see how the companies are, and I will stay by the wireless set.' Half an hour later the Adjutant rang me up to say

221

that the Colonel wasn't feeling at all well and had allowed himself to be evacuated.

The first thing I heard when I got down to C Company was that Porter, another subaltern in D Company, had been killed by the same salvo that hit Grant Peterkin. I was dreadfully sorry about this; he was such a good fellow and had done so well in that night attack with D Company until he was wounded by the schu-mine. His father was a doctor in Southport, and Porter was destined for the same profession but he had wanted to fight with the infantry before starting his medical training. That made seventy officer battle casualties since D-Day.

C Company H.Q. was in the corner house opposite the square, and I decided to run the remainder of the battle from there. A Company was now moving across in the middle to clean up to a line between the church and the station, and D was occupying the houses just east and south of the church. B were then to move forward through C and D to clean up the rest of the waterfront as far as the eastern corner of the town.

It all sounds very easy when one writes it down, but this was far from being so. The clearing of every single house was a separate little military operation requiring a special reconnaissance, plan and execution. And the enemy were resisting fiercely all the time with Spandaus, bazookas and snipers, and only withdrawing a little further back at the last moment when their position became untenable.

When I reached C Company I found them full of enthusiasm for McNair, who was attached to us for the operation with three 3.7 howitzers. These are the little guns that one has seen naval teams take to pieces at Olympia, pass over an obstacle and put together again on the other side. For three years they had been training near Inverness for mountain warfare, and were rushed out here specially for this operation, being the only artillery which was small enough to go in a buffalo. They have a range of 6,000 yards and fire a 21-lb. shell, and much more

222

accurately than any other gun, as they guarantee the strike to within eighty yards.

This was McNair's first action, and such enthusiasm for battle as he showed can seldom have been seen before – in fact it was rather easy for some of our more battle-weary officers to be quite funny about it. For each situation in this street-to-street battle McNair had some excellent suggestion for using his gun. He hauled it over rubble, rushed it round corners, laid it on a house that was giving trouble, dodged back again, prepared his charges and then back to fire them. He even took it to bits and mounted it in an upstairs room. 'Exactly which window is the sniper in?' he said, and then, when the sniper fired at him, 'Oh, that one!' and laid his gun on it. It set houses on fire as well as any crocodile, and the effect on the enemy was devastating.

This very brave officer took incredible risks; finally he ran out into a street which was under fire and pulled in a wounded officer. He and his gun became the talk of the companies, and already, in a few hours, he had become an almost legendary character!

By the evening the enemy had been pushed back to quite a small area, about 200 yards by 200 yards, at the very east end of the town. B Company was trying to clean them up, as indeed they had been trying to do for the last three or four hours, while A, D and the Black Watch to the north were acting as stops to prevent them breaking out.

These Hun parachutists were very tough. They had been chased out of France, Belgium and Holland, into Germany, back over the Rhine, and now street by street across Rees into a corner. Yet they were still fighting it out. B Company had a very difficult fight and the two hours' work cost us three more officers.

That morning I told Halleron that Porter had been killed. He replied: 'Oh, God! He was my greatest friend.' An hour later he himself was killed, shot through the back by a sniper at a street corner. Then MacDonald was hit by a whole burst of Spandau or Schmeisser; he had been evacuated but was paralysed and not expected to live. Then Burrell was shot in the head. He was a spare officer in B Company who had only come up to take over a platoon that day, and off he went to it, full of great enthusiasm, to be hit within the hour.

At 7 p.m. we had a conference of company commanders. George arrived from B, saying: 'Never say steel helmets aren't any good.' He had been hit on his by a glancing bullet from a sniper, just at the join of the crown and the brim where the metal was of double thickness. It undoubtedly saved his life.

The situation now was that the enemy were confined to the last hundred yards, at the very tip of the east end, but they were in a strong position with deep trenches and concrete and any attempts to get at it were met by heavy fire. I was going to make a last effort with C Company, when in came four or five prisoners, including a captain who said he was in command. It appeared that, as soon as it was dark, he had told them all to split up into small groups to try to get through to the German lines. He was marched in front of me as I sat at my table poring over the map, and gave me a spectacular Hitler salute, which I ignored. I was very annoyed that, instead of being killed to a man, they had apparently won out in the end, escaping with their lives after shooting lots of our chaps. He was a nasty piece of work, cocksure and good-looking in a flashy sort of way, but I had to admire the brave resistance which he had put up. The strain of the battle was apparent in the dark black chasms under his eyes. He said that they had left eight badly wounded men in two dug-outs.

'Very well,' I said. 'You will guide C Company to them, and you will have your hands tied behind you so that you do not slip away in the dark.'

He began to complain that the soldiers who had taken him prisoner had stolen his note-case.

'My good man,' I replied, 'the German Army has plundered

everything they could lay their hands on in Europe. You surely don't expect any sympathy from me?'

Then B Company sent word to say that they had entered the strong-point which had caused all the trouble and that it was unoccupied. About the same time we heard that Burrell was not dead, but hit in the back of the neck and had lost a couple of fingers and that they had got him back as soon as it was dark. The doctor later said that he would recover, which was excellent news

It was a great moment when at 10 p.m. we were able to send the signal that the town was clear. We were overloaded with congratulations. The Corps Commander and the Divisional Commander both visited us specially next day, and the Brigadier said he thought it was the finest thing the battalion had ever done. The Corps Commander said that, in his experience, the best troops were whacked after twenty-four hours' street fighting, but we had kept it up for forty-eight hours, against the best part of two enemy battalions of picked parachutists. One could only hope that these congratulations would pay a dividend in the form of a good crop of decorations for the other ranks who had done so splendidly.

I walked round the battlefield in the morning, and was astonished at the strength of the enemy position which had held out for so long at the end of the town. I counted fifteen captured Spandaus in that last 100 yards.

Going round the companies, I found a cocky wee Gordon with his face all cut about, a great little chap named Blackman. I had heard about him at Thomashof, when a solid shot was fired into the room he was in. He continued to keep watch at the window without budging an inch, remarking only 'that one was a little close.' In Rees he was looking out of a window when a Hun fired a bazooka at him, which burst very near, chipping his face with brick fragments. For half an hour he disappeared on a private vendetta of his own to hunt down the firer. Two vacancies now came through for short leave to Paris, and

George told me that he offered one to Blackman but he turned it down, saying the he wasn't going to take any leave until he had caught up with the man with the bazooka.

While I was walking through the town talking to Alastair Duncan-Miller, who commanded our R.E. Field Company, there was a loud bang from up the street. He sprinted off, thinking it was a mine which his sappers had failed to discover, only to find a few Jocks sweating and cussing round the front of a safe which they were trying to open. We heard of two good remarks, operators' chat, on the German R/T from their Rees post which were picked up by our interception. One was: 'I hear old Fritz has been given the Iron Cross. What about us poor so-and-so's in the front line?' The other was: 'What shall we report?' 'Oh, better say "nothing to report" as otherwise they get such wind up behind.'

I was out when the Corps Commander, General Horrocks, visited our H.Q., but I met him in the town later and took him to see the battlefield. He was very interested in it all and most complimentary. Afterwards he took the trouble to explain the situation to the company commanders whom we had picked up in the course of our wanderings, with his big map placed on the bonnet of his jeep. He said that the next week might be bloody since we (ourselves and 43rd Division on our left) had the best German troops in front of us, but that after we had broken them down the armour would go through and, since the Huns had nothing much behind, we should then start motoring.

The most surprising feature of this twenty-four hours was the lack of shelling. I thought that as soon as the Hun was satisfied that his troops in here had been mopped up, we would get hell. After all, Rees was, as it were, the port to which all the bridges came and through which all roads must lead. I mentioned this to Horrocks, who said that the absence of shelling was due to the fine weather, since we were taking air-photos all the time, and as soon as a new battery was spotted about sixty guns opened up on it.

226

Alvar Liddel said in the nine o'clock news: 'It is with great regret that we announce the death of . . .' and I thought at once of our beloved General, but it was only Lloyd George.

We heard that 53rd (Welsh) Division were very annoyed about all the publicity the Highland Division was having. They said it was only because the English papers wanted to increase their circulation in the North of Scotland!

10

The next day, March 28th, was a bad one.

We were ordered to advance beyond 154 Brigade and take a position four and a half miles north of Rees. It was the usual hurried show. I left Brigade with my orders at twelve, making my plan in the jeep on the way back. I had not even met the tank commander until he arrived at 12.20, just as I was about to kick off, but I was immediately heartened to find that he was none other than an old friend, Bill Enderby of the Bays, now commanding a squadron of Sherwood Rangers.

After orders had been given out I went off with the company commanders to find out how the land lay, while Alec brought up the battalion: the companies to rest in some fields and a few buildings, and the vehicles to a park just behind. Newly installed as second-in-command of the Argylls, I found Jim Church, whom I had last seen thirteen years before in Shanghai – what a wonderful freemasonry the peace-time regular Army was! – and he told me that it was quiet there on the whole, though there were sudden spasms of mortaring. We could not make a reconnaissance as the country was dead flat.

There was a good deal of 'orders, counter-orders and dis-order' just before we got off at 5 p.m., as 43rd Division was in front of us on our left and there were conflicting reports as to where exactly they were. So first we were to advance behind a barrage, then it was cancelled as being too dangerous for them, then they weren't there at all and it was put on again.

The first two companies took their objectives without very much opposition (five or six casualties), helped largely by the tanks who were operating in darkness owing to delays caused by mines. What a joy it was to meet a regiment which really went, as we had sometimes been so disappointed by our armoured support. But meanwhile I was having hell as the road was mined and I couldn't get my carrier with its two wireless sets forward, and the company sets seemed to be pretty well out of range.

I kept moving the H.Q. forward each time that the sappers cleared the road. These moves were very exciting as there was a good deal of mortaring. I'd say to my signallers: 'Come on Hastings, Armitage, on we go.' They would take down their aerials and begin to coil up the leads, and Rowbotham would move over towards the dark shape which was the carrier, and then suddenly there would be a shower of stuff and we would all come flying back into the doorway.

Mortaring is not like shelling, you don't hear the distant whistle of the shells coming slowly from afar. There is a sudden swish and a crack as the first bomb arrives, and you have hardly any time before the others land. We would wait a few minutes half-way down the cellar steps and then I would say: 'Come on, chaps, now we'll go.' And then, when half-way over to the carrier, we would hear the swishes and the cracks, and some would drop flat while the others dodged back into the house. But it was not fun at all. In the autumn I had thought it was, but I no longer did so.

But it was far, far worse for the sappers. I took off my hat to them. It was all the same for the assault R.E. – either building bridges or clearing roads of mines in places where the enemy could not fail to know that we needed bridges or roads, and therefore always under fire. It was different for us, who had a job to do and then were able to dig in.

I would have put the unpleasantness, by which I mean the danger, of soldiering in this campaign as: firstly, field companies, R.E.; secondly, infantry; and thirdly, either airborne formations (who had long rests at home between operations) or tank crews (who were not called upon to fight so often as infantry). And the rest (with the German 1944–45 shortage of ammunition) nowhere at all in comparison.

During intervals in the battle, in the cellars that were our H.Q., Bill Enderby and I talked about our time together at Sandhurst, his shamba in Kenya, the Galway Blazers, and the Sherwood Rangers, until 1939 the private regiment, as it were, of Lord Yarborough, my landlord and neighbour. What a change and a joy!

But the battle dragged on. At intervals Alastair Duncan-Miller strolled in to report the progress of his sappers, in a raincoat and soft hat, for all the world as if he were just off to the races. With the signal difficulties and the darkness – it was overcast and men always think and move slowly at night – it took us seven hours to get all our objectives.

Bruce Rae[1] was slightly wounded and for the fourth time, hit by a shell splinter while standing on the top of one of the tanks to get a better view. Our tanks were unfortunate, two officers and the sergeant-major becoming casualties on mines. We also lost a self-propelled gun, and a carrier in which the driver had both legs blown off. The companies took their objectives without much difficulty, though it was nearly daylight before the road was clear and vehicles reached them.

While we were milling about, 5th Black Watch and 5-7th Gordons were getting on well on the right, and 152 Brigade passed up the road through us. Soon after breakfast our artillery

---

[1] Bruce Rae, M.C. and Bar, was perhaps the most outstanding of all the many officers who at one time or another commanded a company in 1st Bn. The Gordon Highlanders in the Desert and North-West Europe. Having survived being wounded four times he was killed a few months after the end of the war when, leaning back in a chair he over-balanced and fell through a window.

began to move up, and before long we found ourselves in the middle of our gun-lines. This had also been part of the enemy gun-lines for the defence of the Rhine, and I went for a walk to look for all the blasted and broken guns I hoped to find from our counter-battery, but not one did I see. They had got them all away. And I saw very few dead Germans (except for a civilian or two; we accidentally killed a woman in the afternoon when we sent tanks out with a small patrol and they shot up a house).

It depressed one and made one think that all we did was to keep driving them back without breaking them and smashing them, and that it would go on for a long time and cost us a lot more good men yet. Every battle we went into I thought of our magnificent company commanders:

George Morrison, Alec Lumsden, Bruce Rae, and 'Casey' Petrie, and dreaded to hear that one of them had got it.

When it was all over I had to face the fact that this little operation took seven hours instead of three or four because I was windy. The mortaring had influenced me to stay at my H.Q. in the orthodox way, instead of being right up behind the leading companies on foot. It was so easy to shirk a little when you were the battalion commander. The truth, I realised, was that by this time I was not half the man I had been six or even three months before and seemed to have lost all my old dash.

Next day Grant Peterkin was back, and he sent me to 33 and 34 Reinforcements Holding Units to try to pick up some Gordon N.C.O.s before the other two battalions took them, and I got five, but all very junior. It was an enjoyable drive. The blossom and spring flowers were now out and one or two front gardens were a mass of hyacinths. Apart from that, the journey was much the same as along all those roads: flat fields with here and there a man or woman behind a plough or harrow, hamlets with blitzed houses, odd graves by the roadside, an occasional blown-up tank or truck. Once I saw the peculiarly sad sight of a burnt-out tank and four crosses beside it. The shell craters in the side roads were most indifferently filled in. They and the twisted and blasted trees above them, the Mines notices and white tape roping in small minefields at the roadside, and occasional dumps of mines which had been lifted and collected together, reminded one continually that fierce fighting took place not so long ago down all these roads and lanes.

I stopped the night with my new-found friends at Oisterwijk, who were surprised and delighted at my unexpected appearance. They complimented me on the exploits of the Highland Division, the fortunes of which they had followed closely in the news.

'But we always thought of the casualties that must have gone with your victories,' said Mr. M. 'I fear that you must have lost some of those fine-looking officers that used to stride up and down this road in their kilts?'

'Yes,' I said. 'Twenty-nine of them.'

'And the young lieutenant who also came to this house?' they asked.

'He was killed at Goch,' I replied, somewhat shortly.

After that we talked about London (Mrs. M. used to show her Airedales at Cruft's every season), and the Riviera and Vienna, and hardly at all about the war. What a joy it was to be with a cultured family once again. Besides, they had a most engaging habit of drinking claret from about seven o'clock right through till bedtime.

When the evening came to an end my hostess took me upstairs to show me my room. As we shook hands and said good-bye (for I was starting at daybreak) she put her other hand over mine and looked at me in a manner which I can only describe as compassionate. She was some ten years older than me and perhaps was thinking 'Shall I ever see this young man again?' She was a woman with great sweetness of character and great charm. For a second, as we stood there looking at each other, I felt that anything might happen. Then the spell was broken. I opened the door of my room and she turned and went downstairs to her husband.

The armour was committed at nine that morning and I returned to the battalion to find it engulfed by a great wave of optimism. Everyone seemed to think the war was over. Apparently we were to follow the Guards Armoured Division and protect the left flank against the three enemy divisions still in Holland. It was said that the armour was not meeting much organised resistance and that it was chiefly blown bridges and craters that were delaying them.

On the following day, April 1st, I was sent off again, this time to Brussels. It was due to our having been told that eleven out of the twelve recommendations for Military Medals which we put in after the Reichswald battle had been turned down. It was simply monstrous and everybody who knew of it was speechless with rage. Especially as four officers had received awards recently – the Colonel, George Morrison, Alec Lumsden and myself. It looked so bad, as if we just wrote citations for each other and did not bother about the men, and it was really only because of their bravery and devotion to duty than an officer could qualify for an award at all. This was really just the last straw to a situation which had been extremely unsatisfactory for a long time.

To give the men a trifle in lieu of the decorations they deserved and could not get, the Colonel had ordered some 'honoris causa' cards to be printed. The wording under the regimental crest was to be 'Awarded to —— in recognition of

S. P. Gun

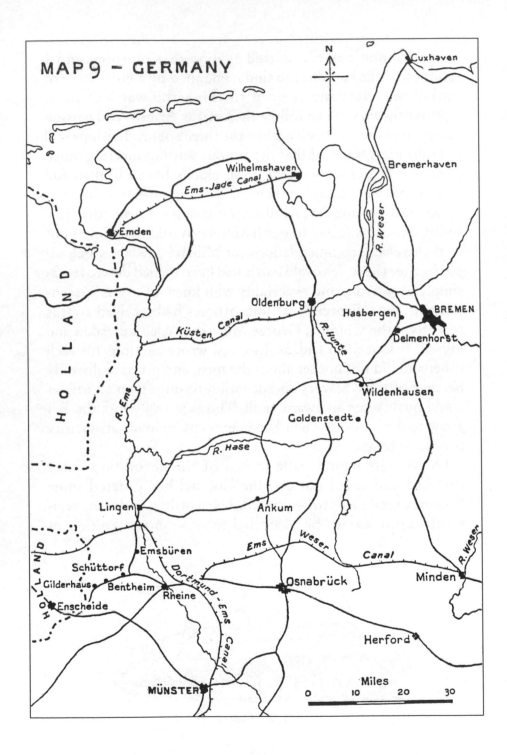

MAP 9 - GERMANY

N

Cuxhaven

Bremerhaven

Wilhelmshaven

Ems-Jade Canal

R. Weser

Emden

HOLLAND

Oldenburg

Hasbergen

BREMEN

Delmenhorst

Küsten Canal

R. Hunte

Wildenhausen

R. Ems

Goldenstedt

R. Hase

Lingen

Ankum

Ems

Weser

Canal

R. Weser

Emsbüren

Schüttorf

Dortmund-Ems Canal

Minden

Gilderhaus

Bentheim

Osnabrück

HOLLAND

Enscheide

Rheine

Herford

MÜNSTER

Miles

0   10   20   30

gallant and distinguished conduct on the battlefield', and we hoped that it would be something which a man would frame and treasure.

We had placed the order in Brussels some weeks ago, with no great results so far, and now with the rejection of these eleven citations the matter had become of a sudden much more pressing. So I went down to Brussels to pass the proof and bring back the printed cards, but when I got there I found that the work was being done in Antwerp, the Brussels shop had not got a proof and, as it was Easter Saturday, nothing more could be done for the moment.

During this pause I visited Harry Cumming-Bruce. He said that the great difference he found on leaving us for 15th Scottish was how much fresher they all were than us, as the result of not having had the desert campaign before this one.

I went on to tea with 6th Royal Scots Fusiliers, which was commanded by Churchill for a time in the 1914–18 war. Ian Mackenzie, who had been C.O. for the last six months, was a great little man. He was only thirty and had done brilliantly. But I would not have recognised him for the gay, handsome chap he was when we two crossed the Channel together on that sunny July day which seemed so many years ago. He looked ten years older; in fact, I had to look at his badges of rank when he came into the room. He admitted that he always felt tired nowadays. Like us, they were resting and wondering what was going to happen next, and hoping nothing.

Late on April 3rd we were put at six hours' notice, so things did not seem to be going too well. Certainly we were all rather disappointed at the short distance the armour had got in four days, but it was very easy to be critical from back there.

I was told to take the companies' advance parties to Enschede in north-east Holland. There we saw something I had never seen before: masses and masses of flowers in the front windows of each house, banked up on the sill like a florist's display, though whether it was for Easter or Eisenhower no man could say. At any rate they had been liberated only two days and this nice little Dutch industrial town (weaving) was full of the usual thrilling stories.

One was of a Dutch girl, the widow of an English colonel who went down in a ship sunk by a U-Boat. She was landed here by parachute with a Dutch officer and a wireless set just before Arnhem, expecting that British forces would get through to them in a fortnight. But we didn't, and she and the Dutch officer transmitted information back until the Huns caught them three months later.

Another was of the underground leader who had done excellent work all the time, but came up prematurely on hearing that the British were around, so that the Huns got him too. And how they surrounded the town in October and took 11,000 men between seventeen and fifty-five to work in Germany. But the story I liked best was that of the German tank colonel. The Dutch had their flags out and were dancing all over the streets, celebrating the departure of the invaders. Then a German tank stopped, a colonel put his head and shoulders out and said pompously: 'My friends, the play is not yet over,' then bobbed back into his tank, slammed down the turret and drove on.

We had a wonderful welcome at Enschede and all the troops would have been very comfortable, billeted two or three in each house, but next day we got word to go on and meet the battalion at Bentheim, thirty miles over the German border.

There were not many signs of fighting having taken place on the way up, but we passed a score of brewed-up lorries and half-tracks which had been ditched at the side of the road after being destroyed by the R.A.F. As we got nearer Bentheim we overtook a number of tanks that had been hit, and heard that the Grenadiers and Irish Guards had lost about six each. The paraboys had again fought fanatically, and a young captain in the Irish Guards with a D.S.O. told me that two of their tank crews which had baled out had been shot, including Fitzherbert, the squadron commander.

236

We began to discuss casualties in general and he was horrified, in fact almost unbelieving, when I told him that we had lost over seventy officers in battle since D-Day. I gathered that the average losses of officers in the armoured divisions was in the twenties or thirties.

We were now for the first time in a German area which was inhabited, and so for the first time put into effect our instructions about turning Germans out of the houses we were to occupy. As I had gone ahead with the advance party this largely fell to me, and I must say I felt a bit of a cad, especially on one occasion when I found that the farmer's wife to whom I was talking was a pleasant young English-woman from Dulwich, whose infant son had been killed by our bombing of Emden.

There were no limits to the brutalities I could have inflicted upon the young males, but it did not seem natural to have to regiment women. It was best to give this job to the Dutch interpreters. They found nothing difficult about it and showed no mercy.

After supper that night we discussed what an extraordinarily efficient machine the British Army was at that time. It was all the more remarkable considering what a small proportion – I think less than five per cent – of officers were regulars. The Army is organised in three broad departments, G, A, and Q. G (General Staff) is operations and training; A (Adjutant-General) is everything to do with personnel, and Q (Quartermaster-General) is supplies of all kinds.

I think most Army officers had great confidence in G and Q. To the ordinary fighting soldier the operational planning and execution of this particular campaign seemed nothing short of brilliant, and we were full of praise for the way the supplies always came up. Shortcomings in equipment such as the defects of our tanks and tank equipment (and it was difficult to put one's finger on any other notable deficiencies) was more the responsibility of the Ministry of Supply than of the Quartermaster-General of the Army. But some of the

237

shortcomings in A could hardly fail to be obvious to every-body. To list a few examples:

(*a*) The monstrously inadequate distribution of awards to other ranks.

(*b*) The bog-up over the 1939–43 Star. The Prime Minister's official announcement in the House of Commons in August, 1943, said that men who had taken part in an evacuation would qualify. It then took the authorities four months to print the ribbon and draft the regulations, and when these were published it was found that only those who had received a deco-ration or mention in despatches in a campaign which ended in evacuation qualified. This mistake caused such an uproar from the scores of thousands who had been promised the ribbon and were now to be excluded that a 'War Office spokesman' was quickly put up to say that new regulations were being prepared.

(*c*) The lack of any effective scheme for posting home tired-out N.C.O.s and men who had done far more than their duty. There had been no such arrangement until very recently, and then it all hung on men coming out from home to take their place, but these replacements just did not arrive.

(*d*) The abortive leave-home-to-breed scheme for Middle East Forces which caused such a clamour that it had to be hurriedly dropped.

(*e*) Desertion in the field of battle and cowardice in the face of the enemy had been treated as comparatively minor military delinquencies, and the men had had every reason to think that these were not regarded as very serious offences. The maximum paper sentence was three years and few men actually served six months. The result was that there were 190 men awaiting trial in the Divisional cage at this time. Now, after ten months, it was suddenly announced that they would serve their sentences (and a court could award up to fifteen years) in full.

(*f*) The refusal to authorise a collar and tie in uniform for other ranks until some quarter of a century after the R.A.F. had had this very much prized privilege.

(g) The regulation that other ranks would salute officers at all times and places; or, if this regulation were necessary, the failure to enforce it. Naval ratings are not expected to salute their officers in the streets of London. Either the Army Council should likewise have qualified the regulation (for example, limit it to other ranks saluting officers of their own corps) or else it should have been rigorously enforced. At the moment two out of three soldiers in any large town, well knowing the orders on the subject, deliberately and flagrantly avoided saluting. This was not good for discipline.

It was a pity that the Army, which showed such great efficiency in so many directions, should sometimes have come such croppers over comparatively small matters in the sphere of human feelings. They caused far more resentment than the loss of battles.

On April 8th we had quite a nice little operation. We left Gilderhaus in the morning and went to a staging area in the top half of Schuttorf, which 5th Black Watch had entered the day before, and where we had an evening meal. We were directed on Emsburen but by a longer route, first going east and then turning northwards, so that we should clean up a wider area. The Reconnaissance Regiment were ahead of us, and Grant Peterkin went off with two companies at about 5 p.m. while I stayed behind, listening on the wireless, and ready to send up what he required. I heard quite a lot of shelling in the distance, which was a sad disappointment as I'd hoped that the Huns had taken all their guns back with them to Bremen.

An hour or two went by, and I did not know what was happening. Then I got word to send up another company and the ambulance (that sounds bad, I thought), and then later to come up myself with Battalion H.Q.

It was now 7.30 and getting pretty dark. I jeeped down a main road for three miles, followed by Jack Johnston in the wireless scout-car, George Forbes with his signallers, and one or two trucks containing a few more hangers-on. At the top of a lane a guide met us, to say that Battalion H.Q. was in the first farm on the left.

I walked down the lane until I saw the shape of it, silhouetted against the pattern of the stars. Then I turned up a path. 'Aye, sir, it's a gey black nicht so ye'd best tak a daunder roon' the byre as the bla' oot ben the hoose is nae saw guid,' said the dark shadow which proved to be McDonald on duty in front of the house. So I went through the cow-house, using my torch to avoid treading on the Jocks who lay sleeping on the hay between the two rows of gleaming eyes; for the cows, too, were all lying down, chewing and slobbering over the cud, flicking their ears and occasionally jerking the chains round their necks. I stepped gingerly over the sprawling bodies that lay there like the dead, and over their rifles and wireless sets, steel helmets and stretchers until I reached the door at the far end, which led directly to the central living-room of the farmhouse.

The Colonel sat at the small kitchen table, which was barely large enough for all that was on it: two maps and two sets of R/T microphones and earphones, a Tilley lamp, his tam o' shanter, field-glasses and gloves, several cups and plates. The small room was already overcrowded, but somebody gave me a chair. As usual, it was indescribably untidy, with all the household chattels that the German family had been using until we turned them out into the house next door. So, mixed up with our weapons and equipment there were dirty dishes, cooking utensils, knitting, underclothing and children's toys. Neil was brewing up. Cornish soon went on the prowl and returned with an enormous basket of eggs which had eluded all previous search parties, and the few of us who kept vigil through the night – Grant Peterkin and I and two or three signallers – had four eggs apiece about 4 a.m., and never have eggs tasted better.

The operation seemed to be going well. Companies moved successively up the roads and lanes, and each one was only moved forward when those in front were firm. There were the usual difficulties of wireless communications, and it was hard to get information, but it became more and more evident that there were very few enemy abroad.

About 4.30 a.m. the Colonel moved forward to C Company's farmhouse, and an hour later came up on the air and said he wanted me. So I drove up the road towards him. By now it was getting light and I saw that it was most attractive country: rolling grassland, woods and fine old farmhouses, surrounded by stately beeches. I met Alec Lumsden at the roadside just in front of C Company's farm, looking down into a slit-trench.

'Look at this sod,' he said. 'The first we knew of him being here was when we were challenged in German. This is where the grenade landed right under his chin.'

Huddled at the bottom of the trench I saw the mess that a few hours before had been a German soldier.

Inside I found the Colonel, and he told me to go down the road and see that the sappers were doing their best to open it up, and then to come back and let him know as soon as transport could get through, so that the companies could have their breakfasts sent up. It was a lovely spring morning and, with the sun rising and the beauty of the countryside, I felt pretty good. So, I think, did Cornish and Ackers.

But we had not gone far before we came upon a brewed-up jeep by a road crater, terribly smashed. Bill McFarlan was trying to salvage what he could of the things that had been blown out when the jeep blew up on a mine. Both his and George's personal kit had been in the jeep, and the company telephone and wireless set and so on. I was horrified to see the damage done to the car and the great pool of blood in the middle of the road. Cornish did not need to be told to put some sand on it. Sandbags had not saved poor Morrison from being killed instantly, such was the damage done by this powerful mine.

Morrison was one of the best type of old soldiers in the battalion and his greatest friend was Neil, the C.O.'s jeep driver. B Company's real jeep driver was Private Watts, M.M., but now he was on leave in Scotland, and Morrison had come up from B Echelon to take his place for a few days. Such are the chances of war!

I wandered up the road on foot to see what obstacles there might be. Then I came across a severed foot in an Army boot. Forty yards further on I found two sappers lifting more mines, and the dreadfully mutilated body of a man by the side of another road crater. One of the mines had been booby-trapped, the sappers explained to me. A string had been tied from the igniter to the bank at the side of the road, and when a man from B Company, who had lost his way, walked along the verge, it was set off.

'I wouldn't care for your job,' I said to them, and walked on a little further. In Emsburen I found 5-7th Gordons, who had entered it from the west.

Emsburen seemed a nice little place and we gathered that we might be there a few days. The sappers were building a bridge beyond it. It was all very peaceful.

We had a nice H.Q. in a modern house, built and owned by a building contractor. It even had a bath in it. The weather was lovely and the war seemed a long way away. There was an un-limited supply of eggs in this part of the country at this season. The Jocks had learnt how high the standing of officers was in Germany, and that it paid a dividend to go round the houses asking for 'eggs for the officer'.

Ewen told me that there was a memorial in the church to all those of this parish who had been killed in this war and the last, with names and dates. It showed that whereas in the last war the death-roll was forty, in this one it was already forty-two (all but three of whom had been killed in Russia). In addition there must also have been a large number of missing who had actu-ally been killed but were not yet shown as such. So if this small village was any guide to German casualties as a whole, they had been at least as heavy in this war as in the last. Whereas ours had fortunately been very much less.

I had a drive round some outlying farms which might have

been missed out, to look for German deserters. We didn't find any, but lots of Polish, French, Italian, Russian, Dutch and even Greek workers. Cornish and I came to the conclusion that most of them were pretty comfortably off in those farms. We took one small porker into protective custody. I was careful to explain that the German Army had stolen everything in Europe, and therefore they had no grounds for complaint.

5th Black Watch lost seven of their pioneers in an unlucky accident. There was a big drive on foot to round up all the Boche mines which were lying at the side of the road, lest 'evilly disposed persons' (as Childs Bank says on the front of their cheque-books) should lay them again in our wake. These men were throwing some mines into a pond when one detonated and exploded the others, killing four men and wounding three more.

11

On April 10th we were still there, and how nice it was!

It was an odd situation, for we did not know whether we had fought our last battle and only a little gentle mopping-up remained, or whether there was still a lot of stiff fighting ahead of us. This might well have been so, since we were routed on Bremen and the Hun was reported to have two para divisions there (even though without their parachutes) and to have brought up a marine division from Hamburg. I felt that we should take the last pockets slowly, and not lose a man more than we could help. By this I meant send over every bomber we possessed until there was nothing left, and then turn to the next place. But I was not sure that this was what the public wanted. They wanted the war to be finished as quickly as possible. Unfortunately they had already been told by the Press that it was virtually over.

It was said that there were 130,000 dozen bottles of bubbly in Bremen, but it was suggested that this was a rumour in order to encourage us to capture the place more quickly.

At this time there was a good deal of chat at all levels about the Army's two most serious problems, fraternisation and looting.

Very strict instructions had been given about fraternisation, which was defined for us as:

(*a*) Talking (except on duty), laughing and eating with Germans.

(*b*) Playing games with them.

(*c*) Giving them food or chocolate, even to children.

(*d*) Shaking hands with them.

(*e*) Allowing children to climb on a car.

(*f*) Sharing a house with them.

All this was quite right and one only hoped it could be enforced as it was completely contrary to the nature of the British soldier.

Looting presented a greater problem since it was so hard to define. Difficulties arose over such articles as cars, food, luxuries like eggs and fruit, prohibited articles such as cameras and shot-guns, and wine. We had more or less come to agreement amongst ourselves that we were going to take only:

(*a*) What was necessary to make ourselves more comfortable, such as bedding or furniture.

(*b*) Luxuries that the Huns could well get on without, e.g. eggs and fruit, but not food such as meat or poultry.

(*c*) Forbidden articles we wanted for our own personal use, such as shot-guns, cartridges, cameras, field-glasses.

(*d*) Wine (which was mostly looted from France already).

There was an anti-looting strafe at Brigade H.Q., and the Commander ordered that nothing which was not an article of Army rations was to be served in their mess. The Brigade Major told me that while the Commander was pinned down as it were, on the throne that morning a Jock of his H.Q. passed his field of vision with a side of bacon, followed shortly after by another with a wireless set, followed a few minutes later by a third with a goose under his arm. Whereupon he rose in his wrath, sent for his Brigade Major and issued several fresh edicts, the effect of which was that there would probably be no looting at Brigade H.Q. for at least a week.

After five days at Emsburen we were on the move again, to Ankum. There the Battalion was installed in most attractive old farmhouses. This was lovely country, like Sussex at its best, and for two or three weeks the weather had been perfect. We gathered that the Canadians were now going to take Bremen and 51st Division Hamburg. Nobody much minded missing Bremen as it looked as if it would be tough. Intelligence said that the Burgomaster was against any further resistance and wanted to surrender the city, but they put in the S.S., who shot him.

Next day we went on again, to Goldenstet. But when we arrived we found that 5th Seaforths were doing an attack from there, starting at 5 p.m. So for a few hours we had to wait outside and then gradually filtered in as they moved out. Our H.Q. farmhouse had great dignity and charm and we would not have minded staying there for a little. It also had electricity run from a mill at the end of the garden.

That evening we had three unusual visitors. The first was a woman to complain that the German Army had stolen her two horses! Then a brace of Communists: they had been in concentration camps off and on for years; in the off periods they had listened to the B.B.C. and been told that as soon as the Allies arrived they should come forward and offer their assistance; they could give us a list of all the strong Nazi types in the district, and only that morning had they seen a perfectly good German soldier walking through the village in civilian clothes.

A German girl said: 'We know quite well that the Highland Division is the Scottish S.S. You needn't think you can hide the fact. But we think you are worse than the S.S., who did at least walk with us in the woods.'

Next day we took over from 2nd Lincolns to allow 3rd Division to concentrate. I had lunch with Firbank, the C.O. We both agreed that we were very tired and, as he put it, rather like steeplechase riders who begin to feel that they are getting stiff and elderly and that it was time to give way to younger men.

The farm we took over was typical of many we had seen, a substantial house built in the nineteen-twenties. Farming would seem to have been prosperous in West Germany: all the farms we saw were in good repair and well stocked (all the cattle being black and white Frisians; I did not see a red cow in Germany). The cottages were all extremely good and a very large number had been built in the thirties: I could think of many farm-workers' cottages in Britain which were a sad sight in comparison.

On April 15th we had to open up the road north of Wildenhausen, twenty miles from Bremen. It took a long time owing to a delaying combination of guns and road mines. In fact, the enemy fought an efficient little rearguard action; how incredible it was that he was still fighting us so energetically right in the heart of Germany, though he well knew that the war was irretrievably lost.

This advance of two or three miles caused us to lose more good men. Howitt was blown up in a carrier and Sergeant Howes was killed, shot through the head. I had taken a great liking to Howitt. He was an elderly subaltern, nearly forty, but his heart was in the right place. He and his brother joined us together on February 14th. Charles was killed four days later and now Jake was dead too. Sergeant Howes was a fine N.C.O. and commanded a platoon in C Company in many actions after his officers had become casualties. He was one of those for whom we tried unsuccessfully to get a Military Medal. We also lost Donald, a stretcher-bearer in C Company since El Alamein, hit in the back of the head by a piece of metal flying from a tank, itself hit by an S.P. gun.

We sat in a garden most of next day, basking in the sun.

The General visited us and said we were now for Hamburg. We were due to start on April 21st, but the General did not think they could make this date, so perhaps it would be the 23rd or 24th. And I was to go on leave on the 26th!

It was noticeable how very slow even the simplest operations had now become, and we thought that because of this we might have a difficult task during the next month. Everybody had a prejudice against being killed in the last month of a six-years' war. So people were playing for safety with one eye upon the clock – no hitting for sixes. But even this did not stop men dying. George Clark, our doctor, said that 5th Black Watch, who were moving forward on our left, had forty-two casualties that day.

It occurred to me to count the number of officers who had served in the battalion since D-Day. Up to March 27th, the end of the Rhine crossing, it was 102 (the average number of officers on the strength of the Battalion at any one time was about 30). I found that we had had 55 officers commanding the twelve rifle platoons, and that their average service with the Battalion was thirty-eight days, or five and a half weeks. Of these fifty-three per cent were wounded, twenty-four per cent killed or died of wounds, fifteen per cent invalided, and five per cent had survived.

43rd Division took over from us and we moved to some nice farmhouses not far away. Arriving there I saw a tank crew sitting in a group round an attractive young woman. I got out of my jeep and went over to them. 'You know this is forbidden,' I said. 'What is your name, Sergeant? Show me your pay-book.'

'Sergeant Clive, sir,' he said, standing very respectfully to attention. And then, when I had written down his number, name and unit, 'She's Russian.' So, after I had satisfied myself that this was indeed the case, I had no option but to apologise!

There was certainly a Great Trek on – the migration of the Russians eastwards. A steady stream of them had been going past all day, little groups of three or four men, carrying their pitiful little bundles or pulling them in handcarts or prams. I wondered whether they knew exactly where they were going and how long it would take, or whether they were just simple folk trekking eastwards by the sun.

The plan changed again and our Brigade was now to take Delmenhorst. This is a fair-sized town, several times the size of Rees, and four or five miles west of Bremen. Unfortunately it was well within range of all the artillery that the Hun had got back and grouped together for the defence of Bremen.

We had been living well lately with the profusion of eggs and, best of all, a good stock of red wine which we had captured at Wildenhausen. The servility of the Germans we had so far met did not suggest that there were administrative difficulties ahead. Wherever I had come upon road-blocks I had ordered the nearest Huns to remove them, and we were all struck by the speed of their compliance – you barely had time to get back into the car before a party was on the way. Their general attitude to some extent surprised us: they obeyed all orders, however unpleasant, with an appearance of willingness. I am sure that English householders, given an hour to move out of a house, would have shown indignation and been quietly obstructive. But the Germans appeared to revel in obedient co-operation.

We appreciated this lovely colourful countryside. The buds on the trees were all beginning to come out and the young leaves of the silver birches were a rich shade of light green. Most of the farm roofs were coral or carmine and the dazzling white blossom of the fruit-trees made a beautiful contrast. To make the picture more perfect, there were great patches of yellow mustard streaked across the green landscape. No painter could have blended the colours more graphically.

There seemed to be a lot of shelling south of Delmenhorst. We heard that 152 Brigade had been having a sticky time with the 15th Panzer Grenadiers in front of them fighting hard.

Then 'No move tomorrow' reached us. This meant that the commanders were all in a huddle, trying to decide what to do next.

But the next was an extraordinary day.

It started with a super-conference at Division. The Corps Commander was present as well as the Divisional Commander and seven brigadiers. After much talk, a tremendous plan was produced for the capture of Delmenhorst. But before they had all dispersed word came in that the town was empty. The Hun had pulled right out during the night, so we in due course were ordered to motor in. We drove into the town and, to our astonishment, found ourselves being waved to and cheered, just as in the old days when we liberated Belgium and Holland. The girls proved to be Russians and Poles, who had been imported to work in the local jute-spinning and aircraft factories.

We expected to get heavily shelled from all the big guns mounted round Bremen, but all was quiet and we wondered why. Later we were told that there were 2,000 wounded Boches in the hospitals here, so they declared it an open town. Anyway we moved in and made ourselves pretty comfortable. Anti-tank guns were pointing down the streets and the foremost section posts were manned, but most other people could sleep in beds. Later in the day there was a little desultory shelling on the exits to the north, but we had only one casualty, a poor lad of nineteen shot through the stomach on a patrol. We had a very nice H.Q. in the house of one Dr. Richter. The Herr Doktor had a most comfortable study, but we were not able to locate his cigars.

About teatime we were told that we probably had to take Hasbergen, a small village two miles to the north-east. We did not much care for the idea as it might easily have meant fifty or sixty casualties, as there were several self-propelled guns up that way, in addition to the usual shelling, mortaring and Spandau fire. Moreover, we could not see much point in it as Hasbergen was a dead-end place, leading nowhere.

So we were overjoyed when the Colonel came back from Brigade to say that all we were now required to do was to patrol forward. Also that 3rd, 43rd and 52nd Divisions were to capture Bremen, and as 12th Corps were taking Hamburg we were not for that either. What a let-off!

I now began to think that I really should make my leave getaway in six days' time. Bruce said that for the first time he saw his sergeant-major duck when a shell came over; then he remembered that he was also in the next leave party!

It was very quiet and peaceful. We did a little patrolling during the next two days, just to keep contact with the enemy.

The Huns were still there in front of us, but not being at all offensive and nor were we, though any undue movement on their part was promptly shelled. A few deserters trickled in from time to time. Two of them were Gef. Berger of 2nd Grenadier Regiment (the present strength of this company was ten, he said, and they were commanded by Lieut. Bloem, but he had not been seen for some days) and Gef. Hauff of 683 Anti-Tank Regiment. The normal establishment of his company, he told us, was thirty-five vehicles and nine 88 mm. guns, but at the moment it had two guns, two trucks and no petrol. The company, forty strong, was put in the line three days ago, but twenty-five had since deserted. From P.O.W. we gathered that the nearest company to us belonged to a marine battalion and was commanded by a U-Boat petty officer. To such shifts was the German Army now reduced.

In the night we fired 4,000 leaflet shells over Bremen, telling them to surrender. At 5 p.m., the first bombing, by several hundred Lancasters and Fortresses, took place. Grant Peterkin, Ewen and I went up to our observation post at the top of a factory to watch it.

Meanwhile the Russians were fighting in the heart of Berlin. Stuttgart and Nuremberg had fallen, so east and west might join up at any moment.

At Delmenhorst we heard that the whole Brigade was allowed only six awards (including officers) for the Rhine crossing and subsequent fighting, so once again our efforts to obtain decorations for the Jocks had been almost entirely frustrated. On top of the February operations from the Reichswald to Goch, for which none of our Jocks had received decorations although twelve were recommended, it was a major scandal.

The magnitude of the scandal can best be shown by a comparison with the R.A.F. 153 Infantry Brigade's assault crossing of the Rhine was as important as any single air operation such as the breaching of the Möhne Dam or the sinking of the *Tirpitz*. I do not know too much about the Möhne Dam, but the sinking of the *Tirpitz* did not affect the end of the war in the same way that the crossing of the Rhine did. During this operation 153 Brigade had, say, 1,500 men in close contact with the enemy, on a calculation of 500 in each of the three infantry battalions, of which 230, or fifteen per cent, became casualties (1st Gordons seventy-eight, 5th Black Watch sixty-five, 5-7th Gordons eighty-seven). Our allowance of six decorations for the whole Brigade was 0.4 per cent of those in close contact. I could not imagine for one moment that only 0.4 per cent or even four percent of the air-crews engaged on either of those two operations were decorated.

Six months later I had a chance to find out. In answer to a question in Parliament on November 26th, 1945, the Under-Secretary of State for Air informed me that immediate awards were granted to 31 per cent of the members of air crews who took part in the operation against the Möhne Dam and to 7 per cent of those who took part in the sinking of the *Tirpitz*.

Bruce Rae told me that quite a nice young German hospital nurse came to see him in his Company H.Q. He showed her the pictures of the Buchenwald concentration camp. She looked horrified, then suddenly her face cleared. 'But it's only the Jews,' she said.

Bill McFarlan had a factory and a lot of foreign workers in his area. One of them asked him whether in England we flogged women who do not work satisfactorily. I visited our Military Government people. They said that any respect they ever possessed for the Germans had entirely gone now.

Freyburg and Frankfurt had fallen and Stuttgart had been entered. We were fighting on the outskirts of Hamburg and Bremen. Patrols had reached the Swiss frontier.

The war in Europe was coming rapidly to an end.

It was midnight, or thereabouts, and I was sitting in the Herr Doktor's study in the nominal capacity of duty officer. But the telephones were silent; at the moment there was no duty to be done. And *in three hours' time* I would start off on leave.

It was a good moment to take stock. For we were coming now to the end of an era. It would be more than a fortnight before I was back from England, and by that time Berlin, Hamburg and Bremen would have fallen and resistance in North Germany would be over. There seemed no doubt that we had fought our last major engagement. When I returned things would have begun to be very different.

The Herr Doktor's study was a good place in which to take stock, for it was symbolic of the school of thought we had come to destroy. The two most prominent pictures in it were Friedrich der Grosse and Kaiser Wilhelm II, but there was an empty nail between them. There can be little doubt that on it had hung Hitler's picture, hastily removed as we drove into the town. But if you talked politics with the Herr Doktor he would tell you that he was not a Nazi and did not like Hitler. It was most odd that of all the Germans I had spoken to, not one had ever been a Nazi. On his desk was a small metal flagstaff – but no flag. The swastika had also been whipped away just in time, but there was no ready means of removing the one painted on the flagstone in front of the house, and there it remained: the crooked symbol of Nazi tyranny. The room was full of military souvenirs, from the 154 Infanterie Regiment epaulettes on the wall to the little bomber paperweight on his desk. Most significant of all, the bookcases against the wall contained a whole library of war books beginning, top left, with *The Battle of Hohenfriedburg, June 4th, 1866*, down through *World War in Pictures, 1914–18*, and ending, bottom right, with a book which we had found in almost every house, which had the sadistic title: *With Bombs and Machine Guns over Poland*.

I had asked the Frau Doktor what kind of doctorate her husband had since there there was no surgery in the house nor any indications of great learning. Her answer, though it was almost inconceivable, was that he was a doktor of philosophy! The fruits of that philosophy could be seen in the pictures of

German concentration camps which had appeared in the last few days: the slaughter yards stained the same dull crimson as the tulips in the room. They, too, were symbolic, for the little metal disc at the end of the row had informed me that those heavy red blooms – grown, you might well think, from blood and iron – were named 'Reichskanzler Bismarck'.

It was just ten and a half months since D-Day. The beaches and orchards of Calvados seemed half a lifetime ago. We had certainly travelled far since then: the break-through south of Caen which took us across the Seine, the reduction of Le Havre, the woods north-west of Eindhoven and northwards from there to the Maas, the canal crossings, our sojourn on the 'Island' north of Nijmegen, the hurried move down into the Ardennes, the break-through into the Reichswald and onwards to Goch, the Rhine crossing, and now the thrust forward into the very heart of Germany.

In the course of these journeyings we had fought some thirty-six actions, in all but two of which the battalion had been attacking. The price had been seventy-five officers and 975[1] other ranks, of whom rather more than one-quarter had been killed or died of wounds. I shall never get over the sadness of these losses. To the day of my death I shall remember David Martin; George Stewart; Arthur Thompson; Donald Howorth, the best platoon commander that ever was; Albert Brown, our doctor; Glass, the young Canadian; Jimmy Graham, my first servant; 'Carrots' Chamberlain, for so long my signaller, and Sergeants Dunlop and Coutts, together with General Thomas Rennie and many others, as gallant and lovely Highlanders as have ever been. I do not believe that anybody can go through a campaign with such men as these, and watch them killed one after the other, and know that their joyous personalities were

---

[1]   The Battalion fought one more small action on April 28th which caused another eleven casualties, making 986 for the whole campaign.

254

now but blackened, broken corpses tied up in a few feet of Army blanket under the damp earth – and remain quite the same. For my part I felt that this had made a mark upon me that will never be effaced. It is as if some spring deep down inside me has run down.

But I refused to let such thoughts depress me now. For I could hear my driver warming up the engine of my borrowed car. Cornish had laid out my kilt and my pack stood there, all ready. It was time to go. In seventy-two hours Joyce would be waiting for me at the Dorchester. Park Lane, Bond Street, Piccadilly, then Long Sleddale with the children.

The ancient village taxi would draw up at the gate. I should walk up the garden path and across the narrow, wooden foot-bridge over the Sprint, pausing a moment to look for trout in the pools and eddies below, then a few more yards up a slight rise to the house. At this time of year there would be great clusters of blue irises, in front of the pale yellow moorland stone. Ronald, Jacynth and young Oliver would be in bed and asleep. But, whatever their mother might say, I should wake them.

I could not remember ever having felt quite so excited before. I was a Gay Gordon indeed.

Glossary of Military Terms and Abbreviations

A Echelon. – The transport of an infantry battalion in the field is normally divided into three Echelons: F, A and B. F (or Fighting) is the minimum number of vehicles needed for battle: jeeps, carriers, anti-tank guns, etc. A Echelon consists mostly of 15-cwt. trucks containing day-to-day requirements such as food, reserve ammunition, blankets or greatcoats, cooking utensils. B Echelon contains all the remaining vehicles of the battalion, chiefly 3-ton lorries with stores, workshops, etc.; it only joins up with the battalion when out of the line for a resting or refitting period.

A.P.M. – Assistant Provost Marshal, the officer on the staff of certain formations who is responsible for disciplinary matters.

Artillery. – Though an infantry brigade may have several field and medium artillery regiments directly supporting it during the different phases of an attack, it has one field regiment (24 guns) permanently at its disposal and the regimental commander functions at Brigade H.Q. during an operation. Similarly each of the three 8-gun batteries in the regiment is allotted to one of the three battalions in the brigade, and the Battery Commander, a major, is at the side of the Battalion Commander throughout the action. He usually has one or two officers up with the companies as Forward Observation Officers (F.O.O.s). These artillery officers are always accompanied by their signallers in direct wireless touch with the guns. Thus, though the guns themselves may be several miles in the rear, the Battery Commander, F.O.O.s and signallers share all the risks of the infantry. 127 Field Regiment supported 153 Brigade from El Alamein onwards and 301 Battery supported 1st Gordons. We thought the world of 'our' gunners.

Avre. – Assault vehicle R.E. (or Petard). An armoured vehicle which fires a block-buster at concrete defences.

Bazooka. – A one-man portable projector which, by means of a spring, projects an anti-tank bomb about 100 yards. The bazooka is the American equivalent of the British piat.

B Echelon. – See A Echelon.

B.M. – Brigade Major, the senior operations staff officer at a Brigade H.Q.

Bofors. – Light anti-aircraft artillery.

Bren. – The British light machine-gun.

Buffalo. – An armoured amphibious transporter. For description see page 113.

B.W. – Black Watch.

Carrier. – A four-man tracked vehicle. A battalion has a platoon of them, each armed with one bren-gun – the 'carrier platoon.' The mortars also move in carriers and the anti-tank guns are towed by them.

C.B. – Counter battery artillery fire.

C.C.P. – Casualty Collecting Point.

C.C.R.A. – Commanding Corps Royal Artillery – a brigadier.

C.C.S. – Casualty Clearing Station.

C.O. – Commanding Officer, usually a Lieut.-Col.'s appointment.

C.R.A. – Commanding Royal Artillery (of a division) – Brigadier.

C.R.E. – Commanding Royal Engineers (of a division) – Lieut.-Col.

Crocodiles – Flame-throwing tanks.

C.S.M. – Company Sergeant-Major.

D.F. – Defensive Fire. Prearranged artillery and/or mortar fire which can be put down quickly in front of forward troops if they call for it. One or more D.F. tasks is often selected to be an S.O.S. task, which means that the weapon is actually laid to shoot there.

D.R. – Despatch Rider.

E. – 18-set. The two-man portable R/t set which was carried by each company. Replaced by the 46-set.

F.D.L.s – Forward Defended Localities.

F Echelon. – See A Echelon.

Flail. – A tank with steel chains rotating in front of it and thrashing the ground in order to explode anti-tank mines.

F.O.O. – See Artillery.

H.E. – High Explosive.

H-Hour. – The same as Zero Hour.

I.O. – Intelligence Officer. A battalion has one I.O. with a section of about six men. He is the C.O.'s assistant in all operational matters.

Kangaroo. – A tank minus turret and innards, used as an armoured transporter.

K.O.S.B. – King's Own Scottish Borderers.

K.S.L.I. – King's Shropshire Light Infantry.

L.M.G. – Light Machine-gun.

L.O. – Liaison Officer.

M.M.G. – Medium Machine-gun.

Mortar. – A projector with the appearance of a short length of steel drain-pipe fitting into a base-plate. A bomb slides down inside it to explode a propelling charge when it reaches the bottom. The 3-inch mortar fires a 10-lb. bomb one and a half miles, and the battalion has six of them.

M.T. – Mechanised Transport.

M.T.O. – Officer in Charge of M.T.

O Group. – Order Group. The Commanders and others in any formation required to receive or listen to orders before an operation. Thus a Brigade O Group consists of the three battalion commanders, the artillery, tank and other supporting arms commanders and the principal staff officers of the Brigade Commander. Similarly, a battlion O Group consists of the company and supporting arms commanders, I.O., S.O., Adjt., M.O., etc.

O.P. – Observation Post.

Other Ranks. – Warrant Officers, N.C.O.s and Privates.

Piat. – Projector infantry anti-tank. The British equivalent of the bazooka (see above).

Priest. – A S.P. gun minus turret and innards, used like the kangaroo as an armoured transporter.

R.A.C. – Royal Armoured Corps. Formed from Cavalry and Yeomanry Regiments and the Royal Tank Corps into regiments or battalions of tanks, flails, crocodiles, buffaloes, kangaroos or priests.

R.A.P. – Regimental Aid Post.

R.E. – Royal Engineers (or Sappers). Each brigade normally has a field company commanded by a Major.

Recce. – Pronounced 'rekky.' Reconnaissance. To make a reconnaissance.

R/T. – Radio telephony (speech by wireless).

R.V. – Rendezvous.

R.W.F. – Royal Welch Fusiliers.

S.A.A. – Small Arms Ammunition.

Schmeisser. – The German equivalent of the Tommy-gun.

Schu-mine. – For description see page 111.

Sitrep. – A situation or progress report.

S.O. – Signal Officer.

S.O.S. – See D.F.

S.L. – Start Line.

S.P. – Self-propelled gun. An armoured field gun or anti-tank gun on a tank chassis. Also Start Point.

Spandau. – The German light machine-gun corresponding to our Bren.

Sten. – The British equivalent of the Tommy-gun.

Tac H.Q. – The C.O.'s battle H.Q., consisting usually of two jeeps or carriers containing his and the battery commander's signallers and wireless sets. When Tac H.Q. moves into a room or dug-out it is usually called a Command Post. Brigade and Divisional H.Q.s also split themselves into Tac and Main H.Q.s during an operation.

Track. – The bearing surface of any vehicle (e.g., tank or carrier) which does not run on wheels. All these are known as 'tracked vehicles.' Half-tracks are those which have tracks behind the driving wheels.

Weasel. – A small tracked vehicle somewhat similar to a carrier.

Index

Certain individuals, units, brigades and divisions are mentioned so frequently that they are not listed in this index in every case.